Python 3 Data Visualization Using ChatGPT / GPT-4

Companion files for this title are available by writing to the publisher at info@merclearning.com.

Python 3 Data Visualization Using ChatGPT / GPT-4

Oswald Campesato

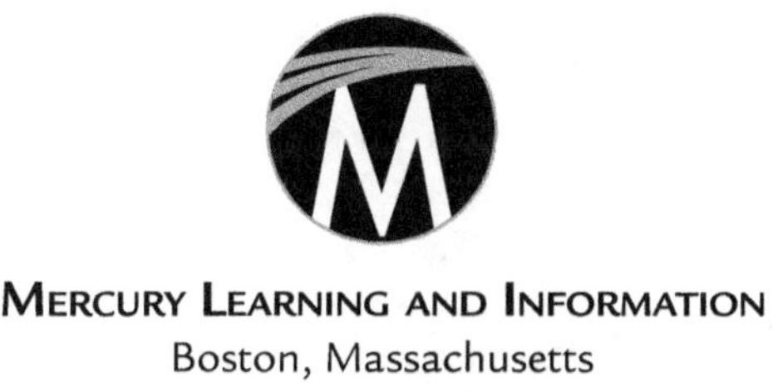

Mercury Learning and Information
Boston, Massachusetts

Publisher: David Pallai
MERCURY LEARNING AND INFORMATION
121 High Street, 3rd Floor
Boston, MA 02110
info@merclearning.com
www.merclearning.com
800-232-0223

O. Campesato. *Python 3 Data Visualization Using ChatGPT / GPT -4.*
ISBN: 978-1-50152-232-1

Library of Congress Control Number: 2023947157
232425321 This book is printed on acid-free paper in the United States of America.

Our titles are available for adoption, license, or bulk purchase by institutions, corporations, etc. For additional information, please contact the Customer Service Dept. at 800-232-0223(toll free).

All of our titles are available in digital format at academiccourseware.com and other digital vendors. *Companion files (code listings) for this title are available by contacting info@merclearning.com.* The sole obligation of MERCURY LEARNING AND INFORMATION to the purchaser is to replace the disc, based on defective materials or faulty workmanship, but not based on the operation or functionality of the product.

I'd like to dedicate this book to my parents
– may this bring joy and happiness into their lives.

Contents

PREFACE

WHAT IS THE PRIMARY VALUE PROPOSITION FOR THIS BOOK?

This book is designed to show readers the concepts of Python 3 programming and the art of data visualization. Chapter 1 introduces the essentials of Python, covering a vast array of topics from basic data types, loops, and functions to more advanced constructs like dictionaries, sets, and matrices. In Chapter 2, the focus shifts to NumPy and its powerful array operations, leading into the world of data visualization using prominent libraries such as Matplotlib. Chapter 6 includes Seaborn's rich visualization tools, offering insights into datasets like Iris and Titanic. Further, the book covers other visualization tools and techniques, including SVG graphics, D3 for dynamic visualizations, and more. Chapter 7 covers information about the main features of ChatGPT and GPT-4, as well as some of their competitors. Chapter 8 contains examples of using `ChatGPT` in order to perform data visualization, such as charts and graphs that are based on datasets (e.g., the Titanic dataset). From foundational Python concepts to the intricacies of data visualization, this book serves as a comprehensive resource for both beginners and seasoned professionals.

THE TARGET AUDIENCE

This book is intended primarily for people who have worked with `Python` and are interested in learning about graphics effects with `Python` libraries. This book is also intended to reach an international audience of readers with highly diverse backgrounds in various age groups. Consequently, this book uses standard English rather than colloquial expressions that might be confusing to those readers. This book provides a comfortable and meaningful learning experience for the intended readers.

WHY ARE THE CODE SAMPLES PRIMARILY IN PYTHON?

Most of the code samples are short (usually less than one page and sometimes less than half a page), and if necessary, you can easily and quickly copy/paste the code into a new Jupyter notebook. For the Python code samples that reference a `csv` file, you do not need any additional code in the corresponding Jupyter notebook to access the `csv` file. Moreover, the code samples execute quickly, so you won't need to avail yourself of the free GPU that is provided in Google Colaboratory.

If you do decide to use Google Colaboratory, you can easily copy/paste the `Python` code into a notebook, and also use the upload feature to upload existing Jupyter notebooks. Keep in mind the following point: if the `Python` code references a `csv` file, make sure that you include the appropriate code snippet (details are available online) to access the `csv` file in the corresponding Jupyter notebook in Google Colaboratory.

WHY DOES THIS BOOK INCLUDE SKLEARN MATERIAL?

First, keep in mind that the Sklearn material in this book is minimalistic because this book is not about machine learning. Second, the Sklearn material is located in Chapter 6 where you will learn about some of the Sklearn built-in datasets. If you decide to delve into machine learning, you will have already been introduced to some aspects of Sklearn.

GETTING THE MOST FROM THIS BOOK

Some programmers learn well from prose, others learn well from sample code (and lots of it), which means that there's no single style that can be used for everyone.

Moreover, some programmers want to run the code first, see what it does, and then return to the code to delve into the details (and others use the opposite approach).

Consequently, there are various types of code samples in this book: some are short, some are long, and other code samples "build" from earlier code samples.

WHAT DO I NEED TO KNOW FOR THIS BOOK?

Current knowledge of `Python` 3.x is the most helpful skill. Knowledge of other programming languages (such as Java) can also be helpful because of the exposure to programming concepts and constructs.

The less technical knowledge that you have, the more diligence will be required in order to understand the various topics that are covered.

As for the non-technical skills, it's important to have a strong desire to learn about data visualization, along with the motivation and discipline to read and understand the code samples.

DO THE COMPANION FILES OBVIATE THE NEED FOR THIS BOOK?

The companion files contain all the code samples to save you time and effort from the error-prone process of manually typing code into a text file. In addition, there are situations in which you might not have easy access to the companion disc. Furthermore, the code samples in the book provide explanations that are not available on the companion files.

DOES THIS BOOK CONTAIN PRODUCTION-LEVEL CODE SAMPLES?

The primary purpose of the code samples in this book is to show you `Python`-based libraries for data visualization. Clarity has higher priority than writing more compact code that is more difficult to understand (and possibly more prone to bugs). If you decide to use any of the code in this book in a production website, you ought to subject that code to the same rigorous analysis as the other parts of your code base.

HOW DO I SET UP A COMMAND SHELL?

If you are a Mac user, there are three ways to do so. The first method is to use `Finder` to navigate to `Applications > Utilities` and then double click on the `Utilities` application. Next, if you already have a command shell available, you can launch a new command shell by typing the following command:

```
open /Applications/Utilities/Terminal.app
```

A second method for Mac users is to open a new command shell on a MacBook from a command shell that is already visible simply by clicking `command+n` in that command shell, and your Mac will launch another command shell.

If you are a PC user, you can install Cygwin (open source *https://cygwin.com/*) that simulates bash commands, or use another toolkit such as MKS (a commercial product). Please read the online documentation that describes the download and installation process. Note that custom aliases are not automatically set if they are defined in a file other than the main start-up file (such as .bash_login).

COMPANION FILES

All the code samples and figures in this book may be obtained by writing to the publisher at *info@merclearning.com*.

WHAT ARE THE "NEXT STEPS" AFTER FINISHING THIS BOOK?

The answer to this question varies widely, mainly because the answer depends heavily on your objectives. If you are interested primarily in NLP, then you can learn more advanced concepts, such as attention, transformers, and the BERT-related models.

If you are primarily interested in machine learning, there are some subfields of machine learning, such as deep learning and reinforcement learning (and deep reinforcement learning) that might appeal to you. Fortunately, there are many resources available, and you can perform an Internet search for those resources. One other point: the aspects of machine learning for you to learn depend on who you are: the needs of a machine learning engineer, data scientist, manager, student or software developer are all different.

O. Campesato
December 2023

CHAPTER 1

INTRODUCTION TO PYTHON

This chapter contains an introduction to Python, with information about useful tools for installing modules, basic constructs, and how to work with some data types.

The first part of this chapter covers how to install Python, some environment variables, and how to use the interpreter. You will see code samples and also how to save code in text files that you can launch from the command line. The second part of this chapter shows you how to work with simple data types, such as numbers, fractions, and strings. The final part of this chapter discusses exceptions and how to use them in scripts.

NOTE *The Python files in this book are for Python 3.x.*

TOOLS FOR PYTHON

The Anaconda Python distribution available for Windows, Linux, and Mac is downloadable at *http://continuum.io/downloads*.

Anaconda is well-suited for modules such as `numpy` and `scipy`, and if you are a Windows user, Anaconda appears to be a better alternative.

easy_install and pip

Both `easy_install` and `pip` are easy to use when you need to install Python modules. Whenever you need to install a module (and there are many in this book), use either `easy_install` or `pip` with the following syntax:

```
easy_install <module-name>
pip install <module-name>
```

NOTE *Python-based modules are easier to install, whereas modules with code written in C are usually faster but more difficult in terms of installation.*

virtualenv

The `virtualenv` tool enables you to create isolated Python environments, and its home page is at *http://www.virtualenv.org/en/latest/virtualenv.html*.

`virtualenv` addresses the problem of preserving the correct dependencies and versions (and indirectly, permissions) for different applications. If you are a Python novice, you might not need `virtualenv` right now, but keep this tool in mind.

IPython

Another very good tool is IPython (which won a Jolt award), and its home page is at *http://ipython.org/install.html*. Two very nice features of IPython are tab expansion and "?" (textual assistance). An example of tab expansion is shown here:

```
python
Python 3.9.1 (v3.9.1:1e5d33e9b9, Dec  7 2020, 12:44:01)
[Clang 12.0.0 (clang-1200.0.32.27)] on darwin
Type "help", "copyright", "credits" or "license" for more
information.

IPython 0.13.2 -- An enhanced Interactive Python.
?          -> Introduction and overview of IPython's
              features.
%quickref -> Quick reference.
help       -> Python's own help system.
object?    -> Details about 'object', use 'object??' for
extra details.

In [1]: di
%dirs    dict     dir      divmod
```

In the preceding session, if you type the characters `di`, IPython responds with the following line that contains all the functions that start with the letters `di`:

```
%dirs    dict     dir      divmod
```

If you enter a question mark ("?"), IPython provides textual assistance, the first part of which is here:

```
IPython -- An enhanced Interactive Python
=========================================

IPython offers a combination of convenient shell features,
special commands and a history mechanism for both input
(command history) and output (results caching, similar
to Mathematica). It is intended to be a fully compatible
replacement for the standard Python interpreter, while
offering vastly improved functionality and flexibility.
```

The next section shows you how to check whether Python is installed on your machine, and also where you can download Python.

PYTHON INSTALLATION

Before you download anything, check if you have Python already installed on your machine (which is likely if you have a MacBook or a Linux machine) by typing the following command in a command shell:

```
python -V
```

The output for the MacBook used in this book is here:

```
Python 3.9.1
```

NOTE *Install Python 3.9 (or as close as possible to this version) on your machine so that you will have the same version of Python that was used to test the Python files in this book.*

If you need to install Python on your machine, navigate to the Python home page and select the downloads link or navigate directly to this website:

http://www.python.org/download/

In addition, PythonWin is available for Windows, and its home page is here:

http://www.cgl.ucsf.edu/Outreach/pc204/pythonwin.html

Use any text editor that can create, edit, and save Python scripts, and save them as plain text files (do not use Microsoft Word). After you have Python installed and configured on your machine, you are ready to work with the Python scripts in this book.

SETTING THE PATH ENVIRONMENT VARIABLE (WINDOWS ONLY)

The `PATH` environment variable specifies a list of directories that are searched whenever you specify an executable program from the command line. The following URL has a useful guide to setting up your environment so that the Python executable is always available in every command shell:

http://www.blog.pythonlibrary.org/2011/11/24/python-101-setting-up-python-on-windows/

LAUNCHING PYTHON ON YOUR MACHINE

There are three different ways to launch Python:

- Use the Python Interactive Interpreter.
- Launch Python scripts from the command line.
- Use an IDE.

The next section shows you how to launch the Python interpreter from the command line, and later in this chapter you will learn how to launch scripts from the command line and also about IDEs.

NOTE *The emphasis in this book is to launch Python scripts from the command line or to enter code in the Python interpreter.*

The Python Interactive Interpreter

Launch the interactive interpreter from the command line by opening a command shell and typing the following command:

```
python
```

You will see the following prompt (or something similar):

```
Python 3.9.1 (v3.9.1:1e5d33e9b9, Dec  7 2020, 12:44:01)
[Clang 12.0.0 (clang-1200.0.32.27)] on darwin
Type "help", "copyright", "credits" or "license" for more information.
>>>
```

Now type the expression `2 + 7` at the prompt:

```
>>> 2 + 7
```

Python displays the following result:

```
9
>>>
```

Press `ctrl-d` to exit the Python shell.

You can launch any Python script from the command line by preceding it with the word "python." For example, if you have a script `myscript.py` that contains commands, launch the script as follows:

```
python myscript.py
```

As a simple illustration, suppose that the script `myscript.py` contains the following code:

```
print('Hello World from Python')
print('2 + 7 = ', 2+7)
```

When you launch the preceding script, you will see the following output:

```
Hello World from Python
2 + 7 =  9
```

PYTHON IDENTIFIERS

An *identifier* is the name of a variable, function, class, module, or other Python object, and a valid identifier conforms to the following rules:

- starts with a letter A to Z or a to z or an underscore (_)
- zero or more letters, underscores, and digits (0 to 9)

NOTE *Python identifiers cannot contain characters such as @, $, and %.*

Python is a case-sensitive language, so `Abc` and `abc` are different identifiers in Python. In addition, Python has the following naming conventions:

- Class names start with an uppercase letter and all other identifiers with a lowercase letter
- An initial underscore is used for private identifiers.
- Two initial underscores are used for strongly private identifiers.

A Python identifier with two initial underscores and two trailing underscore characters indicates a language-defined special name.

LINES, INDENTATION, AND MULTI-LINE COMMENTS

Unlike other programming languages (such as Java or Objective-C), Python uses indentation instead of curly braces for code blocks. Indentation must be consistent in a code block, as shown here:

```
if True:
    print("ABC")
    print("DEF")
else:
    print("ABC")
    print("DEF")
```

Multi-line statements in Python can terminate with a new line or the backslash ("\") character, as shown here:

```
total = x1 + \
        x2 + \
        x3
```

Obviously, you can place `x1, x2`, and `x3` on the same line, so there is no reason to use three separate lines; however, this functionality is available in case you need to add a set of variables that do not fit on a single line.

You can specify multiple statements in one line by using a semicolon (";") to separate each statement, as shown here:

```
a=10; b=5; print(a); print(a+b)
```

The output of the preceding code snippet is here:

```
10
15
```

NOTE *The use of semi-colons and the continuation character are discouraged in Python.*

QUOTATIONS AND COMMENTS IN PYTHON

Python allows single ('), double ("), and triple (''' or """) quotation marks for string literals, provided that they match at the beginning and the end of the string. You can use triple quotation marks for strings that span multiple lines. The following examples are legal Python strings:

```
word = 'word'
line = "This is a sentence."
para = """This is a paragraph. This paragraph contains
more than one sentence."""
```

A string literal that begins with the letter "r" (for "raw") treats everything as a literal character and "escapes" the meaning of meta characters, as shown here:

```
a1 = r'\n'
a2 = r'\r'
a3 = r'\t'
print('a1:',a1,'a2:',a2,'a3:',a3)
```

The output of the preceding code block is here:

```
a1: \n a2: \r a3: \t
```

You can embed a single quotation mark in a pair of double quotation marks (and vice versa) to display a single quotation mark or double quotation marks. Another way to accomplish the same result is to precede single or double quotation marks with a backslash ("\") character. The following code block illustrates these techniques:

```
b1 = "'"
b2 = '"'
b3 = '\''
b4 = "\""
print('b1:',b1,'b2:',b2)
print('b3:',b3,'b4:',b4)
```

The output of the preceding code block is here:

```
b1: ' b2: "
b3: ' b4: "
```

A hash sign (#) that is not inside a string literal is the character that indicates the beginning of a comment. Moreover, all characters after the # and up to the physical line end are part of the comment (and ignored by the Python interpreter). Consider the following code block:

```
#!/usr/bin/python
# First comment
print("Hello, Python!")  # second comment
```

This will produce following result:

```
Hello, Python!
```

A comment may be on the same line after a statement or expression:

```
name = "Tom Jones" # This is also comment
```

You can comment multiple lines as follows:

```
# This is comment one
# This is comment two
# This is comment three
```

A blank line in Python is a line containing only whitespace, a comment, or both.

SAVING YOUR CODE IN A MODULE

Earlier you saw how to launch the Python interpreter from the command line and then enter commands. However, everything you type in the Python interpreter is only valid for the current session: if you exit the interpreter and then launch the interpreter again, your previous definitions are no longer valid. Fortunately, Python enables you to store code in a text file, as discussed in the next section.

A *module* in Python is a text file that contains Python statements. In the previous section, you saw how the interpreter enables you to test code snippets whose definitions are valid for the current session. If you want to retain the code snippets and other definitions, place them in a text file so that you can execute that code outside of the interpreter.

The outermost statements in a Python program are executed from top to bottom when the module is imported for the first time, which will then set up its variables and functions.

A Python module can be run directly from the command line, as shown here:

```
python first.py
```

As an illustration, place the following two statements in a text file called `first.py`:

```
x = 3
print(x)
```

Now type the following command:

```
python first.py
```

The output from the preceding command is `3`, which is the same as executing the preceding code from the interpreter.

When a module is run directly, the special variable `__name__` is set to `__main__`. You will often see the following type of code in a module:

```
if __name__ == '__main__':
    # do something here
    print('Running directly')
```

The preceding code snippet enables Python to determine if a module was launched from the command line or imported into another module.

SOME STANDARD MODULES IN PYTHON

The Python Standard Library provides many modules that can simplify your own scripts. A list of the Standard Library modules is at *http://www.python.org/doc/*.

Some of the most important modules include `cgi`, `math`, `os`, `pickle`, `random`, `re`, `socket`, `sys`, `time`, and `urllib`.

The code samples in this book use the modules `math`, `os`, `random`, `re`, `socket`, `sys`, `time`, and `urllib`. You need to import these modules to use them in your code. For example, the following code block shows you how to import 4 standard Python modules:

```
import datetime
import re
import sys
import time
```

The code samples in this book import one or more of the preceding modules, as well as other Python modules.

THE help() AND dir() FUNCTIONS

An Internet search for Python-related topics usually returns a number of links with useful information. Alternatively, you can check the official Python documentation site: *docs.python.org*.

In addition, Python provides the `help()` and `dir()` functions that are accessible from the interpreter. The `help()` function displays documentation strings, whereas the `dir()` function displays defined symbols.

For example, if you type `help(sys)` you will see documentation for the `sys` module, whereas `dir(sys)` displays a list of the defined symbols.

Type the following command in the interpreter to display the string-related methods in Python:

```
>>> dir(str)
```

The preceding command generates the following output:

```
['__add__', '__class__', '__contains__', '__delattr__',
'__doc__', '__eq__', '__format__', '__ge__', '__
getattribute__', '__getitem__', '__getnewargs__', '__
```

```
getslice__', '__gt__', '__hash__', '__init__', '__le__',
'__len__', '__lt__', '__mod__', '__mul__', '__ne__',
'__new__', '__reduce__', '__reduce_ex__', '__repr__',
'__rmod__', '__rmul__', '__setattr__', '__sizeof__',
'__str__', '__subclasshook__', '_formatter_field_name_
split', '_formatter_parser', 'capitalize', 'center',
'count', 'decode', 'encode', 'endswith', 'expandtabs',
'find', 'format', 'index', 'isalnum', 'isalpha', 'isdigit',
'islower', 'isspace', 'istitle', 'isupper', 'join',
'ljust', 'lower', 'lstrip', 'partition', 'replace',
'rfind', 'rindex', 'rjust', 'rpartition', 'rsplit',
'rstrip', 'split', 'splitlines', 'startswith', 'strip',
'swapcase', 'title', 'translate', 'upper', 'zfill']
```

The preceding list gives you a consolidated "dump" of built-in functions (including some that are discussed later in this chapter). Although the `max()` function obviously returns the maximum value of its arguments, the purpose of other functions such as `filter()` or `map()` is not immediately apparent (unless you have used them in other programming languages). The preceding list provides a starting point for finding out more about various Python built-in functions that are not discussed in this chapter.

Note that while `dir()` does not list the names of built-in functions and variables, you can obtain this information from the standard module `__builtin__` that is automatically imported under the name `__builtins__`:

```
>>> dir(__builtins__)
```

The following command shows you how to get more information about a function:

```
help(str.lower)
```

The output from the preceding command is here:

```
Help on method_descriptor:

lower(...)
    S.lower() -> string

    Return a copy of the string S converted to lowercase.
(END)
```

Check the online documentation and also experiment with `help()` and `dir()` when you need additional information about a particular function or module.

COMPILE TIME AND RUNTIME CODE CHECKING

Python performs some compile-time checking, but most checks (including type, name, and so forth) are *deferred* until code execution. Consequently, if your Python code references a user-defined function that does not exist, the code will compile successfully. In fact, the code will fail with an exception *only* when the code execution path references the non-existent function.

As a simple example, consider the following function `myFunc` that references the non-existent function called `DoesNotExist`:

```
def myFunc(x):
    if x == 3:
        print(DoesNotExist(x))
    else:
        print('x: ',x)
```

The preceding code will only fail when the `myFunc` function has passed the value 3, after which Python raises an error.

In Chapter 2, you will learn how to define and invoke user-defined functions, along with an explanation of the difference between local versus global variables in Python.

Now that you understand some basic concepts (such as how to use the Python interpreter) and how to launch your custom modules, the next section discusses primitive data types.

SIMPLE DATA TYPES

Python supports primitive data types, such as numbers (integers, floating point numbers, and exponential numbers), strings, and dates. Python also supports more complex data types, such as lists (or arrays), tuples, and dictionaries, all of which are discussed in Chapter 3. The next several sections discuss some of the Python primitive data types, along with code snippets that show you how to perform various operations on those data types.

WORKING WITH NUMBERS

Python provides arithmetic operations for manipulating numbers in a straightforward manner that is similar to other programming languages. The following examples involve arithmetic operations on integers:

```
>>> 2+2
4
>>> 4/3
1
>>> 3*8
24
```

The following example assigns numbers to two variables and computes their product:

```
>>> x = 4
>>> y = 7
>>> x * y
28
```

The following examples demonstrate arithmetic operations involving integers:

```
>>> 2+2
4
>>> 4/3
1
>>> 3*8
24
```

Notice that division ("/") of two integers is actually truncation in which only the integer result is retained. The following example converts a floating point number into exponential form:

```
>>> fnum = 0.00012345689000007
>>> "%.14e"%fnum
'1.23456890000070e-04'
```

You can use the `int()` function and the `float()` function to convert strings to numbers:

```
word1 = "123"
word2 = "456.78"
var1 = int(word1)
var2 = float(word2)
print("var1: ",var1," var2: ",var2)
```

The output from the preceding code block is here:

```
var1:  123  var2:  456.78
```

Alternatively, you can use the `eval()` function:

```
word1 = "123"
word2 = "456.78"
var1 = eval(word1)
var2 = eval(word2)
print("var1: ",var1," var2: ",var2)
```

If you attempt to convert a string that is not a valid integer or a floating point number, Python raises an exception, so it is advisable to place your code in a `try/except` block.

Working with Other Bases

Numbers in Python are in base 10 (the default), but you can easily convert numbers to other bases. For example, the following code block initializes the variable x with the value `1234`, and then displays that number in base `2, 8`, and `16`:

```
>>> x = 1234
>>> bin(x) '0b10011010010'
>>> oct(x) '0o2322'
>>> hex(x) '0x4d2' >>>
```

Use the `format()` function if you want to suppress the `0b`, `0o`, or `0x` prefixes, as shown here:

```
>>> format(x, 'b') '10011010010'
>>> format(x, 'o') '2322'
>>> format(x, 'x') '4d2'
```

Negative integers are displayed with a negative sign:

```
>>> x = -1234
>>> format(x, 'b') '-10011010010'
>>> format(x, 'x') '-4d2'
```

The chr() Function

The `chr()` function takes a positive integer as a parameter and converts it to its corresponding alphabetic value (if one exists). The letters A through Z have decimal representation of `65` through `91` (which corresponds to hexadecimal `41` through `5b`), and the lowercase letters `a` through `z` have decimal representation `97` through `122` (hexadecimal `61` through `7b`).

Here is an example of using the `chr()` function to print uppercase `A`:

```
>>> x=chr(65)
>>> x
'A'
```

The following code block prints the ASCII values for a range of integers:

```
result = ""
for x in range(65,91):
  print(x, chr(x))
  result = result+chr(x)+' '
print("result: ",result)
```

NOTE *Python 2 uses ASCII strings whereas Python 3 uses Unicode.*

You can represent a range of characters with the following line:

```
for x in range(65,91):
```

However, the following equivalent code snippet is more intuitive:

```
for x in range(ord('A'), ord('Z')):
```

If you want to display the result for lowercase letters, change the preceding range from `(65,91)` to either of the following statements:

```
for x in range(65,91):
for x in range(ord('a'), ord('z')):
```

The round() Function

The `round()` function enables you to round decimal values to the nearest precision:

```
>>> round(1.23, 1)
1.2
>>> round(-3.42,1)
-3.4
```

Formatting Numbers

Python allows you to specify the number of decimal places of precision to use when printing decimal numbers, as shown here:

```
>>> x = 1.23456
>>> format(x, '0.2f')
'1.23'
>>> format(x, '0.3f')
'1.235'
>>> 'value is {:0.3f}'.format(x) 'value is 1.235'
>>> from decimal import Decimal
>>> a = Decimal('4.2')
>>> b = Decimal('2.1')
>>> a + b
Decimal('6.3')
>>> print(a + b)
6.3
>>> (a + b) == Decimal('6.3')
True
>>> x = 1234.56789
>>> # Two decimal places of accuracy
>>> format(x, '0.2f')
'1234.57'
>>> # Right justified in 10 chars, one-digit accuracy
>>> format(x, '>10.1f')
' 1234.6'
>>> # Left justified
>>> format(x, '<10.1f') '1234.6 '
>>> # Centered
>>> format(x, '^10.1f') ' 1234.6 '
>>> # Inclusion of thousands separator
>>> format(x, ',')
'1,234.56789'
>>> format(x, '0,.1f')
'1,234.6'
```

WORKING WITH FRACTIONS

Python supports the `Fraction()` function (defined in the `fractions` module), which accepts two integers that represent the numerator and the denominator (which must be non-zero) of a fraction. Several examples of defining and manipulating fractions are shown here:

```
>>> from fractions import Fraction
>>> a = Fraction(5, 4)
>>> b = Fraction(7, 16)
>>> print(a + b)
27/16
>>> print(a * b) 35/64
>>> # Getting numerator/denominator
>>> c = a * b
```

```
>>> c.numerator
35
>>> c.denominator 64
>>> # Converting to a float >>> float(c)
0.546875
>>> # Limiting the denominator of a value
>>> print(c.limit_denominator(8))
4
>>> # Converting a float to a fraction >>> x = 3.75
>>> y = Fraction(*x.as_integer_ratio())
>>> y
Fraction(15, 4)
```

Before delving into code samples that work with strings, the next section briefly discusses Unicode and UTF-8, both of which are character encodings.

UNICODE AND UTF-8

A Unicode string consists of a sequence of numbers that are between `0` and `0x10ffff`, where each number represents a group of bytes. An *encoding* is the manner in which a Unicode string is translated into a sequence of bytes. Among the various encodings, UTF-8 ("Unicode Transformation Format") is perhaps the most common, and it is also the default encoding for many systems. The digit 8 in UTF-8 indicates that the encoding uses 8-bit numbers, whereas UTF-16 uses 16-bit numbers (but this encoding is less common).

The ASCII character set is a subset of UTF-8, so a valid ASCII string can be read as a UTF-8 string without any re-encoding required. In addition, a Unicode string can be converted into a UTF-8 string.

WORKING WITH UNICODE

Python supports Unicode, which means that you can render characters in different languages. Unicode data can be stored and manipulated in the same way as strings. Create a Unicode string by prepending the letter `u`, as shown here:

```
>>> u'Hello from Python!'
u'Hello from Python!'
```

Special characters can be included in a string by specifying their Unicode value. For example, the following Unicode string embeds a space (which has the Unicode value 0x0020) in a string:

```
>>> u'Hello\u0020from Python!'
u'Hello from Python!'
```

Listing 1.1 displays the content of `unicode1.py` that illustrates how to display a string of characters in Japanese and another string of characters in Chinese (Mandarin).

LISTING 1.1: unicode1.py

```
chinese1 = u'\u5c07\u63a2\u8a0e HTML5 \u53ca\u5176\u4ed6'
hiragana = u'D3 \u306F \u304B\u3063\u3053\u3043\u3043 \
u3067\u3059!'

print('Chinese:',chinese1)
print('Hiragana:',hiragana)
```

The output of Listing 1.2 is here:

```
Chinese: 將探討 HTML5 及其他
Hiragana: D3 は かっこぃぃ です!
```

The next portion of this chapter shows you how to "slice and dice" text strings with built-in Python functions.

WORKING WITH STRINGS

You can concatenate two strings using the "+" operator. The following example prints a string and then concatenates two single-letter strings:

```
>>> 'abc'
'abc'
>>> 'a' + 'b'
'ab'
```

You can use "+" or "*" to concatenate identical strings, as shown here:

```
>>> 'a' + 'a' + 'a'
'aaa'
>>> 'a' * 3
'aaa'
```

You can assign strings to variables and print them using the `print()` command:

```
>>> print('abc')
abc
>>> x = 'abc'
>>> print(x)
abc
>>> y = 'def'
>>> print(x + y)
abcdef
```

You can "unpack" the letters of a string and assign them to variables, as shown here:

```
>>> str = "World"
>>> x1,x2,x3,x4,x5 = str
>>> x1
```

```
'W'
>>> x2
'o'
>>> x3
'r'
>>> x4
'l'
>>> x5
'd'
```

The preceding code snippets show you how easy it is to extract the letters in a text string, and in Chapter 3 you will learn how to "unpack" other data structures.

You can extract substrings of a string as shown in the following examples:

```
>>> x = "abcdef"
>>> x[0]
'a'
>>> x[-1]
'f'
>>> x[1:3]
'bc'
>>> x[0:2] + x[5:]
'abf'
```

However, you will cause an error if you attempt to "subtract" two strings:

```
>>> 'a' - 'b'
Traceback (most recent call last):
  File "<stdin>", line 1, in <module>
TypeError: unsupported operand type(s) for -: 'str' and
'str'
```

The `try/except` construct enables you to handle the preceding type of exception gracefully.

Comparing Strings

You can use the methods `lower()` and `upper()` to convert a string to lowercase and uppercase, respectively, as shown here:

```
>>> 'Python'.lower()
'python'
>>> 'Python'.upper()
'PYTHON'
>>>
```

The methods `lower()` and `upper()` are useful for performing a case-insensitive comparison of two ASCII strings. Listing 1.2 displays the content of `compare.py` that uses the `lower()` function to compare two ASCII strings.

LISTING 1.2: compare.py

```
x = 'Abc'
y = 'abc'

if(x == y):
  print('x and y: identical')
elif (x.lower() == y.lower()):
  print('x and y: case insensitive match')
else:
  print('x and y: different')
```

Since `x` contains mixed case letters and `y` contains lowercase letters, Listing 1.2 displays the following output:

```
x and y: different
```

Formatting Strings

Python provides the functions `string.lstring()`, `string.rstring()`, and `string.center()` for positioning a text string so that it is left-justified, right-justified, and centered, respectively. As you saw in a previous section, Python also provides the `format()` method for advanced interpolation features.

Now enter the following commands in the interpreter:

```
import string

str1 = 'this is a string'
print(string.ljust(str1, 10))
print(string.rjust(str1, 40))
print(string.center(str1,40))
```

The output is shown here:

```
this is a string
                        this is a string
            this is a string
```

The next portion of this chapter shows you how to "slice and dice" text strings with built-in functions.

SLICING AND SPLICING STRINGS

Python enables you to extract substrings of a string (called "slicing") using array notation. Slice notation is `start:stop:step`, where the start, stop, and step values are integers that specify the start value, end value, and the increment value, respectively. The interesting part about slicing in Python is that you can use the value `-1`, which operates from the right-side instead of the left-side of a string.

Some examples of slicing a string are here:

```
text1 = "this is a string"
print('First 7 characters:',text1[0:7])
print('Characters 2-4:',text1[2:4])
print('Right-most character:',text1[-1])
print('Right-most 2 characters:',text1[-3:-1])
```

The output from the preceding code block is here:

```
First 7 characters: this is
Characters 2-4: is
Right-most character: g
Right-most 2 characters: in
```

Later in this chapter, you will see how to insert a string in the middle of another string.

Testing for Digits and Alphabetic Characters

Python enables you to examine each character in a string and then test whether that character is a bona fide digit or an alphabetic character. This section provides a precursor to regular expressions that are discussed in Chapter 4.

Listing 1.3 displays the content of `char_types.py` that illustrates how to determine if a string contains digits or characters. In case you are unfamiliar with the conditional "if" statement in Listing 1.3, more detailed information is available in Chapter 2.

LISTING 1.3: char_types.py

```
str1 = "4"
str2 = "4234"
str3 = "b"
str4 = "abc"
str5 = "a1b2c3"

if(str1.isdigit()):
  print("this is a digit:",str1)

if(str2.isdigit()):
  print("this is a digit:",str2)

if(str3.isalpha()):
  print("this is alphabetic:",str3)

if(str4.isalpha()):
  print("this is alphabetic:",str4)

if(not str5.isalpha()):
  print("this is not pure alphabetic:",str5)

print("capitalized first letter:",str5.title())
```

Listing 1.3 initializes some variables, followed by 2 conditional tests that check whether `str1` and `str2` are digits using the `isdigit()` function. The next portion of Listing 1.3 checks if `str3`, `str4`, and `str5` are alphabetic strings using the `isalpha()` function. The output of Listing 1.3 is here:

```
this is a digit: 4
this is a digit: 4234
this is alphabetic: b
this is alphabetic: abc
this is not pure alphabetic: a1b2c3
capitalized first letter: A1B2C3
```

SEARCH AND REPLACE A STRING IN OTHER STRINGS

Python provides methods for searching and replacing a string in a second text string. Listing 1.4 displays the content of `find_pos1.py` that shows you how to use the find function to search for the occurrence of one string in another string.

LISTING 1.4: find_pos1.py

```
item1 = 'abc'
item2 = 'Abc'
text = 'This is a text string with abc'

pos1 = text.find(item1)
pos2 = text.find(item2)

print('pos1=',pos1)
print('pos2=',pos2)
```

Listing 1.4 initializes the variables `item1`, `item2`, and `text`, and then searches for the index of the contents of `item1` and `item2` in the string text. The `find()` function returns the column number where the first successful match occurs; otherwise, the `find()` function returns a `-1` if a match is unsuccessful.

The output from launching Listing 1.4 is here:

```
pos1= 27
pos2= -1
```

In addition to the `find()` method, you can use the `in` operator when you want to test for the presence of an element, as shown here:

```
>>> lst = [1,2,3]
>>> 1 in lst
True
```

Listing 1.5 displays the content of `replace1.py` that shows you how to replace one string with another string.

LISTING 1.5: replace1.py

```
text = 'This is a text string with abc'
print('text:',text)
text = text.replace('is a', 'was a')
print('text:',text)
```

Listing 1.5 starts by initializing the variable text and then printing its contents. The next portion of Listing 1.5 replaces the occurrence of "is a" with "was a" in the string text, and then prints the modified string. The output from launching Listing 1.5 is here:

```
text: This is a text string with abc
text: This was a text string with abc
```

REMOVE LEADING AND TRAILING CHARACTERS

Python provides the functions `strip()`, `lstrip()`, and `rstrip()` to remove characters in a text string. Listing 1.6 displays the content of `remove1.py` that shows you how to search for a string.

LISTING 1.6: remove1.py

```
text = '   leading and trailing white space    '
print('text1:','x',text,'y')

text = text.lstrip()
print('text2:','x',text,'y')

text = text.rstrip()
print('text3:','x',text,'y')
```

Listing 1.6 starts by concatenating the letter x and the contents of the variable `text`, and then printing the result. The second part of Listing 1.6 removes the leading white spaces in the string `text` and then appends the result to the letter x. The third part of Listing 1.6 removes the trailing white spaces in the string `text` (note that the leading white spaces have already been removed) and then appends the result to the letter x.

The output from launching Listing 1.6 is here:

```
text1: x    leading and trailing white space    y
text2: x leading and trailing white space    y
text3: x leading and trailing white space y
```

If you want to remove extra white spaces inside a text string, use the `replace()` function, as discussed in the previous section. The following example illustrates how this can be accomplished, which also contains the `re` module as a "preview" for what you will learn in Chapter 4:

```
import re
text = 'a    b'
```

```
a = text.replace(' ', '')
b = re.sub('\s+', ' ', text)

print(a)
print(b)
```

The result is here:

```
ab
a b
```

Chapter 2 shows you how to use the `join()` function to remove extra white spaces in a text string.

PRINTING TEXT WITHOUT NEWLINE CHARACTERS

If you need to suppress white space and a newline between objects output with multiple `print()` statements, you can use concatenation or the `write()` function.

The first technique is to concatenate the string representations of each object using the `str()` function prior to printing the result. For example, run the following statement in `Python`:

```
x = str(9)+str(0xff)+str(-3.1)
print('x: ',x)
```

The output is shown here:

```
x:  9255-3.1
```

The preceding line contains the concatenation of the numbers `9` and `255` (which is the decimal value of the hexadecimal number `0xff`) and `-3.1`.

Incidentally, you can use the `str()` function with modules and user-defined classes. An example involving the Python built-in module `sys` is here:

```
>>> import sys
>>> print(str(sys))
<module 'sys' (built-in)>
```

The following code snippet illustrates how to use the `write()` function to display a string:

```
import sys
write = sys.stdout.write
write('123')
write('123456789')
```

The output is here:

```
123123456789
```

TEXT ALIGNMENT

Python provides the methods `ljust()`, `rjust()`, and `center()` for aligning text. The `ljust()` and `rjust()` functions left justify and right justify a text string, respectively, whereas the `center()` function will center a string. An example is shown in the following code block:

```
text = 'Hello World'
text.ljust(20)
'Hello World '
>>> text.rjust(20)
' Hello World'
>>> text.center(20)
' Hello World '
```

You can use the `format()` function to align text. Use the <, >, or ^ characters, along with a desired width, in order to right justify, left justify, and center the text, respectively. The following examples illustrate how you can specify text justification:

```
>>> format(text, '>20')
'         Hello World'
>>>
>>> format(text, '<20')
'Hello World         '
>>>
>>> format(text, '^20')
'    Hello World     '
>>>
```

WORKING WITH DATES

Python provides a rich set of date-related functions. Listing 1.7 displays the content of the script `date_time2.py` that displays various date-related values, such as the current date and time; the day of the week, month, and year; and the time in seconds since the epoch.

LISTING 1.7: date_time2.py

```
import time
import datetime

print("Time in seconds since the epoch: %s" %time.time())
print("Current date and time: " , datetime.datetime.now())
print("Or like this: " ,datetime.datetime.now().
strftime("%y-%m-%d-%H-%M"))

print("Current year: ", datetime.date.today().
strftime("%Y"))
print("Month of year: ", datetime.date.today().
strftime("%B"))
```

```
print("Week number of the year: ", datetime.date.today().
strftime("%W"))
print("Weekday of the week: ", datetime.date.today().
strftime("%w"))
print("Day of year: ", datetime.date.today().
strftime("%j"))
print("Day of the month : ", datetime.date.today().
strftime("%d"))
print("Day of week: ", datetime.date.today().
strftime("%A"))
```

Listing 1.8 displays the output generated by running the code in Listing 1.7.

LISTING 1.8 datetime2.out

```
Time in seconds since the epoch: 1375144195.66
Current date and time:  2013-07-29 17:29:55.664164
Or like this:  13-07-29-17-29
Current year:  2013
Month of year:  July
Week number of the year:  30
Weekday of the week:  1
Day of year:  210
Day of the month :  29
Day of week:  Monday
```

Python allows you to perform arithmetic calculates with date-related values, as shown in the following code block:

```
>>> from datetime import timedelta
>>> a = timedelta(days=2, hours=6)
>>> b = timedelta(hours=4.5)
>>> c = a + b
>>> c.days
2
>>> c.seconds
37800
>>> c.seconds / 3600
10.5
>>> c.total_seconds() / 3600
58.5
```

Converting Strings to Dates

Listing 1.9 displays the content of `string2date.py` that illustrates how to convert a string to a date, and also how to calculate the difference between two dates.

LISTING 1.9: string2date.py

```
from datetime import datetime

text = '2014-08-13'
y = datetime.strptime(text, '%Y-%m-%d')
```

```
z = datetime.now()
diff = z - y
print('Date difference:',diff)
```

The output from Listing 1.9 is shown here:

```
Date difference: -210 days, 18:58:40.197130
```

EXCEPTION HANDLING IN PYTHON

Unlike JavaScript, you cannot add a number and a string in Python. However, you can detect an illegal operation using the `try/except` construct in Python, which is similar to the `try/catch` construct in languages such as JavaScript and Java.

An example of a `try/except` block is here:

```
try:
  x = 4
  y = 'abc'
  z = x + y
except:
  print('cannot add incompatible types:', x, y)
```

When you run the preceding code, the `print()` statement in the `except` code block is executed because the variables `x` and `y` have incompatible types.

Earlier in the chapter, you also saw that subtracting two strings throws an exception:

```
>>> 'a' - 'b'
Traceback (most recent call last):
  File "<stdin>", line 1, in <module>
TypeError: unsupported operand type(s) for -: 'str' and
'str'
```

A simple way to handle this situation is to use a `try/except` block:

```
>>> try:
...   print('a' - 'b')
... except TypeError:
...   print('TypeError exception while trying to subtract
two strings')
... except:
...   print('Exception while trying to subtract two
strings')
...
```

The output from the preceding code block is here:

```
TypeError exception while trying to subtract two strings
```

As you can see, the preceding code block specifies the finer-grained exception called `TypeError`, followed by a generic `except` code block to handle all other exceptions that might occur during the execution of your Python code. This style is similar to the exception handling in Java code.

Listing 1.10 displays the content of `exception1.py` that illustrates how to handle various types of exceptions.

LISTING 1.10: exception1.py

```
import sys

try:
    f = open('myfile.txt')
    s = f.readline()
    i = int(s.strip())
except IOError as err:
    print("I/O error: {0}".format(err))
except ValueError:
    print("Could not convert data to an integer.")
except:
    print("Unexpected error:", sys.exc_info()[0])
    raise
```

Listing 1.10 contains a `try` block followed by three `except` statements. If an error occurs in the `try` block, the first `except` statement is compared with the type of exception that occurred. If there is a match, then the subsequent `print()` statement is executed, and the program terminates. If not, a similar test is performed with the second `except` statement. If neither `except` statement matches the exception, the third `except` statement handles the exception, which involves printing a message and then "raising" an exception. Note that you can also specify multiple exception types in a single statement, as shown here:

```
except (NameError, RuntimeError, TypeError):
    print('One of three error types occurred')
```

The preceding code block is more compact, but you do not know which of the three error types occurred. Python allows you to define custom exceptions, but this topic is beyond the scope of this book.

HANDLING USER INPUT

Python enables you to read user input from the command line via the `input()` function or the `raw_input()` function. Typically, you assign user input to a variable, which will contain all characters that users enter from the keyboard. User input terminates when users press the `<return>` key (which is included with the input characters). Listing 1.11 displays the content of `user_input1.py` that prompts users for their name and then uses interpolation to display a response.

LISTING 1.11: user_input1.py

```
userInput = input("Enter your name: ")
print ("Hello %s, my name is Python" % userInput)
```

The output of Listing 1.11 is here (assume that the user entered the word `Dave`):

```
Hello Dave, my name is Python
```

The `print()` statement in Listing 1.11 uses string interpolation via `%s`, which substitutes the value of the variable after the `%` symbol. This functionality is obviously useful when you want to specify something that is determined at run-time.

User input can cause exceptions (depending on the operations that your code performs), so it is important to include exception-handling code.

Listing 1.12 displays the content of `user_input2.py` that prompts users for a string and attempts to convert the string to a number in a `try/except` block.

LISTING 1.12: user_input2.py

```
userInput = input("Enter something: ")

try:
  x = 0 + eval(userInput)
  print('you entered the number:',userInput)
except:
  print(userInput,'is a string')
```

Listing 1.12 adds the number `0` to the result of converting a user's input to a number. If the conversion was successful, a message with the user's input is displayed. If the conversion failed, the `except` code block consists of a `print()` statement that displays a message.

NOTE *This code sample uses the* `eval()` *function, which should be avoided so that your code does not evaluate arbitrary (and possibly destructive) commands.*

Listing 1.13 displays the content of `user_input3.py` that prompts users for two numbers and attempts to compute their sum in a pair of `try/except` blocks.

LISTING 1.13: user_input3.py

```
sum = 0

msg = 'Enter a number:'
val1 = input(msg)
```

```
try:
  sum = sum + eval(val1)
except:
  print(val1,'is a string')

msg = 'Enter a number:'
val2 = input(msg)

try:
  sum = sum + eval(val2)
except:
  print(val2,'is a string')

print('The sum of',val1,'and',val2,'is',sum)
```

Listing 1.13 contains two `try` blocks, each of which is followed by an `except` statement. The first `try` block attempts to add the first user-supplied number to the variable `sum`, and the second `try` block attempts to add the second user-supplied number to the previously entered number. An error message occurs if either input string is not a valid number; if both are valid numbers, a message is displayed containing the input numbers and their sum. Be sure to read the caveat regarding the `eval()` function that is mentioned earlier in this chapter.

COMMAND-LINE ARGUMENTS

Python provides a `getopt` module to parse command-line options and arguments, and the `sys` module provides access to any command-line arguments via the `sys.argv`. This serves two purposes:

1. `sys.argv` is the list of command-line arguments.
2. `len(sys.argv)` is the number of command-line arguments.

Here, `sys.argv[0]` is the program name, so if the program is called `test.py`, it matches the value of `sys.argv[0]`.

Now you can provide input values for a Python program on the command line instead of providing input values by prompting users for their input.

As an example, consider the script `test.py` shown here:

```
#!/usr/bin/python
import sys
print('Number of arguments:',len(sys.argv),'arguments')
print('Argument List:', str(sys.argv))
```

Now run above script as follows:

```
python test.py arg1 arg2 arg3
```

This will produce following result:

```
Number of arguments: 4 arguments.
Argument List: ['test.py', 'arg1', 'arg2', 'arg3']
```

The ability to specify input values from the command line provides useful functionality. For example, suppose that you have a custom Python class that contains the methods add and subtract to add and subtract a pair of numbers.

You can use command-line arguments to specify which method to execute on a pair of numbers, as shown here:

```
python MyClass add 3 5
python MyClass subtract 3 5
```

This functionality is very useful because you can programmatically execute different methods in a Python class, which means that you can write unit tests for your code as well. Read Chapter 8 to learn how to create custom classes.

Listing 1.14 displays the content of hello.py that shows you how to use sys.argv to check the number of command line parameters.

LISTING 1.14: hello.py

```
import sys

def main():
  if len(sys.argv) >= 2:
    name = sys.argv[1]
  else:
    name = 'World'
  print('Hello', name)

# Standard boilerplate to invoke the main() function
if __name__ == '__main__':
  main()
```

Listing 1.14 defines the main() function that checks the number of command-line parameters: if this value is at least 2, then the variable name is assigned the value of the second parameter (the first parameter is hello.py), otherwise name is assigned the value Hello. The print() statement then prints the value of the variable name.

The final portion of Listing 1.14 uses conditional logic to determine whether to execute the main() function.

SUMMARY

This chapter showed you how to work with numbers and perform arithmetic operations on numbers, and then you learned how to work with strings and use string operations. You also learned how to use the try/except construct to handle exceptions that might occur in your Python code. The next chapter shows you how to work with conditional statements, loops, and user-defined functions.

CHAPTER 2

INTRODUCTION TO NUMPY

This chapter provides a quick introduction to the Python NumPy package, which provides very useful functionality, not only for "regular" Python scripts, but also for Python-based scripts with TensorFlow. For instance, you will see NumPy code samples containing loops, arrays, and lists. You will also learn about dot products, the `reshape()` method (very useful!), how to plot with Matplotlib (discussed in more detail in Chapter 4), and examples of linear regression.

The first part of this chapter briefly discusses NumPy and some of its useful features. The second part contains examples of working arrays in NumPy, and contrasts some of the APIs for lists with the same APIs for arrays. In addition, you will see how easy it is to compute the exponent-related values (square, cube, and so forth) of elements in an array.

The second part of the chapter introduces subranges, which are very useful (and frequently used) for extracting portions of datasets in machine learning tasks. In particular, you will see code samples that handle negative (-1) subranges for vectors as well as for arrays, because they are interpreted one way for vectors and a different way for arrays.

The third part of this chapter delves into other NumPy methods, including the `reshape()` method, which is useful (and very common) when working with image files: some TensorFlow APIs require converting a 2D array of `(R,G,B)` values into a corresponding one-dimensional vector.

The fourth part of this chapter delves into linear regression, the mean squared error (MSE), and how to calculate MSE with the NumPy `linspace()` API.

WHAT IS NUMPY?

NumPy is a Python library that provides many convenient methods and improved code performance. NumPy contains a core library for scientific computing in Python, with performant multi-dimensional arrays and vectorized math functions, along with support for linear algebra and random numbers.

NumPy is modeled after MatLab, with support for lists, arrays, and so forth. NumPy is easier to use than MatLab, and it is very common in TensorFlow code as well as Python code.

Useful NumPy Features

The NumPy package contains the *ndarray* object, which encapsulates *multi-dimensional* arrays of homogeneous data types. Many `ndarray` operations are performed in compiled code to improve performance.

There are important differences between NumPy arrays and standard Python sequences. First, NumPy arrays have a fixed size, whereas Python lists can expand dynamically. Second, NumPy arrays are homogeneous, which means that the elements in a NumPy array must have the same data type. Third, NumPy arrays support more efficient execution (and require less code) of various types of operations on large amounts of data.

Now that you have a general idea about NumPy, let's delve into some examples that illustrate how to work with NumPy arrays, which is the topic of the next section.

WHAT ARE NUMPY ARRAYS?

An *array* is a set of consecutive memory locations used to store data. Each item in the array is called an *element*. The number of elements in an array is called the *dimension* of the array. A typical array declaration is shown here:

```
arr1 = np.array([1,2,3,4,5])
```

The preceding code snippet declares `arr1` as an array of five elements, which you can access via `arr1[0]` through `arr1[4]`. Notice that the first element has an index value of 0, the second element has an index value of 1, and so forth. Thus, if you declare an array of 100 elements, then the 100th element has an index value of 99.

NOTE *The first position in a NumPy array has the index "0."*

NumPy treats arrays as vectors. Math operations are performed element-by-element. Remember the following difference: "doubling" an array *multiplies* each element by 2, whereas "doubling" a list *appends* a list to itself.

Listing 2.1 displays the content of `nparray1.py` that illustrates some operations on a NumPy array.

LISTING 2.1: nparray1.py

```
import numpy as np

list1 = [1,2,3,4,5]
print(list1)
```

```
arr1  = np.array([1,2,3,4,5])
print(arr1)

list2 = [(1,2,3),(4,5,6)]
print(list2)

arr2  = np.array([(1,2,3),(4,5,6)])
print(arr2)
```

Listing 2.1 defines the variables `list1` and `list2` (which are Python lists), as well as the variables `arr1` and `arr2` (which are arrays) and prints their values. The output from launching Listing 2.1 is here:

```
[1, 2, 3, 4, 5]
[1 2 3 4 5]
[(1, 2, 3), (4, 5, 6)]
[[1 2 3]
 [4 5 6]]
```

As you can see, Python lists and arrays are easy to define. Now, we are ready to look at some loop operations for lists and arrays.

WORKING WITH LOOPS

Listing 2.2 displays the content of `loop1.py` that illustrates how to iterate through the elements of a NumPy array and a Python list.

LISTING 2.2: loop1.py

```
import numpy as np

list = [1,2,3]
arr1 = np.array([1,2,3])

for e in list:
  print(e)

for e in arr1:
  print(e)
```

Listing 2.2 initializes the variable `list`, which is a Python list, and also the variable `arr1`, which is a NumPy array. The next portion of Listing 2.2 contains two loops, each of which iterates through the elements in `list` and `arr1`. As you can see, the syntax is identical in both loops. The output from launching Listing 2.2 is here:

```
1
2
3
1
2
3
```

APPENDING ELEMENTS TO ARRAYS (1)

Listing 2.3 displays the content of `append1.py` that illustrates how to append elements to a NumPy array and a Python list.

LISTING 2.3: append1.py

```
import numpy as np

arr1 = np.array([1,2,3])

# these do not work:
#arr1.append(4)
#arr1 = arr1 + [5]

arr1 = np.append(arr1,4)
arr1 = np.append(arr1,[5])

for e in arr1:
  print(e)

arr2 = arr1 + arr1

for e in arr2:
  print(e)
```

Listing 2.3 initializes the variable `arr1`, which is a NumPy array, and also initialize `arr2`, which is another NumPy array. The output from launching Listing 2.3 is here:

```
1
2
3
4
5
2
4
6
8
10
```

APPENDING ELEMENTS TO ARRAYS (2)

Listing 2.4 displays the content of `append2.py` that illustrates how to append elements to a NumPy array and a Python list.

LISTING 2.4: append2.py

```
import numpy as np

arr1 = np.array([1,2,3])
arr1 = np.append(arr1,4)
```

```
for e in arr1:
  print(e)

arr1 = np.array([1,2,3])
arr1 = np.append(arr1,4)

arr2 = arr1 + arr1

for e in arr2:
  print(e)
```

Listing 2.4 initializes the variable `arr1`, which is a NumPy array. Notice that NumPy arrays do not have an "append" method: this method is available through NumPy itself. Another important difference between Python lists and NumPy arrays is that the "+" operator *concatenates* Python lists, whereas this operator *doubles* the elements in a NumPy array. The output from launching Listing 2.4 is here:

```
1
2
3
4
2
4
6
8
```

MULTIPLYING LISTS AND ARRAYS

Listing 2.5 displays the content of `multiply1.py` that illustrates how to multiply elements in a Python list and a NumPy array.

LISTING 2.5: multiply1.py

```
import numpy as np

list1 = [1,2,3]
arr1  = np.array([1,2,3])
print('list:  ',list1)
print('arr1:  ',arr1)
print('2*list:',2*list)
print('2*arr1:',2*arr1)
```

Listing 2.5 contains a Python list called list and a NumPy array called `arr1`. The `print()` statements display the contents of `list1` and `arr1`, as well as the result of doubling `list1` and `arr1`. Recall that "doubling" a Python list is different from doubling a Python array, which you can see in the output from launching Listing 2.5:

```
('list:  ', [1, 2, 3])
('arr1:  ', array([1, 2, 3]))
('2*list:', [1, 2, 3, 1, 2, 3])
('2*arr1:', array([2, 4, 6]))
```

DOUBLING THE ELEMENTS IN A LIST

Listing 2.6 displays the content of `double_list1.py` that illustrates how to double the elements in a Python list.

LISTING 2.6: double_list1.py

```
import numpy as np

list1 = [1,2,3]
list2 = []

for e in list1:
  list2.append(2*e)

print('list1:',list1)
print('list2:',list2)
```

Listing 2.6 contains a Python list called `list1` and an empty Python list called `list2`. The next code snippet iterates through the elements of `list1` and appends them to the variable `list2`. The pair of `print()` statements display the contents of `list1` and `list2` to show you that they are the same. The output from launching Listing 2.6 is here:

```
('list: ', [1, 2, 3])
('list2:', [2, 4, 6])
```

LISTS AND EXPONENTS

Listing 2.7 displays the content of `exponent_list1.py` that illustrates how to compute exponents of the elements in a Python list.

LISTING 2.7: exponent_list1.py

```
import numpy as np

list1 = [1,2,3]
list2 = []

for e in list1:
  list2.append(e*e) # e*e = squared

print('list1:',list1)
print('list2:',list2)
```

Listing 2.7 contains a Python list called `list1` and an empty Python list called `list2`. The next code snippet iterates through the elements of `list1` and appends the square of each element to the variable `list2`. The pair of `print()` statements displays the contents of `list1` and `list2`. The output from launching Listing 2.7 is here:

```
('list1:', [1, 2, 3])
('list2:', [1, 4, 9])
```

ARRAYS AND EXPONENTS

Listing 2.8 displays the content of `exponent_array1.py` that illustrates how to compute exponents of the elements in a NumPy array.

LISTING 2.8: exponent_array1.py

```
import numpy as np

arr1 = np.array([1,2,3])
arr2 = arr1**2
arr3 = arr1**3

print('arr1:',arr1)
print('arr2:',arr2)
print('arr3:',arr3)
```

Listing 2.8 contains a NumPy array called `arr1` followed by two NumPy arrays called `arr2` and `arr3`. Notice the compact manner in which the NumPy `arr2` is initialized with the square of the elements in in `arr1`, followed by the initialization of the NumPy array `arr3` with the cube of the elements in `arr1`. The three `print()` statements display the contents of `arr1`, `arr2`, and `arr3`. The output from launching Listing 2.8 is here:

```
('arr1:', array([1, 2, 3]))
('arr2:', array([1, 4, 9]))
('arr3:', array([ 1,  8, 27]))
```

MATH OPERATIONS AND ARRAYS

Listing 2.9 displays the content of `mathops_array1.py` that illustrates how to compute exponents of the elements in a NumPy array.

LISTING 2.9: mathops_array1.py

```
import numpy as np

arr1 = np.array([1,2,3])
sqrt = np.sqrt(arr1)
log1 = np.log(arr1)
exp1 = np.exp(arr1)

print('sqrt:',sqrt)
print('log1:',log1)
print('exp1:',exp1)
```

Listing 2.9 contains a NumPy array called `arr1` followed by three NumPy arrays called `sqrt`, `log1`, and `exp1` that are initialized with the square root, log, and exponential value of the elements in `arr1`, respectively. The three `print()` statements display the contents of `sqrt`, `log1`, and `exp1`. The output from launching Listing 2.9 is here:

```
('sqrt:', array([1.        , 1.41421356, 1.73205081]))
('log1:', array([0.        , 0.69314718, 1.09861229]))
('exp1:', array([2.71828183, 7.3890561,  20.08553692]))
```

WORKING WITH "–1" SUBRANGES WITH VECTORS

Listing 2.10 displays the content of `npsubarray2.py` that illustrates how to compute exponents of the elements in a NumPy array.

LISTING 2.10: npsubarray2.py

```
import numpy as np

# -1 => "all except the last element in …" (row or col)

arr1   = np.array([1,2,3,4,5])
print('arr1:',arr1)
print('arr1[0:-1]:',arr1[0:-1])
print('arr1[1:-1]:',arr1[1:-1])
print('arr1[::-1]:', arr1[::-1]) # reverse!
```

Listing 2.10 contains a NumPy array called `arr1` followed by four `print()` statements, each of which displays a different subrange of values in `arr1`. The output from launching Listing 2.10 is here:

```
('arr1:',       array([1, 2, 3, 4, 5]))
('arr1[0:-1]:', array([1, 2, 3, 4]))
('arr1[1:-1]:', array([2, 3, 4]))
('arr1[::-1]:', array([5, 4, 3, 2, 1]))
```

WORKING WITH "–1" SUBRANGES WITH ARRAYS

Listing 2.11 displays the content of `np2darray2.py` that illustrates how to compute exponents of the elements in a NumPy array.

LISTING 2.11: np2darray2.py

```
import numpy as np

# -1 => "the last element in …" (row or col)

arr1   = np.array([(1,2,3),(4,5,6),(7,8,9),(10,11,12)])
print('arr1:',          arr1)
print('arr1[-1,:]:',    arr1[-1,:])
print('arr1[:,-1]:',    arr1[:,-1])
print('arr1[-1:,-1]:',arr1[-1:,-1])
```

Listing 2.11 contains a NumPy array called `arr1` followed by four `print()` statements, each of which displays a different subrange of values in `arr1`. The output from launching Listing 2.11 is here:

```
(arr1:', array([[1,  2,  3],
                [4,  5,  6],
                [7,  8,  9],
                [10, 11, 12]]))
(arr1[-1,:]]',   array([10, 11, 12]))
(arr1[:,-1]:',   array([3,  6,  9, 12]))
(arr1[-1:,-1]]', array([12]))
```

OTHER USEFUL NUMPY METHODS

In addition to the NumPy methods that you saw in the code samples prior to this section, the following NumPy methods are also useful.

- The method `np.zeros()` initializes an array with 0 values.
- The method `np.ones()` initializes an array with 1 value.
- The method `np.empty()` initializes an array with 0 values.
- The method `np.arange()` provides a range of numbers.
- The method `np.shape()` displays the shape of an object.
- The method `np.reshape()` <= *very useful!*
- The method `np.linspace()` <= *useful in regression*
- The method `np.mean()` computes the mean of a set of numbers.
- The method `np.std()` computes the standard deviation of a set of numbers.

Although the `np.zeros()` and `np.empty()` both initialize a `2D` array with 0, `np.zeros()` requires less execution time. You could also use `np.full(size, 0)`, but this method is the slowest of all three methods.

The `reshape()` method and the `linspace()` method are very useful for changing the dimensions of an array and generating a list of numeric values, respectively. The `reshape()` method often appears in TensorFlow code, and the `linspace()` method is useful for generating a set of numbers in linear regression. More details about the methods `np.reshape()` and `np.linspace()` are provided later in this chapter.

The `mean()` and `std()` methods are useful for calculating the mean and the standard deviation of a set of numbers, respectively. For example, you can use these two methods to resize the values in a Gaussian distribution so that their mean is 0 and the standard deviation is 1. This process is called *standardizing* a Gaussian distribution.

ARRAYS AND VECTOR OPERATIONS

Listing 2.12 displays the content of `array_vector.py` that illustrates how to perform vector operations on the elements in a NumPy array.

LISTING 2.12: array_vector.py

```
import numpy as np

a = np.array([[1,2], [3, 4]])
b = np.array([[5,6], [7,8]])

print('a:         ', a)
print('b:         ', b)
print('a + b:     ', a+b)
print('a - b:     ', a-b)
print('a * b:     ', a*b)
print('a / b:     ', a/b)
print('b / a:     ', b/a)
print('a.dot(b):',a.dot(b))
```

Listing 2.12 contains two NumPy arrays called `a` and `b` followed by eight `print()` statements, each of which displays the result of "applying" a different arithmetic operation to the NumPy arrays `a` and `b`. The output from launching Listing 2.12 is here:

```
('a    :    ', array([[1, 2], [3, 4]]))
('b    :    ', array([[5, 6], [7, 8]]))
('a + b:    ', array([[ 6,  8], [10, 12]]))
('a - b:    ', array([[-4, -4], [-4, -4]]))
('a * b:    ', array([[ 5, 12], [21, 32]]))
('a / b:    ', array([[0, 0], [0, 0]]))
('b / a:    ', array([[5, 3], [2, 2]]))
('a.dot(b):', array([[19, 22], [43, 50]]))
```

NUMPY AND DOT PRODUCTS (1)

Listing 2.13 displays the content of `dotproduct1.py` that illustrates how to perform the dot product on the elements in a NumPy array.

LISTING 2.13: dotproduct1.py

```
import numpy as np

a = np.array([1,2])
b = np.array([2,3])

dot2 = 0
for e,f in zip(a,b):
  dot2 += e*f
```

```
print('a:    ',a)
print('b:    ',b)
print('a*b:  ',a*b)
print('dot1:',a.dot(b))
print('dot2:',dot2)
```

Listing 2.13 contains two NumPy arrays called `a` and `b` followed by a simple loop that computes the dot product of `a` and `b`. The next section contains five `print()` statements that display the contents of `a` and `b`, as well as their inner product that is calculated in three different ways. The output from launching Listing 2.13 is here:

```
('a:    ', array([1, 2]))
('b:    ', array([2, 3]))
('a*b:  ', array([2, 6]))
('dot1:', 8)
('dot2:', 8)
```

NUMPY AND DOT PRODUCTS (2)

NumPy arrays support a "dot" method for calculating the inner product of an array of numbers, which uses the same formula used for calculating the inner product of a pair of vectors. Listing 2.14 displays the content of `dotproduct2.py` that illustrates how to calculate the dot product of two NumPy arrays.

LISTING 2.14: dotproduct2.py

```
import numpy as np

a = np.array([1,2])
b = np.array([2,3])

print('a:             ',a)
print('b:             ',b)
print('a.dot(b):      ',a.dot(b))
print('b.dot(a):      ',b.dot(a))
print('np.dot(a,b):',np.dot(a,b))
print('np.dot(b,a):',np.dot(b,a))
```

Listing 2.14 contains two NumPy arrays called `a` and `b` followed by six `print()` statements that display the contents of `a` and `b`, as well as their inner product that is calculated in three different ways. The output from launching Listing 2.14 is here:

```
('a:             ', array([1, 2]))
('b:             ', array([2, 3]))
('a.dot(b):      ', 8)
('b.dot(a):      ', 8)
('np.dot(a,b):', 8)
('np.dot(b,a):', 8)
```

NUMPY AND THE LENGTH OF VECTORS

The *norm* of a vector (or an array of numbers) is the length of a vector, which is the square root of the dot product of a vector with itself. NumPy also provides the "sum" and "square" functions that you can use to calculate the norm of a vector.

Listing 2.15 displays the content of `array_norm.py` that illustrates how to calculate the magnitude ("norm") of a NumPy array of numbers.

LISTING 2.15: array_norm.py

```
import numpy as np

a = np.array([2,3])
asquare = np.square(a)
asqsum  = np.sum(np.square(a))
anorm1  = np.sqrt(np.sum(a*a))
anorm2  = np.sqrt(np.sum(np.square(a)))
anorm3  = np.linalg.norm(a)

print('a:       ',a)
print('asquare:',asquare)
print('asqsum: ',asqsum)
print('anorm1: ',anorm1)
print('anorm2: ',anorm2)
print('anorm3: ',anorm3)
```

Listing 2.15 contains an initial NumPy array called `a`, followed by the NumPy array `asquare` and the numeric values `asqsum`, `anorm1`, `anorm2`, and `anorm3`. The NumPy array `asquare` contains the square of the elements in the NumPy array `a`, and the numeric value `asqsum` contains the sum of the elements in the NumPy array `asquare`.

Next, the numeric value `anorm1` equals the square root of the sum of the square of the elements in `a`. The numeric value `anorm2` is the same as `anorm1`, computed in a slightly different fashion. Finally, the numeric value `anorm3` is equal to `anorm2`, but as you can see, `anorm3` is calculated via a single NumPy method, whereas `anorm2` requires a succession of NumPy methods.

The last portion of Listing 2.15 consists of six `print()` statements, each of which displays the computed values. The output from launching Listing 2.15 is here:

```
('a:       ', array([2, 3]))
('asquare:', array([4, 9]))
('asqsum: ', 13)
('anorm1: ', 3.605551275463989)
('anorm2: ', 3.605551275463989)
('anorm3: ', 3.605551275463989)
```

NUMPY AND OTHER OPERATIONS

NumPy provides the "*" operator to multiply the components of two vectors to produce a third vector whose components are the products of the corresponding components of the initial pair of vectors. This operation is called a *Hadamard product*, which is the name of a famous mathematician. If you then add the components of the third vector, the sum is equal to the inner product of the initial pair of vectors.

Listing 2.16 displays the content of `otherops.py` that illustrates how to perform other operations on a NumPy array.

LISTING 2.16: otherops.py

```
import numpy as np

a = np.array([1,2])
b = np.array([3,4])

print('a:              ',a)
print('b:              ',b)
print('a*b:            ',a*b)
print('np.sum(a*b):  ',np.sum(a*b))
print('(a*b.sum()):  ',(a*b).sum())
```

Listing 2.16 contains two NumPy arrays called `a` and `b` followed five `print()` statements that display the contents of `a` and `b`, their Hadamard product, and their inner product that is calculated in two different ways. The output from launching Listing 2.16 is here:

```
('a:             ', array([1, 2]))
('b:             ', array([3, 4]))
('a*b:           ', array([3, 8]))
('np.sum(a*b): ', 11)
('(a*b.sum()): ', 11)
```

NUMPY AND THE RESHAPE() METHOD

NumPy arrays support the `reshape()` method, which allows you to restructure the dimensions of an array of numbers. In general, if a NumPy array contains `m` elements, where `m` is a positive integer, then that array can be restructured as an `m1` x `m2` NumPy array, where `m1` and `m2` are positive integers such that `m1*m2 = m`.

Listing 2.17 displays the content of `numpy_reshape.py` that illustrates how to use the `reshape()` method on a NumPy array.

LISTING 2.17: numpy_reshape.py

```
import numpy as np

x = np.array([[2, 3], [4, 5], [6, 7]])
print(x.shape) # (3, 2)

x = x.reshape((2, 3))
print(x.shape) # (2, 3)
print('x1:',x)

x = x.reshape((-1))
print(x.shape) # (6,)
print('x2:',x)

x = x.reshape((6, -1))
print(x.shape) # (6, 1)
print('x3:',x)

x = x.reshape((-1, 6))
print(x.shape) # (1, 6)
print('x4:',x)
```

Listing 2.17 contains a NumPy array called `x` whose dimensions are 3x2, followed by a set of invocations of the `reshape()` method that reshapes the contents of `x`. The first invocation of the `reshape()` method changes the shape of `x` from 3x2 to 2x3. The second invocation changes the shape of `x` from 2x3 to 6x1. The third invocation changes the shape of `x` from 1x6 to 6x1. The final invocation changes the shape of `x` from 6x1 to 1x6 again.

Each invocation of the `reshape()` method is followed by a `print()` statement so that you can see the effect of the invocation. The output from launching Listing 2.17 is here:

```
(3, 2)
(2, 3)
('x1:', array([[2, 3, 4],
       [5, 6, 7]]))
(6,)
('x2:', array([2, 3, 4, 5, 6, 7]))
(6, 1)
('x3:', array([[2],
       [3],
       [4],
       [5],
       [6],
       [7]]))
(1, 6)
```

CALCULATING THE MEAN AND STANDARD DEVIATION

If you need to review these concepts from statistics (and perhaps also the mean, median, and mode as well), please read the appropriate online tutorials.

NumPy provides various built-in functions that perform statistical calculations, such as the following list of methods:

```
np.linspace() <= useful for regression
np.mean()
np.std()
```

The `np.linspace()` method generates a set of equally-spaced numbers between a lower bound and an upper bound. The `np.mean()` and `np.std()` methods calculate the mean and standard deviation, respectively, of a set of numbers. Listing 2.18 displays the content of `sample_mean_std.py` that illustrates how to calculate statistical values from a NumPy array.

LISTING 2.18: sample_mean_std.py

```
import numpy as np

x2 = np.arange(8)
print('mean = ',x2.mean())
print('std  = ',x2.std())

x3 = (x2 - x2.mean())/x2.std()
print('x3 mean = ',x3.mean())
print('x3 std  = ',x3.std())
```

Listing 2.18 contains a NumPy array `x2` that consists of the first eight integers. Next, the `mean()` and `std()` "associated" with `x2` are invoked to calculate the mean and standard deviation, respectively, of the elements of `x2`. The output from launching Listing 2.18 is here:

```
('a:              ', array([1, 2]))
('b:              ', array([3, 4]))
```

CODE SAMPLE WITH MEAN AND STANDARD DEVIATION

The code sample in this section extends the code sample in the previous section with additional statistical values, and the code in Listing 2.19 can be used for any data distribution. Keep in mind that the code sample uses random numbers simply for the purposes of illustration: after you have launched the code sample, replace those numbers with values from a CSV file or some other dataset containing meaningful values.

Moreover, this section does not provide details regarding the meaning of quartiles, but you can learn about quartiles at *https://en.wikipedia.org/wiki/Quartile*.

Listing 2.19 displays the content of `stat_values.py` that illustrates how to display various statistical values from a NumPy array of random numbers.

LISTING 2.19: stat_values.py

```
import numpy as np

from numpy import percentile
from numpy.random import rand

# generate data sample
data = np.random.rand(1000)

# calculate quartiles, min, and max
quartiles = percentile(data, [25, 50, 75])
data_min, data_max = data.min(), data.max()

# print summary information
print('Minimum:  %.3f' % data_min)
print('Q1 value: %.3f' % quartiles[0])
print('Median:   %.3f' % quartiles[1])
print('Mean Val: %.3f' % data.mean())
print('Std Dev:  %.3f' % data.std())
print('Q3 value: %.3f' % quartiles[2])
print('Maximum:  %.3f' % data_max)
```

The data sample (shown in bold) in Listing 2.19 is from a uniform distribution between 0 and 1. The NumPy `percentile()` function calculates a linear interpolation (average) between observations, which is needed to calculate the median on a sample with an even number of values. As you can surmise, the NumPy functions `min()` and `max()` calculate the smallest and largest values in the data sample. The output from launching Listing 2.19 is here:

```
Minimum:  0.000
Q1 value: 0.237
Median:   0.500
Mean Val: 0.495
Std Dev:  0.295
Q3 value: 0.747
Maximum:  0.999
```

Trimmed Mean and Weighted Mean

In addition to the arithmetic mean, there are variants that are known as the trimmed mean (also called the "truncated mean") and the weighted mean.

A *trimmed mean* is a robust estimate (i.e., a metric that is not sensitive to outliers). As a simple example of a trimmed mean, suppose that you have five scores for the evaluation of a product: simply drop the highest and lowest scores and then compute the average of the remaining three scores. If you have multiple sets of five scores, repeat the preceding process and then compute the average of the set of trimmed mean values.

A *weighted mean* is useful when sample data does not represent different groups in a dataset. Assigning a larger weight to groups that are under-represented yields a weighted mean that more accurately represents the various groups in the dataset. However, keep in mind that outliers can affect the mean as well as the weighted mean.

The weighted mean is the same as the expected value. If you are unfamiliar with the notion of an expected value, suppose that the set `P = {p1,p2,...,pn}` is a probability distribution, which means that the numeric values in the set `P` must be non-negative and have a sum equal to 1. In addition, suppose that `V = {v1,v2,...,vn}` is a set of numeric scores that are assigned to `n` features of a product `M`. For example, the values in the set V could be positive integers in some range (e.g., between 1 and 10) that represent "rewards".

Then the *expected value* `E` for that product is computed as follows:

```
E = p1*v1 + p2*v2 + ... + pn*vn
```

The Python code samples in the next several sections contain some rudimentary APIs from Matplotlib. The code samples start with simple examples of line segments, followed by an introduction to Linear Regression.

WORKING WITH LINES IN THE PLANE (OPTIONAL)

This section contains a short review of lines in the Euclidean plane, so you can skip this section if you are comfortable with this topic. A minor point that is often overlooked is that lines in the Euclidean plane have infinite length. If you select two distinct points of a line, then all the points between those two selected points are a *line segment*. A *ray* is a "half infinite" line: when you select one point as an endpoint, then all the points on one side of the line constitute a ray.

For example, the points in the plane whose y-coordinate is 0 form a line along the x-axis, whereas the points between (0,0) and (1,0) on the x-axis form a line segment. In addition, the points on the x-axis that are to the right of (0,0) form a ray, and the points on the x-axis that are to the left of (0,0) also form a ray.

For simplicity and convenience, in this book we will use the terms "line" and "line segment" interchangeably. Now, let's delve into the details of lines in the Euclidean plane. Here is the equation of a (non-vertical) line in the Euclidean plane:

```
y = m*x + b
```

The value of `m` is the slope of the line and the value of `b` is the y-intercept (i.e., the place where the non-vertical line intersects the y-axis). The following form for a line in the plane is a general equation that includes vertical lines:

```
a*x + b*y + c = 0
```

However, we will not be working with vertical lines, so we will continue using the first formula. Figure 2.1 displays three horizontal lines whose equations (from top to bottom) are `y = 3`, `y = 0`, and `y = -3`.

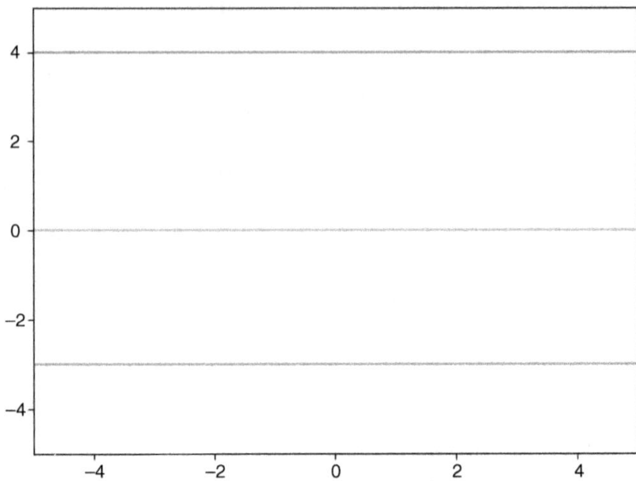

FIGURE 2.1 A graph of three horizontal line segments

Figure 2.2 displays two slanted lines whose equations are y = x and y = -x.

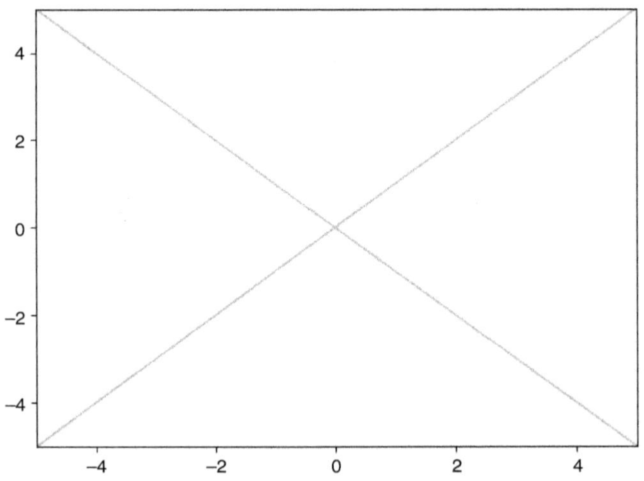

FIGURE 2.2 A graph of two diagonal line segments

Figure 2.3 displays two slanted parallel lines whose equations are `y = 2*x` and `y = 2*x+3`.

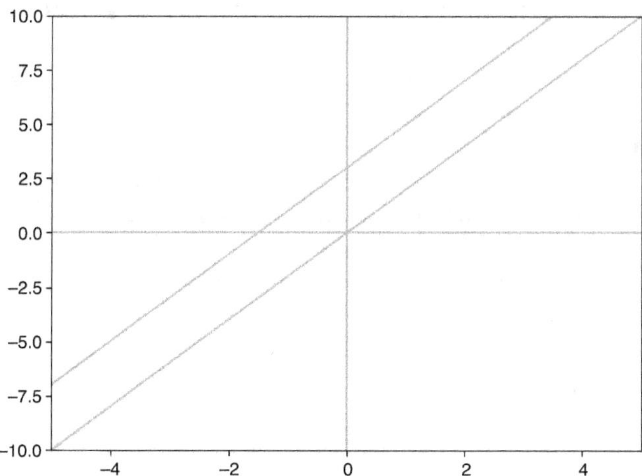

FIGURE 2.3 A graph of two slanted parallel line segments

Figure 2.4 displays a piece-wise linear graph consisting of connected line segments.

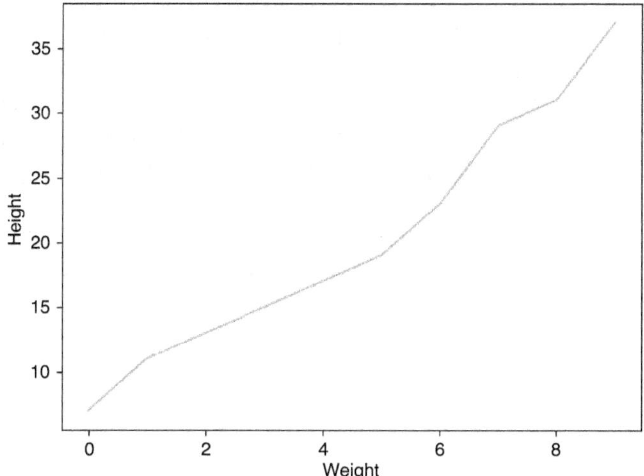

FIGURE 2.4 A piece-wise linear graph of line segments

Now that you have seen some basic examples of lines in the Euclidean plane, let's look at some code samples that use NumPy and Matplotlib to display scatterplots of points in the plane.

PLOTTING RANDOMIZED POINTS WITH NUMPY AND MATPLOTLIB

The previous section contains simple examples of line segments, but the code is deferred until Chapter 7. This section and the next section contain code samples with Matplotlib APIs that are not discussed; however, the code is straightforward, so you can infer its purpose. In addition, you can learn more about Matplotlib in Chapter 7 (which focuses on data visualization) or read a short online tutorial for more details.

Listing 2.20 displays the content of `np_plot.py` that illustrates how to plot multiple points on a line in the plane.

LISTING 2.20: np_plot.py

```
import numpy as np
import matplotlib.pyplot as plt

x = np.random.randn(15,1)
y = 2.5*x + 5 + 0.2*np.random.randn(15,1)

plt.scatter(x,y)
plt.show()
```

Listing 2.20 starts with two `import` statements, followed by the initialization of `x` as a set of random values via the NumPy `randn()` API. Next, `y` is assigned a range of values that consist of two parts: a linear equation with input values from the `x` values, which is combined with a randomization factor. Figure 2.5 displays the output generated by the code in Listing 2.20.

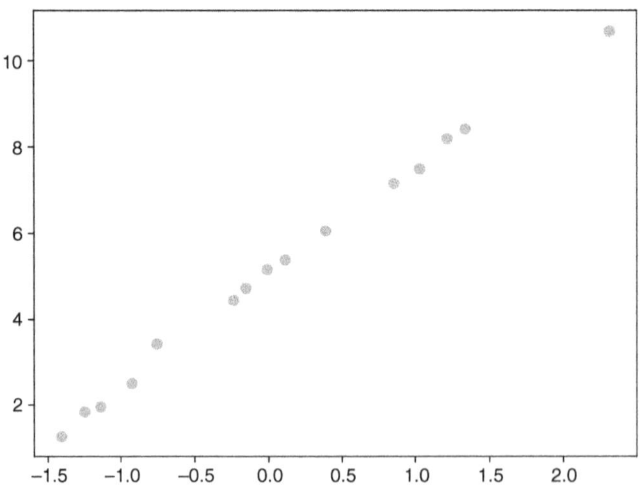

FIGURE 2.5 Datasets with potential linear regression

PLOTTING A QUADRATIC WITH NUMPY AND MATPLOTLIB

Listing 2.21 displays the content of `np_plot_quadratic.py` that illustrates how to plot a quadratic function in the plane.

LISTING 2.21: np_plot_quadratic.py

```
import numpy as np
import matplotlib.pyplot as plt

x = np.linspace(-5,5,num=100)[:,None]
y = -0.5 + 2.2*x +0.3*x**3+ 2*np.random.randn(100,1)

plt.plot(x,y)
plt.show()
```

Listing 2.21 starts with two `import` statements, followed by the initialization of `x` as a range of values via the NumPy `linspace()` API. Next, `y` is assigned a range of values that fit a quadratic equation, which are based on the values for the variable `x`. Figure 2.6 displays the output generated by the code in Listing 2.21.

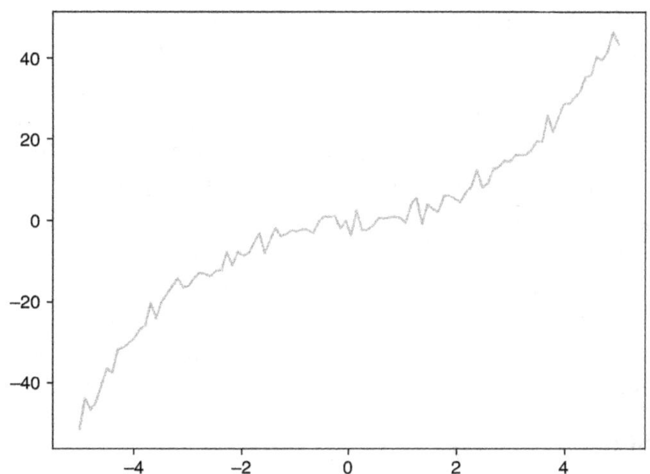

FIGURE 2.6 Datasets with potential linear regression, showing the output generated by the code in Listing 2.21

Now that you have seen an assortment of line graphs and scatterplots, let's delve into linear regression, which is the topic of the next section.

WHAT IS LINEAR REGRESSION?

Linear regression was created in 1805, and it is an important algorithm in statistical analysis and machine learning. Any decent statistical package supports linear regression and invariably supports polynomial regression. Linear regression involves lines, which are polynomials with degree one, whereas polynomial regression involves fitting polynomials of degrees greater than one to a dataset.

In general terms, linear regression finds the equation of the best-fitting hyperplane that approximates a dataset, where the hyperplane has degree one less than the dimensionality of the dataset. In particular, if the dataset is in the Euclidean plane, the hyperplane is simply a line; if the dataset is in 3D, the hyperplane is a "regular" plane.

Linear regression is suitable when the points in a dataset are distributed in such a way that they can reasonably be approximated by a hyperplane. If not, then you can try to fit other types of multi-variable polynomial surfaces to the points in the dataset.

Keep in mind two other details. First, the best-fitting hyperplane does not necessarily intersect all (or even most of) the points in the dataset. In fact, the best-fitting hyperplane might not intersect *any* points in the dataset. The purpose of a best-fitting hyperplane is to *approximate* the points in dataset as closely as possible. Second, linear regression is *not* the same as curve fitting, which attempts to find a polynomial that passes through a set of points.

Some details about curve fitting are as follows. Given `n` points in the plane (no two of which have the same `x` value), there is a polynomial of degree less than or equal to `n-1` that passes through those points. Thus, a line (which has degree 1) will pass through any pair of non-vertical points in the plane. For any triple of points in the plane, there is a quadratic equation or a line that passes through those points.

In some cases, a lower degree polynomial is available. For instance, consider the set of 100 points in which the `x` value equals the `y` value: clearly the line `y = x` (a polynomial of degree 1) passes through all of those points.

However, the extent to which a line "represents" a set of points in the plane depends on how closely those points can be approximated by a line.

What is Multivariate Analysis?

Multivariate analysis generalizes the equation of a line in the Euclidean plane, and it has the following form:

```
y = w1*x1 + w2*x2 + . . . + wn*xn + b
```

The preceding equation contains a linear combination of the variables `x1`, `x2`, . . ., `xn`. In this book we will usually work with datasets that involve lines in the Euclidean plane.

What about Non-Linear Datasets?

Simple linear regression finds the line that best fits a dataset, but what happens if the dataset does not fit a line in the plane? This is an excellent point! In such a scenario, we look for other curves to approximate the dataset, such as quadratic, cubic, or higher-degree polynomials. However, these alternatives involve trade-offs, as we will discuss later.

Another possibility is to use a continuous piece-wise linear function, which is a function that comprises a set of line segments, where adjacent line segments are connected. If one or more pairs of adjacent line segments are not connected, then it is a piece-wise linear function (i.e., the function is discontinuous). In either case, line segments have degree one, which involves lower computational complexity than higher order polynomials.

Thus, given a set of points in the plane, try to find the best-fitting line that fits those points after addressing the following questions:

1. How do we know that a line "fits" the data?
2. What if a different type of curve is a better fit?
3. What does "best fit" mean?

One way to check if a line fits the data well is through a simple visual check: display the data in a graph and if the data conforms to the shape of a line reasonably well, then a line might be a good fit. However, this is a subjective decision, and a sample dataset that does not fit a line is displayed in Figure 2.7.

Figure 2.7 displays a dataset containing four points that do not fit a line.

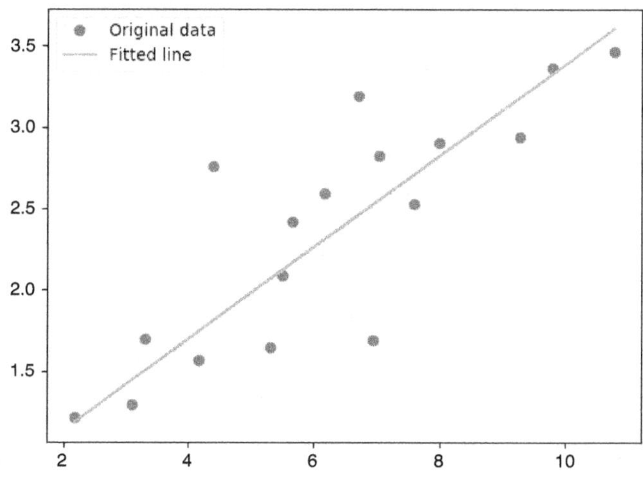

FIGURE 2.7 A non-linear dataset

However, if a line does not appear to be a good fit for the data, then perhaps a quadratic or cubic (or even higher degree) polynomial has the potential of being a better fit. Let's defer the non-linear scenario and make the assumption that a line would be a good fit for the data. There is a well-known technique for finding the best-fitting line for such a dataset: the Mean Squared Error (MSE).

THE MSE (MEAN SQUARED ERROR) FORMULA

Figure 2.8 displays the formula for the MSE. The MSE is the sum of the squares of the difference between an *actual* y value and the *predicted* y value, divided by the number of points. Note that the predicted y value is the y value that each data point would have if that data point were actually on the best-fitting line.

In general, the goal is to minimize the error, which determines the best-fitting line in the case of linear regression. However, you might be satisfied with a "good enough" value when the time and/or cost for any additional reduction in the error is deemed prohibitive, which means that this decision is not a purely programmatic decision.

Figure 2.8 displays the formula for the MSE for calculating the best-fitting line for a set of points in the plane.

$$\text{MSE} = \frac{1}{n}\sum_{i=1}^{n}(Y_i - \hat{Y_i})^2.$$

FIGURE 2.8 The MSE formula

Other Error Types

Although we only discuss the MSE for linear regression in this book, there are other types of formulas for errors that you can use for linear regression, some of which are listed here:

- MAE
- RMSE
- RMSPROP
- MAE

The MSE is the basis for the preceding error types. For example, the RMSE is the Root Mean Squared Error, which is the square root of the MSE.

The MAE is the Mean Absolute Error, which is *the sum of the absolute value of the differences of the y terms* (not the square of the differences of the y terms).

The RMSProp optimizer utilizes the magnitude of recent gradients to normalize the gradients. Maintain a moving average over the RMS (root mean squared, which is the square root of the MSE) gradients, and then divide that term by the current gradient.

Although it is easier to compute the derivative of the MSE (because it is a differentiable function), it is also true that the MSE is more susceptible to outliers, more so than the MAE. The reason is simple: a squared term can be significantly larger than adding the absolute value of a term. For example, if a difference term is 10, then the squared term 100 is added to the MSE, whereas only 10 is added to the MAE. Similarly, if a difference term is -20, then the squared term 400 is added to the MSE, whereas only 20 (which is the absolute value of -20) is added to the MAE.

Non-Linear Least Squares

When predicting housing prices, where the dataset contains a wide range of values, techniques such as linear regression or random forests can cause the model to "overfit" the samples with the highest values in order to reduce quantities such as the mean absolute error.

In this scenario, you probably want an error metric, such as relative error, that reduces the importance of fitting the samples with the largest values. This technique is called *non-linear least squares*, which may use a log-based transformation of labels and predicted values.

CALCULATING THE MSE MANUALLY

Let's look at two simple graphs, each of which contains a line that approximates a set of points in a scatterplot. Notice that the line segment is the same for both sets of points, but the datasets are slightly different. We will manually calculate the MSE for both datasets and determine which value of the MSE is smaller.

Figure 2.9 displays a set of points and a line that is a potential candidate for best-fitting line for the data.

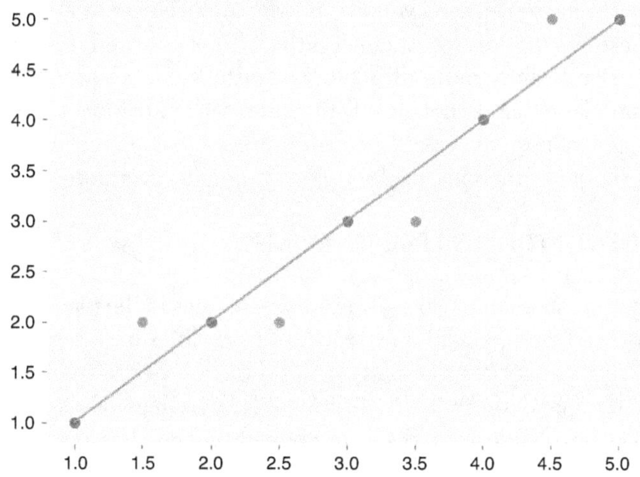

FIGURE 2.9 A line graph that approximates the points of a scatterplot

The MSE for the line in Figure 2.9 is computed as follows:

```
MSE = 1*1 + (-1)*(-1) + (-1)*(-1) + 1*1 = 4
```

Now look at Figure 2.10, which also displays a set of points and a line that is a potential candidate for the best-fitting line of the data.

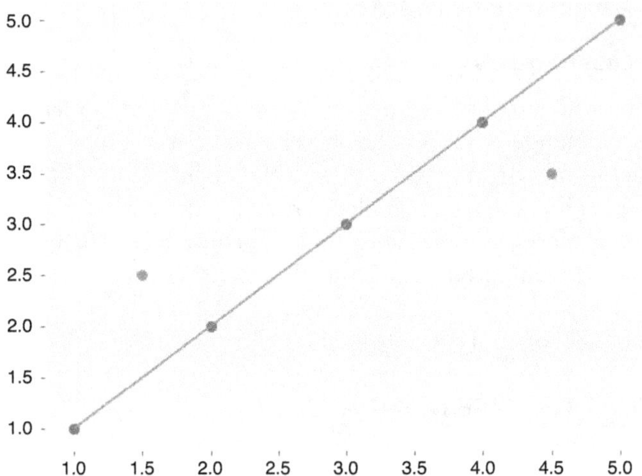

FIGURE 2.10 A line graph that approximates the points of a scatterplot

The `MSE` for the line in Figure 2.10 is computed as follows:

```
MSE = (-2)*(-2) + 2*2 = 8
```

Thus, the line in Figure 2.10 has a smaller `MSE` than the line in Figure 2.9, which might have surprised you (or did you guess correctly?)

In these two figures we calculated the MSE easily and quickly, but in general, it is significantly more difficult. For instance, if we plot 10 points in the Euclidean plane that do not closely fit a line, with individual terms that involve non-integer values, we would probably need a calculator. A better solution involves NumPy functions, as discussed in the next section.

FIND THE BEST-FITTING LINE IN NUMPY

Earlier in this chapter, you saw examples of lines in the plane, including horizontal, slanted, and parallel lines. Most of those lines have a positive slope and a non-zero value for their y-intercept. Although there are scatterplots of data points in the plane where the best-fitting line has a negative slope, the examples in this book involve scatterplots whose best-fitting line has a positive slope.

Listing 2.22 displays the content of `find_best_fit.py` that illustrates how to determine the best-fitting line for a set of points in the Euclidean plane. The solution is based on "closed form" formulas, which are available from statistics.

LISTING 2.22: find_best_fit.py

```
import numpy as np

xs = np.array([1,2,3,4,5], dtype=np.float64)
ys = np.array([1,2,3,4,5], dtype=np.float64)

def best_fit_slope(xs,ys):
  m = (((np.mean(xs)*np.mean(ys))-np.mean(xs*ys)) /
       ((np.mean(xs)**2) - np.mean(xs**2)))
  b = np.mean(ys) - m * np.mean(xs)

  return m, b

m,b = best_fit_slope(xs,ys)
print('m:',m,'b:',b)
```

Listing 2.22 starts with two NumPy arrays `xs` and `ys` that are initialized with the first five positive integers. The Python function `best_fit_slope()` calculates the optimal values of `m` (the slope) and `b` (the y-intercept) of a set of numbers. The output from Listing 2.22 is here:

```
m: 1.0 b: 0.0
```

Notice that the NumPy arrays `xs` and `ys` are identical, which means that these points lie on the identity function whose slope is 1. By simple extrapolation, the point (0,0) is also a point on the same line. Hence, the y-intercept of this line must equal 0.

If you are interested, you can search online to find the derivation for the values of `m` and `b`. In this chapter, we will skip the derivation and proceed with examples of calculating the MSE. The first example involves calculating the MSE manually, followed by an example that uses NumPy formulas to perform the calculations.

CALCULATING THE MSE BY SUCCESSIVE APPROXIMATION (1)

This section contains a code sample that uses a simple technique for successively determining better approximations for the slope and y-intercept of the best-fitting line. Recall that an approximation of a derivative is the ratio of "delta y" divided by "delta x." The "delta" values calculate the difference of the y values and the difference of the x values, respectively, of two nearby points `(x1,y1)` and `(x2,y2)` on a function. Hence, the delta-based approximation ratio is `(y2-y1)/(x2-x1)`.

The technique in this section involves a simplified approximation for the "delta" values: we assume that the denominators are equal to 1. As a result, we need only calculate the numerators of the "delta" values: in this code sample, those numerators are the variables `dw` and `db`.

Listing 2.23 displays the content of `plain_linreg1.py` that illustrates how to compute the MSE with simulated data.

LISTING 2.23: plain_linreg1.py

```
import numpy as np
import matplotlib.pyplot as plt

X = [0,0.12,0.25,0.27,0.38,0.42,0.44,0.55,0.92,1.0]
Y = [0,0.15,0.54,0.51,0.34,0.1, 0.19,0.53,1.0,0.58]

losses = []
#Step 1: Parameter initialization
W = 0.45 # the initial slope
b = 0.75 # the initial y-intercept

for i in range(1, 100):
  #Step 2: Calculate Loss
  Y_pred = np.multiply(W, X) + b
  loss_error = 0.5 * (Y_pred - Y)**2
  loss = np.sum(loss_error)/10

  #Step 3: Calculate dw and db
  db = np.sum((Y_pred - Y))
  dw = np.dot((Y_pred - Y), X)
  losses.append(loss)

  #Step 4: Update parameters:
  W = W - 0.01*dw
  b = b - 0.01*db

  if i%10 == 0:
    print("Loss at", i,"iteration = ", loss)

#Step 5: Repeat via a for loop with 1000 iterations

#Plot loss versus # of iterations
print("W = ", W,"& b = ",  b)
plt.plot(losses)
plt.ylabel('loss')
plt.xlabel('iterations (per tens)')
plt.show()
```

Listing 2.23 defines the variables `X` and `Y` that are simple arrays of numbers (this is our dataset). Next, the losses array is initialized as an empty array, and we will append successive loss approximations to this array. The variables `W` and `b` correspond to the slope and y-intercept, and they are initialized with the values 0.45 and 0.75, respectively (feel free to experiment with these values).

The next portion of Listing 2.23 is a for loop that executes 100 times. During each iteration, the variables `Y_pred`, `loss_error`, and `loss` are computed, and they correspond to the predicted value, the error, and the loss, respectively (remember: we are performing linear regression). The value of `loss` (which is the error for the current iteration) is then appended to the `losses` array.

Next, the variables dw and db are calculated: these correspond to the "delta w" and "delta b" that we will use to update the values of W and b, respectively. The code is reproduced here:

```
#Step 4: Update parameters:
W = W - 0.01*dw
b = b - 0.01*db
```

Notice that dw and db are both multiplied by the value 0.01, which is the value of our "learning rate" (experiment with this value as well).

The next code snippet displays the current cost, which is performed every tenth iteration through the loop. When the loop finishes execution, the values of W and b are displayed, and a plot is displayed that shows the cost values on the vertical axis and the loop iterations on the horizontal axis. The output from Listing 2.23 is here:

```
Loss at 10 iteration =  0.04114630674619491
Loss at 20 iteration =  0.026706242729839395
Loss at 30 iteration =  0.024738889446900423
Loss at 40 iteration =  0.023850565034634254
Loss at 50 iteration =  0.0231499048706651
Loss at 60 iteration =  0.02255361434242207
Loss at 70 iteration =  0.0220425055291673
Loss at 80 iteration =  0.021604128492245713
Loss at 90 iteration =  0.021228111750568435
W =  0.47256473531193927 & b =  0.19578262688662174
```

Figure 2.11 displays the plot of cost-versus-iterations for Listing 2.23.

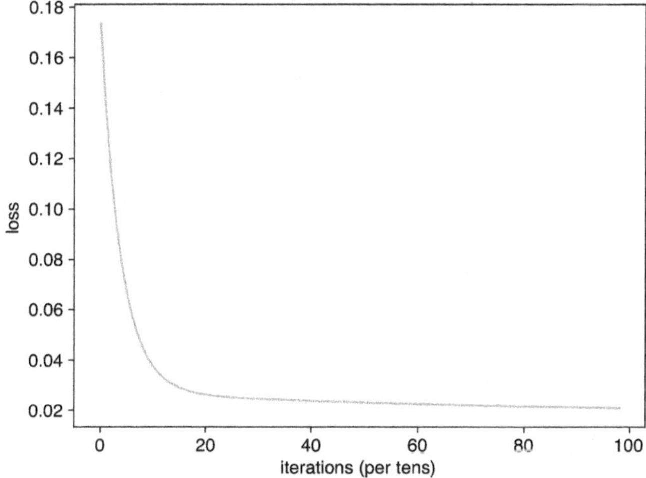

FIGURE 2.11 A plot of cost-versus-iterations

CALCULATING THE MSE BY SUCCESSIVE APPROXIMATION (2)

In the previous section, you saw how to calculate "delta" approximations to determine the equation of a best-fitting line for a set of points in a 2D plane. The example in this section generalizes the code in the previous section by adding an outer loop that represents the number of epochs. The number of epochs specifies the number of times that an inner loop is executed.

Listing 2.24 displays the content of `plain_linreg2.py` that illustrates how to compute the MSE with simulated data.

LISTING 2.24: plain_linreg2.py

```
import numpy as np
import matplotlib.pyplot as plt

# %matplotlib inline
X = [0,0.12,0.25,0.27,0.38,0.42,0.44,0.55,0.92,1.0]
Y = [0,0.15,0.54,0.51, 0.34,0.1,0.19,0.53,1.0,0.58]

#uncomment to see a plot of X versus Y values
#plt.plot(X,Y)
#plt.show()

losses = []
#Step 1: Parameter initialization
W = 0.45
b = 0.75

epochs = 100
lr = 0.001

for j in range(1, epochs):
  for i in range(1, 100):
    #Step 2: Calculate Loss
    Y_pred = np.multiply(W, X) + b
    Loss_error = 0.5 * (Y_pred - Y)**2
    loss = np.sum(Loss_error)/10

    #Step 3: Calculate dW and db
    db = np.sum((Y_pred - Y))
    dw = np.dot((Y_pred - Y), X)
    losses.append(loss)

    #Step 4: Update parameters:
    W = W - lr*dw
    b = b - lr*db

    if i%50 == 0:
      print("Loss at epoch", j,"= ", loss)

#Plot loss versus # of iterations
print("W = ", W,"& b = ",  b)
```

```
plt.plot(losses)
plt.ylabel('loss')
plt.xlabel('iterations (per tens)')
plt.show()
```

Compare the new contents of Listing 2.24 (shown in bold) with the contents of Listing 2.23: the changes are minimal, and the main difference is to execute the inner loop 100 times for each iteration of the outer loop, which also executes 100 times. The output from Listing 2.24 is here:

```
('Loss at epoch', 1, '= ', 0.07161762489862147)
('Loss at epoch', 2, '= ', 0.030073922512586938)
('Loss at epoch', 3, '= ', 0.02541552899298472)
('Loss at epoch', 4, '= ', 0.024227826373677794)
('Loss at epoch', 5, '= ', 0.02346241967071181)
('Loss at epoch', 6, '= ', 0.022827707922883803)
('Loss at epoch', 7, '= ', 0.022284262669854064)
('Loss at epoch', 8, '= ', 0.02181735173716673)
('Loss at epoch', 9, '= ', 0.021416050179776294)
('Loss at epoch', 10, '= ', 0.021071125409343844)
// details omitted for brevity
('Loss at epoch', 90, '= ', 0.018960749188638278)
('Loss at epoch', 91, '= ', 0.01896074755776306)
('Loss at epoch', 92, '= ', 0.018960746155994725)
('Loss at epoch', 93, '= ', 0.018960744951148113)
('Loss at epoch', 94, '= ', 0.018960743915559485)
('Loss at epoch', 95, '= ', 0.018960743025451313)
('Loss at epoch', 96, '= ', 0.018960742260386375)
('Loss at epoch', 97, '= ', 0.018960741602798474)
('Loss at epoch', 98, '= ', 0.018960741037589136)
('Loss at epoch', 99, '= ', 0.018960740551780944)
('W = ', 0.6764145874436108, '& b = ', 0.09976839618922698)
```

Figure 2.12 displays the plot of loss-versus-iterations for Listing 2.24.

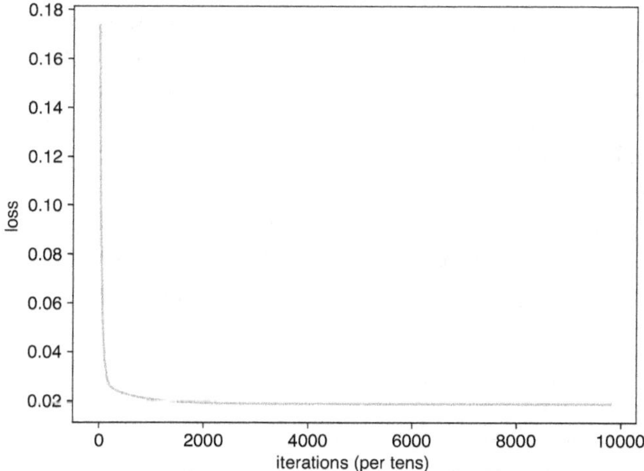

FIGURE 2.12 A plot of loss-versus-iterations

Notice that Figure 2.12 has 10,000 iterations on the horizontal axis, whereas Figure 2.11 has only 100 iterations on the horizontal axis.

GOOGLE COLABORATORY

Depending on the hardware, GPU-based TF 2 code is typically at least 15 times faster than CPU-based TF 2 code. However, the cost of a good GPU can be a significant factor. Although NVIDIA provides GPUs, those consumer-based GPUs are not optimized for multi-GPU support (which *is* supported by TF 2).

Fortunately, Google Colaboratory is an affordable alternative that provides free GPU support, and also runs as a Jupyter notebook environment. In addition, Google Colaboratory executes your code in the cloud and involves zero configuration, and it is available at *https://colab.research.google.com/notebooks/welcome.ipynb*.

The Jupyter notebook is suitable for training simple models and testing ideas quickly. Google Colaboratory makes it easy to upload local files, install software in Jupyter notebooks, and even connect Google Colaboratory to a Jupyter runtime on your local machine.

Some of the supported features of Colaboratory include TF 2 execution with GPUs, visualization using Matplotlib, and the ability to save a copy of your Google Colaboratory notebook to Github by using `File > Save a copy to GitHub`.

Moreover, you can load any `.ipynb` on GitHub by just adding the path to the URL *colab.research.google.com/github/* (see the Colaboratory website for details).

Google Colaboratory has support for other technologies, such as HTML and SVG, enabling you to render SVG-based graphics in notebooks that are in Google Colaboratory. Remember that any software you install in a Google Colaboratory notebook is only available on a per-session basis: if you log out and log in again, you need to perform the same installation steps that you performed during your earlier Google Colaboratory session.

There is one other *very* nice feature of Google Colaboratory: you can execute code on a GPU for up to twelve hours per day for free. This free GPU support is extremely useful for people who do not have a suitable GPU on their local machine (which is probably the majority of users). Now, they can launch TF 2 code to train neural networks in less than 20 or 30 minutes, a process that would otherwise require multiple hours of CPU-based execution time.

You can launch Tensorboard inside a Google Colaboratory notebook with the following command (replace the specified directory with your own location):

```
%tensorboard --logdir /logs/images
```

Keep in mind the following details about Google Colaboratory. First, whenever you connect to a server in Google Colaboratory, you start a *session*.

You can execute the code in a session with a CPU (the default), GPU, or TPU (which is available for free), and you can execute your code without any time limit for your session. However, if you select the GPU option for your session, *only the first 12 hours of GPU execution time are free*. Any additional GPU time during that same session incurs a small charge (see the website for those details).

The other point to keep in mind is that any software that you install in a Jupyter notebook during a given session will *not* be saved when you exit that session. For example, the following code snippet installs `TFLearn` in a Jupyter notebook:

```
!pip install tflearn
```

When you exit the current session and later, start a new session, you need to install `TFLearn` again, as well as any other software (such as Github repositories) that you also installed in any previous session.

Incidentally, you can also run TF 2 code and TensorBoard in Google Colaboratory. Navigate to this URL for more information:

https://www.tensorflow.org/tensorboard/r2/tensorboard_in_notebooks

Uploading CSV Files in Google Colaboratory

Listing 2.25 displays the content `upload_csv_file.ipynb` that illustrates how to upload a CSV file in a Google Colaboratory notebook.

LISTING 2.25: upload_csv_file.ipynb

```
import pandas as pd

from google.colab import files
uploaded = files.upload()

df = pd.read_csv("weather_data.csv")
print("dataframe df:")
df
```

Listing 2.25 uploads the CSV file `weather_data.csv` whose contents are not shown because they are not important for this example. The code shown in bold is the Colaboratory-specific code that is required to upload the CSV file. When you launch this code, you will see a small button labeled "Browse," which you must click and then select the CSV file that is listed in the code snippet. After doing so, the rest of the code is executed and you will see the contents of the CSV file displayed in your browser session.

NOTE *You must supply the CSV file* `weather_data.csv` *if you want to launch this Jupyter notebook successfully in Google Colaboratory.*

SUMMARY

This chapter introduced you to the NumPy library for Python. You learned how to write Python scripts containing loops, arrays, and lists. You also saw how to work with dot products, the `reshape()` method, plotting with Matplotlib (discussed in more detail in Chapter 6), and examples of linear regression.

Then you learned how to work with subranges of arrays, and also negative subranges of vectors and arrays, both of which are very useful for extracting portions of datasets in machine learning tasks. You also saw various other NumPy operations, such as the `reshape()` method, which is useful when working with image files.

Next, you learned how to use NumPy for linear regression, the mean squared error (MSE), and how to calculate the MSE with the NumPy `linspace()` method. Finally, you had an introduction Google Colaboratory, where you can take advantage of the free GPU time when you launch Jupyter notebooks.

CHAPTER 3

PANDAS AND DATA VISUALIZATION

This chapter introduces the Pandas library and contains various code samples that illustrate some useful Pandas features. As you will see, the title of each section clearly indicates its contents, so you can easily scan this chapter for those sections that contain material that is new to you. This approach will help you make efficient use of your time when you read the contents of this chapter.

The first part of this chapter contains a brief introduction to Pandas, followed by code samples that illustrate how to define Pandas DataFrames and also display their attributes. Please keep in mind that this chapter is devoted to Pandas DataFrames. There is one code block that illustrates how to define a Pandas Series, and if you want to learn more about this Pandas Series, you can search online for more information.

The second part of this chapter discusses various types of DataFrames that you can create, such as numeric and Boolean DataFrames. In addition, you will see examples of creating DataFrames with NumPy functions and random numbers. You will also see examples of converting between Python dictionaries and JSON-based data, and also how to create a Pandas DataFrame from JSON-based data.

WHAT IS PANDAS?

Pandas is a Python library that is compatible with other Python libraries, such as NumPy, Matplotlib, and so forth. Install Pandas by opening a command shell and invoking this command for Python 3.x:

```
pip3 install pandas
```

In many ways the Pandas library has the semantics of a spreadsheet, and it also works with various file types, such as xsl, xml, html, csv files. Pandas provides a data type called a `DataFrame` (similar to a `Python` dictionary) with extremely powerful functionality (similar to the functionality of a spreadsheet).

Pandas DataFrames

In simplified terms, a `Pandas DataFrame` is a two-dimensional data structure, and it's convenient to think of the data structure in terms of rows and columns. `DataFrames` can be labeled (rows as well as columns), and the columns can contain different data types. The source of the dataset can be a data file, database tables, Web service, and so forth. `Pandas DataFrame` features include:

- data frame methods
- data frame statistics
- grouping, pivoting, and reshaping
- handle missing data
- join data frames

Dataframes and Data Cleaning Tasks

The specific tasks that you need to perform depend on the structure and contents of a dataset. In general, you will perform a workflow with the following steps (not necessarily always in this order), all of which can be performed with a `Pandas DataFrame`:

- read data into a DataFrame
- display top of DataFrame
- display column data types
- display non-missing values
- replace NA with a value
- iterate through the columns
- statistics for each column
- find missing values
- total missing values
- percentage of missing values
- sort table values
- print summary information
- columns with > 50% missing values
- rename columns

A PANDAS DATAFRAME EXAMPLE

Listing 3.1 displays the contents of `pandas_df.py` that illustrates how to define several `Pandas DataFrames` and display their contents.

LISTING 3.1: pandas_df.py

```
import pandas as pd
import numpy as np
```

```
myvector1 = np.array([1,2,3,4,5])
print("myvector1:")
print(myvector1)
print()

mydf1 = pd.DataFrame(myvector1)
print("mydf1:")
print(mydf1)
print()

myvector2 = np.array([i for i in range(1,6)])
print("myvector2:")
print(myvector2)
print()

mydf2 = pd.DataFrame(myvector2)
print("mydf2:")
print(mydf2)
print()

myarray = np.array([[10,30,20],
[50,40,60],[1000,2000,3000]])
print("myarray:")
print(myarray)
print()

mydf3 = pd.DataFrame(myarray)
print("mydf3:")
print(mydf3)
print()
```

Listing 3.1 starts with a standard `import` statement for `Pandas` and `NumPy`, followed by the definition of two one-dimensional `NumPy` arrays and a two-dimensional `NumPy` array. The `NumPy` syntax ought to be familiar to you (many basic tutorials are available online). Each `NumPy` variable is followed by a corresponding `Pandas DataFrame` `mydf1`, `mydf2`, and `mydf3`. Now launch the code in Listing 3.1 and you will see the following output, and you can compare the `NumPy` arrays with the `Pandas DataFrames`:

```
myvector1:
[1 2 3 4 5]

mydf1:
   0
0  1
1  2
2  3
3  4
4  5

myvector2:
[1 2 3 4 5]
```

```
mydf2:
   0
0  1
1  2
2  3
3  4
4  5
myarray:
[[10   30   20]
 [50   40   60]
 [1000 2000 3000]]

mydf3:
      0     1     2
0    10    30    20
1    50    40    60
2  1000  2000  3000
```

In addition, the following code block illustrates how to construct a `Pandas DataFrame` from two Pandas `Pandas Series`:

```
names = pd.Series(['SF', 'San Jose', 'Sacramento'])
sizes = pd.Series([852469, 1015785, 485199])
df = pd.DataFrame({'Cities': names, 'Size': sizes})
print(df)
```

Create a `Python` file with the preceding code (along with the required `import` statement) and when you launch that code you will see the following output:

```
    City name    sizes
0          SF   852469
1    San Jose  1015785
2  Sacramento   485199
```

DESCRIBING A PANDAS DATAFRAME

Listing 3.2 displays the contents of `pandas_df_describe.py` that illustrates how to define a `Pandas DataFrame` that contains a 3x3 `NumPy` array of integer values, where the rows and columns of the DataFrame are labeled. Various other aspects of the DataFrame are also displayed.

LISTING 3.2: pandas_df_describe.py

```
import numpy as np
import pandas as pd

myarray = np.array([[10,30,20],
[50,40,60],[1000,2000,3000]])

rownames = ['apples', 'oranges', 'beer']
colnames = ['January', 'February', 'March']
```

```
mydf = pd.DataFrame(myarray, index=rownames,
columns=colnames)
print("contents of df:")
print(mydf)
print()

print("contents of January:")
print(mydf['January'])
print()

print("Number of Rows:")
print(mydf.shape[0])
print()

print("Number of Columns:")
print(mydf.shape[1])
print()

print("Number of Rows and Columns:")
print(mydf.shape)
print()

print("Column Names:")
print(mydf.columns)
print()

print("Column types:")
print(mydf.dtypes)
print()

print("Description:")
print(mydf.describe())
print()
```

Listing 3.2 starts with two standard `import` statements followed by the variable `myarray`, which is a 3x3 `NumPy` array of numbers. The variables `rownames` and `colnames` provide names for the rows and columns, respectively, of the `Pandas DataFrame` `mydf`, which is initialized as a `Pandas DataFrame` with the specified datasource (i.e., `myarray`).

The first portion of the output below requires a single `print` statement (which simply displays the contents of `mydf`). The second portion of the output is generated by invoking the `describe()` method that is available for any `NumPy DataFrame`. The `describe()` method is very useful: you will see various statistical quantities, such as the mean, standard deviation minimum, and maximum performed column wise (not row wise), along with values for the 25th, 50th, and 75th percentiles. The output of Listing 3.2 is here:

```
contents of df:
         January  February  March
apples        10        30     20
oranges       50        40     60
beer        1000      2000   3000
```

```
contents of January:
apples       10
oranges      50
beer       1000
Name: January, dtype: int64

Number of Rows:
3

Number of Columns:
3

Number of Rows and Columns:
(3, 3)

Column Names:
Index(['January', 'February', 'March'], dtype='object')

Column types:
January     int64
February    int64
March       int64
dtype: object

Description:
           January     February        March
count     3.000000     3.000000     3.000000
mean    353.333333   690.000000  1026.666667
std     560.386771  1134.504297  1709.073823
min      10.000000    30.000000    20.000000
25%      30.000000    35.000000    40.000000
50%      50.000000    40.000000    60.000000
75%     525.000000  1020.000000  1530.000000
max    1000.000000  2000.000000  3000.000000
```

PANDAS BOOLEAN `DataFrames`

`Pandas` supports Boolean operations on `DataFrames`, such as the logical or, the logical and, and the logical negation of a pair of `DataFrames`. Listing 3.3 displays the contents of `pandas_boolean_df.py` that illustrates how to define a `Pandas DataFrame` whose rows and columns are Boolean values.

LISTING 3.3: pandas_boolean_df.py

```
import pandas as pd

df1 = pd.DataFrame({'a': [1, 0, 1], 'b': [0, 1, 1] },
dtype=bool)
df2 = pd.DataFrame({'a': [0, 1, 1], 'b': [1, 1, 0] },
dtype=bool)

print("df1 & df2:")
print(df1 & df2)
```

```
print("df1 | df2:")
print(df1 | df2)

print("df1 ^ df2:")
print(df1 ^ df2)
```

Listing 3.3 initializes the `DataFrames` `df1` and `df2`, and then computes `df1 & df2`, df1 `| df2`, `df1 ^ df2`, which represent the logical `AND`, the logical `OR`, and the logical negation, respectively, of `df1` and `df2`. The output from launching the code in Listing 3.3 is here:

```
df1 & df2:
       a      b
0  False  False
1  False   True
2   True  False
df1 | df2:
      a     b
0  True  True
1  True  True
2  True  True
df1 ^ df2:
       a      b
0   True   True
1   True  False
2  False   True
```

Transposing a Pandas DataFrame

The `T` attribute (as well as the transpose function) enables you to generate the transpose of a `Pandas DataFrame`, similar to a `NumPy ndarray`.

For example, the following code snippet defines a `Pandas DataFrame` `df1` and then displays the transpose of `df1`:

```
df1 = pd.DataFrame({'a': [1, 0, 1], 'b': [0, 1, 1]},
dtype=int)

print("df1.T:")
print(df1.T)
```

The output is here:

```
df1.T:
   0  1  2
a  1  0  1
b  0  1  1
```

The following code snippet defines `Pandas DataFrames` `df1` and `df2` and then displays their sum:

```
df1 = pd.DataFrame({'a' : [1, 0, 1], 'b' : [0, 1, 1]},
dtype=int)
```

```
df2 = pd.DataFrame({'a' : [3, 3, 3], 'b' : [5, 5, 5]},
dtype=int)

print("df1 + df2:")
print(df1 + df2)
```

The output is here:

```
df1 + df2:
   a  b
0  4  5
1  3  6
2  4  6
```

PANDAS DATAFRAMES AND RANDOM NUMBERS

Listing 3.4 displays the contents of `pandas_random_df.py` that illustrates how to create a `Pandas DataFrame` with random numbers.

LISTING 3.4: pandas_random_df.py

```
import pandas as pd
import numpy as np

df = pd.DataFrame(np.random.randint(1, 5, size=(5, 2)),
columns=['a','b'])
df = df.append(df.agg(['sum', 'mean']))

print("Contents of data frame:")
print(df)
```

Listing 3.4 defines the `Pandas DataFrame` `df` that consists of 5 rows and 2 columns of random integers between 1 and 5. Notice that the columns of `df` are labeled "a" and "b." In addition, the next code snippet appends two rows consisting of the sum and the mean of the numbers in both columns. The output of Listing 3.4 is here:

```
a       b
0       1.0  2.0
1       1.0  1.0
2       4.0  3.0
3       3.0  1.0
4       1.0  2.0
sum    10.0  9.0
mean    2.0  1.8
```

Listing 3.5 displays the contents of `pandas_combine_df.py` that illustrates how to define a `Pandas DataFrame` that is based on two `NumPy` arrays of numbers.

LISTING 3.5: pandas_combine_df.py

```
import pandas as pd
import numpy as np
```

```
df = pd.DataFrame({'foo1' : np.random.randn(5),
                   'foo2' : np.random.randn(5)})

print("contents of df:")
print(df)

print("contents of foo1:")
print(df.foo1)

print("contents of foo2:")
print(df.foo2)
```

Listing 3.5 defines the `Pandas DataFrame df` that consists of 5 rows and 2 columns (labeled "`foo1`" and "`foo2`") of random real numbers between 0 and 5. The next portion of Listing 3.5 displays the contents of `df` and `foo1`. The output of Listing 3.5 is here:

```
contents of df:
       foo1      foo2
0  0.274680 -0.848669
1 -0.399771 -0.814679
2  0.454443 -0.363392
3  0.473753  0.550849
4 -0.211783 -0.015014
contents of foo1:
0    0.256773
1    1.204322
2    1.040515
3   -0.518414
4    0.634141
Name: foo1, dtype: float64
contents of foo2:
0   -2.506550
1   -0.896516
2   -0.222923
3    0.934574
4    0.527033
Name: foo2, dtype: float64
```

CONVERTING CATEGORICAL DATA TO NUMERIC DATA

One common task in machine learning involves converting a feature containing character data into a feature that contains numeric data.

Listing 3.6 displays the contents of `sometext.tsv` that contains labeled data (spam or ham), which is used in the code sample displayed in Listing 3.7 (displayed after Listing 3.6).

LISTING 3.6: sometext.tsv

```
type    text
ham     I'm telling the truth
spam    What a deal such a deal!
```

```
spam    Free vacation for your family
ham     Thank you for your help
spam    Spring break next week!
ham     I received the documents
spam    One million dollars for you
ham     My wife got covid19
spam    You might have won the prize
ham     Everyone is in good health
```

Listing 3.7 displays the contents of `cat2numeric.py` that illustrates how to replace a text field with a corresponding numeric field.

LISTING 3.7: cat2numeric.py

```
import pandas as pd
import numpy as np

df = pd.read_csv('sometext.tsv', delimiter='\t')

print("=> First five rows (before):")
print(df.head(5))
print("-------------------------")

# map ham/spam to 0/1 values:
df['type'] = df['type'].map( {'ham':0 , 'spam':1} )

print("=> First five rows (after):")
print(df.head(5))
print("-------------------------")
```

Listing 3.7 initializes the `DataFrame` `df` with the contents of the `csv` file `sometext.tsv`, and then displays the contents of the first five rows by invoking `df.head(5)`, which is also the default number of rows to display. The next code snippet in Listing 3.7 invokes the `map()` method to replace occurrences of `ham` with 0 and replace occurrences of `spam` with 1 in the column labeled type, as shown here:

```
df['type'] = df['type'].map( {'ham':0 , 'spam':1} )
```

The last portion of Listing 3.7 invokes the `head()` method again to display the first five rows of the dataset after having renamed the contents of the column type. Launch the code in Listing 3.7 and you will see the following output:

```
=> First five rows (before):
   type                          text
0   ham       Available only for today
1   ham            I'm joking with you
2  spam    Free entry in 2 a wkly comp
3   ham          U dun say so early hor
4   ham  I don't think he goes to usf
-------------------------
=> First five rows (after):
   type                          text
```

```
0      0      Available only for today
1      0           I'm joking with you
2      1   Free entry in 2 a wkly comp
3      0          U dun say so early hor
4      0  I don't think he goes to usf
-------------------------
```

As another example, Listing 3.8 displays the contents of `shirts.csv` and Listing 3.9 displays the contents of `shirts.py` that illustrates four techniques for converting categorical data to numeric data.

LISTING 3.8: shirts.csv

```
type,ssize
shirt,xxlarge
shirt,xxlarge
shirt,xlarge
shirt,xlarge
shirt,xlarge
shirt,large
shirt,medium
shirt,small
shirt,small
shirt,xsmall
shirt,xsmall
shirt,xsmall
```

LISTING 3.9: shirts.py

```
import pandas as pd

shirts = pd.read_csv("shirts.csv")
print("shirts before:")
print(shirts)
print()

# TECHNIQUE #1:
#shirts.loc[shirts['ssize']=='xxlarge','size'] = 4
#shirts.loc[shirts['ssize']=='xlarge', 'size'] = 4
#shirts.loc[shirts['ssize']=='large',  'size'] = 3
#shirts.loc[shirts['ssize']=='medium', 'size'] = 2
#shirts.loc[shirts['ssize']=='small',  'size'] = 1
#shirts.loc[shirts['ssize']=='xsmall', 'size'] = 1

# TECHNIQUE #2:
#shirts['ssize'].replace('xxlarge', 4, inplace=True)
#shirts['ssize'].replace('xlarge',  4, inplace=True)
#shirts['ssize'].replace('large',   3, inplace=True)
#shirts['ssize'].replace('medium',  2, inplace=True)
#shirts['ssize'].replace('small',   1, inplace=True)
#shirts['ssize'].replace('xsmall',  1, inplace=True)

# TECHNIQUE #3:
#shirts['ssize'] = shirts['ssize'].apply({'xxlarge':4,
'xlarge':4, 'large':3, 'medium':2, 'small':1, 'xsmall':1}.get)
```

```
# TECHNIQUE #4:
shirts['ssize'] = shirts['ssize'].replace(regex='xlarge',
value=4)
shirts['ssize'] = shirts['ssize'].replace(regex='large',
value=3)
shirts['ssize'] = shirts['ssize'].replace(regex='medium',
value=2)
shirts['ssize'] = shirts['ssize'].replace(regex='small',
value=1)

print("shirts after:")
print(shirts)
```

Listing 3.9 starts with a code block of six statements that uses direct comparison with strings to make numeric replacements. For example, the following code snippet replaces all occurrences of the string `xxlarge` with the value 4:

```
shirts.loc[shirts['ssize']=='xxlarge','size'] = 4
```

The second code block consists of six statements that use the `replace()` method to perform the same updates, an example of which is shown here:

```
shirts['ssize'].replace('xxlarge', 4, inplace=True)
```

The third code block consists of a single statement that use the `apply()` method to perform the same updates, as shown here:

```
shirts['ssize'] = shirts['ssize'].apply({'xxlarge':4,
'xlarge':4, 'large':3, 'medium':2, 'small':1, 'xsmall':1}.
get)
```

The fourth code block consists of four statements that use regular expressions to perform the same updates, an example of which is shown here:

```
shirts['ssize'] = shirts['ssize'].replace(regex='xlarge',
value=4)
```

Since the preceding code snippet matches `xxlarge` as well as `xlarge`, we only need four statements instead of six statements. If you are unfamiliar with regular expressions, you can find online articles that can introduce you to regular expressions. Now launch the code in Listing 3.9 and you will see the following output:

```
shirts before
    type     size
0  shirt  xxlarge
1  shirt  xxlarge
2  shirt   xlarge
3  shirt   xlarge
4  shirt   xlarge
5  shirt    large
6  shirt   medium
7  shirt    small
```

```
8    shirt     small
9    shirt    xsmall
10   shirt    xsmall
11   shirt    xsmall

shirts after:
     type  size
0    shirt     4
1    shirt     4
2    shirt     4
3    shirt     4
4    shirt     4
5    shirt     3
6    shirt     2
7    shirt     1
8    shirt     1
9    shirt     1
10   shirt     1
11   shirt     1
```

MATCHING AND SPLITTING STRINGS IN PANDAS

Listing 3.10 displays the contents of `shirts_str.py` that illustrates how to match a column value with an initial string and also how to split a column value based on a letter.

LISTING 3.10: shirts_str.py

```
import pandas as pd

shirts = pd.read_csv("shirts.csv")
print("shirts:")
print(shirts)
print()

print("shirts starting with xl:")
print(shirts[shirts.ssize.str.startswith('xl')])
print()

print("Exclude 'xlarge' shirts:")
print(shirts[shirts['ssize'] != 'xlarge'])
print()

print("first three letters:")
shirts['sub1'] = shirts['ssize'].str[:3]
print(shirts)
print()

print("split ssize on letter 'a':")
shirts['sub2'] = shirts['ssize'].str.split('a')
print(shirts)
print()
```

```
print("Rows 3 through 5 and column 2:")
print(shirts.iloc[2:5, 2])
print()
```

Listing 3.10 initializes the `DataFrame` `df` with the contents of the `CSV` file `shirts.csv`, and then displays the contents of the `DataFrame`. The next code snippet in Listing 3.10 uses the `startswith()` method to match the shirt types that start with the letters `xl`, followed by a code snippet that displays the shorts whose size does not equal the string `xlarge`.

The next code snippet uses the construct `str[:3]` to display the first three letters of the shirt types, followed by a code snippet that uses the `split()` method to split the shirt types based on the letter "a." The final code snippet invokes `iloc[2:5,2]` to display the contents of rows 3 through 5 inclusive, and only the second column. The output of Listing 3.10 is here:

```
shirts:
      type    ssize
0    shirt  xxlarge
1    shirt  xxlarge
2    shirt   xlarge
3    shirt   xlarge
4    shirt   xlarge
5    shirt    large
6    shirt   medium
7    shirt    small
8    shirt    small
9    shirt   xsmall
10   shirt   xsmall
11   shirt   xsmall

shirts starting with xl:
    type   ssize
2  shirt  xlarge
3  shirt  xlarge
4  shirt  xlarge

Exclude 'xlarge' shirts:
      type    ssize
0    shirt  xxlarge
1    shirt  xxlarge
5    shirt    large
6    shirt   medium
7    shirt    small
8    shirt    small
9    shirt   xsmall
10   shirt   xsmall
11   shirt   xsmall

first three letters:
      type    ssize sub1
0    shirt  xxlarge  xxl
1    shirt  xxlarge  xxl
```

```
2    shirt   xlarge  xla
3    shirt   xlarge  xla
4    shirt   xlarge  xla
5    shirt    large  lar
6    shirt   medium  med
7    shirt    small  sma
8    shirt    small  sma
9    shirt   xsmall  xsm
10   shirt   xsmall  xsm
11   shirt   xsmall  xsm

split ssize on letter 'a':
      type    ssize sub1         sub2
0    shirt  xxlarge  xxl  [xxl, rge]
1    shirt  xxlarge  xxl  [xxl, rge]
2    shirt   xlarge  xla   [xl, rge]
3    shirt   xlarge  xla   [xl, rge]
4    shirt   xlarge  xla   [xl, rge]
5    shirt    large  lar    [l, rge]
6    shirt   medium  med    [medium]
7    shirt    small  sma    [sm, ll]
8    shirt    small  sma    [sm, ll]
9    shirt   xsmall  xsm   [xsm, ll]
10   shirt   xsmall  xsm   [xsm, ll]
11   shirt   xsmall  xsm   [xsm, ll]

Rows 3 through 5 and column 2:
2     xlarge
3     xlarge
4     xlarge
Name: ssize, dtype: object
```

MERGING AND SPLITTING COLUMNS IN PANDAS

Listing 3.11 displays the contents of `employees.csv` and Listing 3.12 displays the contents of `emp_merge_split.py` that illustrates how to merge columns and split columns of a `CSV` file.

LISTING 3.11: employees.csv

```
name,year,month
Jane-Smith,2015,Aug
Dave-Smith,2020,Jan
Jane-Jones,2018,Dec
Jane-Stone,2017,Feb
Dave-Stone,2014,Apr
Mark-Aster,,Oct
Jane-Jones,NaN,Jun
```

LISTING 3.12: emp_merge_split.py

```
import pandas as pd

emps = pd.read_csv("employees.csv")
print("emps:")
```

```
print(emps)
print()

emps['year']  = emps['year'].astype(str)
emps['month'] = emps['month'].astype(str)

# separate column for first name and for last name:
emps['fname'],emps['lname'] = emps['name'].str.
split("-",1).str

# concatenate year and month with a "#" symbol:
emps['hdate1'] = emps['year'].
astype(str)+"#"+emps['month'].astype(str)

# concatenate year and month with a "-" symbol:
emps['hdate2'] = emps[['year','month']].agg('-'.join,
axis=1)

print(emps)
print()
```

Listing 3.12 initializes the `DataFrame` `df` with the contents of the `CSV` file `employees.csv`, and then displays the contents of the `DataFrame`. The next pair of code snippets invoke the `astype()` method to convert the contents of the `year` and `month` columns to strings.

The next code snippet in Listing 3.12 uses the `split()` method to split the name column into the columns `fname` and `lname` that contain the first name and last name, respectively, of each employee's name:

```
emps['fname'],emps['lname'] = emps['name'].str.
split("-",1).str
```

The next code snippet concatenates the contents of the year and month string with a "#" character to create a new column called `hdate1`, as shown here:

```
emps['hdate1'] = emps['year'].
astype(str)+"#"+emps['month'].astype(str)
```

The final code snippet concatenates the contents of the `year` and `month` string with a "-" to create a new column called `hdate2`, as shown here:

```
emps['hdate2'] = emps[['year','month']].agg('-'.join,
axis=1)
```

Now launch the code in Listing 3.12 and you will see the following output:

```
emps:
         name    year month
0  Jane-Smith  2015.0   Aug
1  Dave-Smith  2020.0   Jan
2  Jane-Jones  2018.0   Dec
3  Jane-Stone  2017.0   Feb
```

```
4   Dave-Stone  2014.0    Apr
5   Mark-Aster     NaN    Oct
6   Jane-Jones     NaN    Jun

          name    year month fname  lname       hdate1       hdate2
0   Jane-Smith  2015.0   Aug  Jane  Smith  2015.0#Aug  2015.0-Aug
1   Dave-Smith  2020.0   Jan  Dave  Smith  2020.0#Jan  2020.0-Jan
2   Jane-Jones  2018.0   Dec  Jane  Jones  2018.0#Dec  2018.0-Dec
3   Jane-Stone  2017.0   Feb  Jane  Stone  2017.0#Feb  2017.0-Feb
4   Dave-Stone  2014.0   Apr  Dave  Stone  2014.0#Apr  2014.0-Apr
5   Mark-Aster     nan   Oct  Mark  Aster     nan#Oct     nan-Oct
6   Jane-Jones     nan   Jun  Jane  Jones     nan#Jun     nan-Jun
```

One other detail regarding the following code snippet:

```
emps['fname'],emps['lname'] = emps['name'].str.
split("-",1).str
```

The following deprecation message is displayed:

```
#FutureWarning: Columnar iteration over characters
#will be deprecated in future releases.
```

COMBINING PANDAS DATAFRAMES

Pandas supports the "concat" method in DataFrames in order to concatenate DataFrames. Listing 3.13 displays the contents of concat_frames.py that illustrates how to combine two Pandas DataFrames.

LISTING 3.13: concat_frames.py

```
import pandas as pd

can_weather = pd.DataFrame({
    "city": ["Vancouver","Toronto","Montreal"],
    "temperature": [72,65,50],
    "humidity": [40, 20, 25]
})

us_weather = pd.DataFrame({
    "city": ["SF","Chicago","LA"],
    "temperature": [60,40,85],
    "humidity": [30, 15, 55]
})

df = pd.concat([can_weather, us_weather])
print(df)
```

The first line in Listing 3.13 is an import statement, followed by the definition of the Pandas DataFrames can_weather and us_weather that contain weather-related information for cities in Canada and the United States, respectively. The Pandas DataFrame df is the concatenation of can_weather and us_weather. The output from Listing 3.13 is here:

```
0  Vancouver       40         72
1    Toronto       20         65
2   Montreal       25         50
0         SF       30         60
1    Chicago       15         40
2         LA       55         85
```

DATA MANIPULATION WITH PANDAS DATAFRAMES

As a simple example, suppose that we have a two-person company that keeps track of income and expenses on a quarterly basis, and we want to calculate the profit/loss for each quarter, and also the overall profit/loss.

Listing 3.14 displays the contents of pandas_quarterly_df1.py that illustrates how to define a Pandas DataFrame consisting of income-related values.

LISTING 3.14: pandas_quarterly_df1.py

```
import pandas as pd

summary = {
    'Quarter': ['Q1', 'Q2', 'Q3', 'Q4'],
    'Cost':    [23500, 34000, 57000, 32000],
    'Revenue': [40000, 40000, 40000, 40000]
}

df = pd.DataFrame(summary)

print("Entire Dataset:\n",df)
print("Quarter:\n",df.Quarter)
print("Cost:\n",df.Cost)
print("Revenue:\n",df.Revenue)
```

Listing 3.14 defines the variable summary that contains hard-coded quarterly information about cost and revenue for our two-person company. In general, these hard-coded values would be replaced by data from another source (such as a CSV file), so think of this code sample as a simple way to illustrate some of the functionality that is available in Pandas DataFrames.

The variable df is a Pandas DataFrame based on the data in the summary variable. The three print() statements display the quarters, the cost per quarter, and the revenue per quarter. The output from Listing 3.14 is here:

```
Entire Dataset:
     Cost Quarter  Revenue
0  23500       Q1    40000
1  34000       Q2    60000
```

```
2  57000       Q3    50000
3  32000       Q4    30000
Quarter:
0     Q1
1     Q2
2     Q3
3     Q4
Name: Quarter, dtype: object
Cost:
0     23500
1     34000
2     57000
3     32000
Name: Cost, dtype: int64
Revenue:
0     40000
1     60000
2     50000
3     30000
Name: Revenue, dtype: int64
```

DATA MANIPULATION WITH PANDAS DATAFRAMES (2)

In this section, let's suppose that we have a two-person company that keeps track of income and expenses on a quarterly basis, and we want to calculate the profit/loss for each quarter, and also the overall profit/loss.

Listing 3.15 displays the contents of `pandas_quarterly_df1.py` that illustrates how to define a `Pandas DataFrame` consisting of income-related values.

LISTING 3.15: pandas_quarterly_df2.py

```
import pandas as pd

summary = {
    'Quarter': ['Q1', 'Q2', 'Q3', 'Q4'],
    'Cost':    [-23500, -34000, -57000, -32000],
    'Revenue': [40000, 40000, 40000, 40000]
}
df = pd.DataFrame(summary)
print("First Dataset:\n",df)

df['Total'] = df.sum(axis=1)
print("Second Dataset:\n",df)
```

Listing 3.15 defines the variable `summary` that contains quarterly information about cost and revenue for our two-person company. The variable `df` is a `Pandas DataFrame` based on the data in the `summary` variable. The three `print` statements display the quarters, the cost per quarter, and the revenue per quarter. The output from Listing 3.15 is here:

```
First Dataset:
     Cost Quarter  Revenue
0 -23500      Q1    40000
1 -34000      Q2    60000
2 -57000      Q3    50000
3 -32000      Q4    30000
Second Dataset:
     Cost Quarter  Revenue  Total
0 -23500      Q1    40000  16500
1 -34000      Q2    60000  26000
2 -57000      Q3    50000  -7000
3 -32000      Q4    30000  -2000
```

DATA MANIPULATION WITH PANDAS DATAFRAMES (3)

Let's start with the same assumption as the previous section: we have a two-person company that keeps track of income and expenses on a quarterly basis, and we want to calculate the profit/loss for each quarter, and also the overall profit/loss. In addition, we want to compute column totals and row totals.

Listing 3.16 displays the contents of `pandas_quarterly_df1.py` that illustrates how to define a `Pandas DataFrame` consisting of income-related values.

LISTING 3.16: pandas_quarterly_df3.py

```
import pandas as pd

summary = {
    'Quarter': ['Q1', 'Q2', 'Q3', 'Q4'],
    'Cost':    [_23500, _34000, _57000, _32000],
    'Revenue': [40000, 40000, 40000, 40000]
}

df = pd.DataFrame(summary)
print("First Dataset:\n",df)

df['Total'] = df.sum(axis=1)
df.loc['Sum'] = df.sum()
print("Second Dataset:\n",df)

# or df.loc['avg'] / 3
#df.loc['avg'] = df[:3].mean()
#print("Third Dataset:\n",df)
```

Listing 3.16 defines the variable `summary` that contains quarterly information about cost and revenue for our two-person company. The variable `df` is a `Pandas DataFrame` based on the data in the `summary` variable. The three `print` statements display the quarters, the cost per quarter, and the revenue per quarter. The output from Listing 3.16 is here:

```
First Dataset:
     Cost Quarter  Revenue
0 -23500      Q1    40000
1 -34000      Q2    60000
2 -57000      Q3    50000
3 -32000      Q4    30000
Second Dataset:
        Cost    Quarter  Revenue  Total
0     -23500         Q1    40000  16500
1     -34000         Q2    60000  26000
2     -57000         Q3    50000  -7000
3     -32000         Q4    30000  -2000
Sum -146500   Q1Q2Q3Q4   180000  33500
```

PANDAS DATAFRAMES AND CSV FILES

The code samples in several earlier sections contain hard-coded data inside the Python scripts. However, it's also very common to read data from a CSV file. You can use the Python csv.reader() function, the NumPy loadtxt() function, or the Pandas function read_csv() function (shown in this section) to read the contents of CSV files.

Listing 3.17 displays the contents of the CSV file weather_data.csv and Listing 3.18 displays the contents of weather_data.py that illustrates how to read the CSV weather_data.csv.

LISTING 3.17: weather_data.csv

```
day,temperature,windspeed,event
7/1/2018,42,16,Rain
7/2/2018,45,3,Sunny
7/3/2018,78,12,Snow
7/4/2018,74,9,Snow
7/5/2018,42,24,Rain
7/6/2018,51,32,Sunny
```

LISTING 3.18: weather_data.py

```
import pandas as pd

df = pd.read_csv("weather_data.csv")

print(df)
print(df.shape)  # rows, columns
print(df.head()) # df.head(3)
print(df.tail())
print(df[1:3])
print(df.columns)
print(type(df['day']))
print(df[['day','temperature']])
print(df['temperature'].max())
```

Listing 3.18 invokes the Pandas read_csv() function to read the contents of the CSV file weather_data.csv, followed by a set of Python print()

statements that display various portions of the CSV file. The output from Listing 3.18 is here:

```
         day  temperature  windspeed     event
0  7/1/2018           42         16    Rain
1  7/2/2018           45          3   Sunny
2  7/3/2018           78         12    Snow
3  7/4/2018           74          9   Snow
4  7/5/2018           42         24    Rain
5  7/6/2018           51         32     Sunny
(6, 4)
         day  temperature  windspeed     event
0  7/1/2018           42         16    Rain
1  7/2/2018           45          3   Sunny
2  7/3/2018           78         12    Snow
3  7/4/2018           74          9   Snow
4  7/5/2018           42         24    Rain
         day  temperature  windspeed     event
1  7/2/2018           45          3   Sunny
2  7/3/2018           78         12    Snow
3  7/4/2018           74          9   Snow
4  7/5/2018           42         24    Rain
5  7/6/2018           51         32     Sunny
         day  temperature  windspeed     event
1  7/2/2018           45          3   Sunny
2  7/3/2018           78         12    Snow
Index(['day', 'temperature', 'windspeed', 'event'],
dtype='object')
<class 'pandas.core.series.Series'>
         day  temperature
0  7/1/2018           42
1  7/2/2018           45
2  7/3/2018           78
3  7/4/2018           74
4  7/5/2018           42
5  7/6/2018           51
78
```

In some situations, you might need to apply Boolean conditional logic to "filter out" some rows of data, based on a conditional condition that's applied to a column value.

Listing 3.19 displays the contents of the CSV file `people.csv` and Listing 3.20 displays the contents of `people_pandas.py` that illustrates how to define a `Pandas DataFrame` that reads the CSV file and manipulates the data.

LISTING 3.19: people.csv

```
fname,lname,age,gender,country
john,smith,30,m,usa
jane,smith,31,f,france
jack,jones,32,m,france
```

```
dave,stone,33,m,italy
sara,stein,34,f,germany
eddy,bower,35,m,spain
```

LISTING 3.20: people_pandas.py

```
import pandas as pd

df = pd.read_csv('people.csv')
df.info()
print('fname:')
print(df['fname'])
print('____________')
print('age over 33:')
print(df['age'] > 33)
print('____________')
print('age over 33:')
myfilter = df['age'] >  33
print(df[myfilter])
```

Listing 3.20 populate the `Pandas DataFrame df` with the contents of the `CSV` file `people.csv`. The next portion of Listing 3.20 displays the structure of `df`, followed by the first names of all the people. The next portion of Listing 3.20 displays a tabular list of six rows containing either True or False depending on whether a person is over 33 or at most 33, respectively. The final portion of Listing 3.20 displays a tabular list of two rows containing all the details of the people who are over 33. The output from Listing 3.20 is here:

```
myfilter = df['age'] >  33
<class 'pandas.core.frame.DataFrame'>
RangeIndex: 6 entries, 0 to 5
Data columns (total 5 columns):
fname       6 non_null object
lname       6 non_null object
age         6 non_null int64
gender      6 non_null object
country     6 non_null object
dtypes: int64(1), object(4)
memory usage: 320.0+ bytes
fname:
0    john
1    jane
2    jack
3    dave
4    sara
5    eddy
Name: fname, dtype: object
____________
age over 33:
0    False
1    False
2    False
3    False
```

```
4      True
5      True
Name: age, dtype: bool
______________
age over 33:
  fname  lname  age gender country
4  sara  stein   34      f  france
5  eddy  bower   35      m  france
```

PANDAS DATAFRAMES AND EXCEL SPREADSHEETS

Listing 3.21 displays the contents of `write_people_xlsx.py` that illustrates how to read data from a `CSV` file and then create an Excel spreadsheet with that data.

LISTING 3.21: write_people_xlsx.py

```
import pandas as pd

df1 = pd.read_csv("people.csv")
df1.to_excel("people.xlsx")

#optionally specify the sheet name:
#df1.to_excel("people.xlsx", sheet_name='Sheet_name_1')
```

Listing 3.21 initializes the Pandas DataFrame `df1` with the contents of the `CSV` file `people.csv`, and then invokes the `to_excel()` method in order to save the contents of the DataFrame to the Excel spreadsheet `people.xlsx`.

Listing 3.22 displays the contents of `read_people_xlsx.py` that illustrates how to read data from the Excel spreadsheet `people.xlsx` and create a `Pandas DataFrame` with that data.

LISTING 3.22: read_people_xlsx.py

```
import pandas as pd

df = pd.read_excel("people.xlsx")
print("Contents of Excel spreadsheet:")
print(df)
```

Listing 3.22 is straightforward: the `Pandas DataFrame` `df` is initialized with the contents of the spreadsheet `people.xlsx` (whose contents are the same as `people.csv`) via the `Pandas` function `read_excel()`. The output from Listing 3.22 is here:

```
df1:
   Unnamed: 0 fname  lname  age gender  country
0           0  john  smith   30      m      usa
1           1  jane  smith   31      f   france
2           2  jack  jones   32      m   france
```

```
3           3  dave   stone    33       m     italy
4           4  sara   stein    34       f   germany
5           5  eddy   bower    35       m     spain
```

SELECT, ADD, AND DELETE COLUMNS IN `DataFrames`

This section contains short code blocks that illustrate how to perform operations on a `DataFrame` that resemble the operations on a `Python` dictionary. For example, getting, setting, and deleting columns works with the same syntax as the analogous Python `dict` operations, as shown here:

```
df = pd.DataFrame.from_dict(dict([('A',[1,2,3]),(
'B',[4,5,6])]),
                orient='index', columns=['one', 'two',
'three'])

print(df)
```

The output from the preceding code snippet is here:

```
   one  two  three
A    1    2      3
B    4    5      6
```

Now look at the following operation that appends a new column to the contents of the `DataFrame df`:

```
df['four'] = df['one'] * df['two']
print(df)
```

The output from the preceding code block is here:

```
   one  two  three  four
A    1    2      3     2
B    4    5      6    20
```

The following operation squares the contents of a column in the `DataFrame df`:

```
df['three'] = df['two'] * df['two']
print(df)
```

The output from the preceding code block is here:

```
   one  two  three  four
A    1    2      4     2
B    4    5     25    20
```

The following operation inserts a column of random numbers in index position 1 (which is the second column) in the `DataFrame df`:

```
import numpy as np
rand = np.random.randn(2)
df.insert(1, 'random', rand)
print(df)
```

The output from the preceding code block is here:

```
   one    random  two  three  four
A    1 -1.703111    2      4     2
B    4  1.139189    5     25    20
```

The following operation appends a new column called flag that contains True or False, based on whether or not the numeric value in the "one" column is greater than 2:

```
import numpy as np
rand = np.random.randn(2)
df.insert(1, 'random', rand)
print(df)
```

The output from the preceding code block is here:

```
   one    random  two  three  four   flag
A    1 -1.703111    2      4     2  False
B    4  1.139189    5     25    20   True
```

Columns can be deleted, as shown in following code snippet that deletes the "two" column:

```
del df['two']
print(df)
```

The output from the preceding code block is here:

```
one      random  three  four   flag
A    1 -0.460401      4     2  False
B    4  1.211468     25    20   True
```

Columns can be deleted via the `pop()` method, as shown in following code snippet that deletes the "three" column:

```
three = df.pop('three')
print(df)
```

```
   one    random  four   flag
A    1 -0.544829     2  False
B    4  0.581476    20   True
```

When inserting a scalar value, it will naturally be propagated to fill the column:

```
df['foo'] = 'bar'
print(df)
```

The output from the preceding code snippet is here:

```
   one    random  four   flag  foo
A    1 -0.187331     2  False  bar
B    4 -0.169672    20   True  bar
```

HANDLING OUTLIERS IN PANDAS

If you are unfamiliar with outliers and anomalies, please search for an online article that discusses these two concepts because this section uses `Pandas` to find outliers in a dataset. The key idea involves finding the "z score" of the values in the dataset, which involves calculating the mean `sigma` and standard deviation `std`, and then mapping each value `x` in the dataset to the value `(x-sigma)/std`.

Next, you specify a value of `z` (such as 3) and find the rows whose z score is greater than 3. These are the rows that contain values that are considered outliers. *Note that a suitable value for the z score is your decision (not some other external factor).*

Listing 3.23 displays the contents of `outliers_zscores.py` that illustrates how to find rows of a dataset whose `z-score` greater than (or less than) a specified value.

LISTING 3.23: outliers_zscores.py

```
import numpy as np
import pandas as pd
from scipy import stats
from sklearn import datasets

df = datasets.load_iris()
columns = df.feature_names
iris_df = pd.DataFrame(df.data)
iris_df.columns = columns

print("=> iris_df.shape:",iris_df.shape)
print(iris_df.head())
print()

z = np.abs(stats.zscore(iris_df))
print("z scores for iris:")
print("z.shape:",z.shape)

upper = 2.5
lower = 0.01
print("=> upper outliers:")
print(z[np.where(z > upper)])
print()

outliers = iris_df[z < lower]
print("=> lower outliers:")
print(outliers)
print()
```

Listing 3.23 initializes the variable `df` with the contents of the built-in `Iris` dataset. Next, the variable columns is initialized with the column names, and the DataFrame `iris_df` is initialized from the contents of `df.data` that contains the actual data for the `Iris` dataset. In addition, `iris_df.columns` is initialized with the contents of the variable `columns`.

The next portion of Listing 3.23 displays the shape of the DataFrame `iris_df`, followed by the `z-score` of the `iris_df` DataFrame, which is computed by subtracting the mean and then dividing by the standard deviation (performed for each row).

The last two portions of Listing 3.23 display the outliers (if any) whose `z-score` is outside the interval [0.01, 2.5]. Launch the code in Listing 3.23 and you will see the following output:

```
=> iris_df.shape: (150, 4)
  sepal length (cm) sepal width (cm)   petal length (cm) petal width (cm)
0                5.1              3.5                1.4              0.2
1                4.9              3.0                1.4              0.2
2                4.7              3.2                1.3              0.2
3                4.6              3.1                1.5              0.2
4                5.0              3.6                1.4              0.2

z scores for iris:
z.shape: (150, 4)

=> upper outliers:
[3.09077525 2.63038172]

=> lower outliers:
sepal length (cm)  sepal width (cm)  petal length (cm)  petal width (cm)
73                6.1               2.8               4.7              1.2
82                5.8               2.7               3.9              1.2
90                5.5               2.6               4.4              1.2
92                5.8               2.6               4.0              1.2
95                5.7               3.0               4.2              1.2
```

PANDAS DATAFRAMES AND SCATTERPLOTS

Listing 3.24 displays the contents of `pandas_scatter_df.py` that illustrates how to generate a scatterplot from a `Pandas DataFrame`.

LISTING 3.24: pandas_scatter_df.py

```
import numpy as np
import pandas as pd
import matplotlib.pyplot as plt
from pandas import read_csv
from pandas.plotting import scatter_matrix

myarray = np.array([[10,30,20],
[50,40,60],[1000,2000,3000]])
rownames = ['apples', 'oranges', 'beer']
colnames = ['January', 'February', 'March']
```

```
mydf = pd.DataFrame(myarray, index=rownames,
columns=colnames)

print(mydf)
print(mydf.describe())

scatter_matrix(mydf)
plt.show()
```

Listing 3.24 starts with various `import` statements, followed by the definition of the `NumPy` array `myarray`. Next, the variables `myarray` and `colnames` are initialized with values for the rows and columns, respectively. The next portion of Listing 3.24 initializes the `Pandas DataFrame mydf` so that the rows and columns are labeled in the output, as shown here:

```
January  February  March
apples         10          30        20
oranges        50          40        60
beer         1000        2000      3000
             January      February         March
count       3.000000      3.000000      3.000000
mean      353.333333    690.000000   1026.666667
std       560.386771   1134.504297   1709.073823
min        10.000000     30.000000     20.000000
25%        30.000000     35.000000     40.000000
50%        50.000000     40.000000     60.000000
75%       525.000000   1020.000000   1530.000000
max      1000.000000   2000.000000   3000.0000000
```

PANDAS DATAFRAMES AND SIMPLE STATISTICS

Listing 3.25 displays the contents of `housing_stats.py` that illustrates how to gather basic statistics from data in a `Pandas DataFrame.`

LISTING 3.25: housing_stats.py

```
import pandas as pd

df = pd.read_csv("housing.csv")

minimum_bdrms = df["bedrooms"].min()
median_bdrms  = df["bedrooms"].median()
maximum_bdrms = df["bedrooms"].max()

print("minimum # of bedrooms:",minimum_bdrms)
print("median  # of bedrooms:",median_bdrms)
print("maximum # of bedrooms:",maximum_bdrms)
print("")

print("median values:",df.median().values)
print("")
```

```
prices = df["price"]
print("first 5 prices:")
print(prices.head())
print("")

median_price = df["price"].median()
print("median price:",median_price)
print("")

corr_matrix = df.corr()
print("correlation matrix:")
print(corr_matrix["price"].sort_values(ascending=False))
```

Listing 3.25 initializes the `Pandas DataFrame df` with the contents of the `CSV` file `housing.csv`. The next three variables are initialized with the minimum, median, and maximum number of bedrooms, respectively, and then these values are displayed.

The next portion of Listing 3.25 initializes the variable `prices` with the contents of the `prices` column of the `Pandas DataFrame df`. Next, the first five rows are printed via the `prices.head()` statement, followed by the median value of the prices.

The final portion of Listing 3.25 initializes the variable `corr_matrix` with the contents of the correlation matrix for the `Pandas DataFrame df`, and then displays its contents. The output from Listing 3.25 is here:

```
Apples
10
```

FINDING DUPLICATE ROWS IN PANDAS

Listing 3.26 displays the contents of `duplicates.csv` and Listing 3.27 displays the contents of `duplicates.py` that illustrates how to find duplicate rows in a `Pandas DataFrame`.

LISTING 3.26: duplicates.csv

```
fname,lname,level,dept,state
Jane,Smith,Senior,Sales,California
Dave,Smith,Senior,Devel,California
Jane,Jones,Year1,Mrktg,Illinois
Jane,Jones,Year1,Mrktg,Illinois
Jane,Stone,Senior,Mrktg,Arizona
Dave,Stone,Year2,Devel,Arizona
Mark,Aster,Year3,BizDev,Florida
Jane,Jones,Year1,Mrktg,Illinois
```

LISTING 3.27: duplicates.py

```
import pandas as pd

df = pd.read_csv("duplicates.csv")
print("Contents of data frame:")
```

```
print(df)
print()

print("Duplicate rows:")
#df2 = df.duplicated(subset=None)
df2 = df.duplicated(subset=None, keep='first')
print(df2)
print()

print("Duplicate first names:")
df3 = df[df.duplicated(['fname'])]
print(df3)
print()

print("Duplicate first name and level:")
df3 = df[df.duplicated(['fname','level'])]
print(df3)
print()
```

Listing 3.27 initializes the `DataFrame df` with the contents of the `CSV` file `duplicates.csv`, and then displays the contents of the DataFrame. The next portion of Listing 3.27 displays the duplicate rows by invoking the `duplicated()` method, whereas the next portion of Listing 3.27 displays only the first name `fname` of the duplicate rows. The final portion of Listing 3.27 displays the first name `fname` as well as the level of the duplicate rows. Launch the code in Listing 3.27 and you will see the following output:

```
Contents of data frame:
  fname  lname   level    dept       state
0  Jane  Smith  Senior   Sales  California
1  Dave  Smith  Senior   Devel  California
2  Jane  Jones   Year1   Mrktg    Illinois
3  Jane  Jones   Year1   Mrktg    Illinois
4  Jane  Stone  Senior   Mrktg     Arizona
5  Dave  Stone   Year2   Devel     Arizona
6  Mark  Aster   Year3  BizDev     Florida
7  Jane  Jones   Year1   Mrktg    Illinois

Duplicate rows:
0    False
1    False
2    False
3     True
4    False
5    False
6    False
7     True
dtype: bool

Duplicate first names:
  fname  lname   level   dept     state
2  Jane  Jones   Year1  Mrktg  Illinois
3  Jane  Jones   Year1  Mrktg  Illinois
4  Jane  Stone  Senior  Mrktg   Arizona
```

```
5   Dave   Stone    Year2  Devel    Arizona
7   Jane   Jones    Year1  Mrktg   Illinois

Duplicate first name and level:
  fname  lname   level   dept      state
3  Jane  Jones   Year1  Mrktg  Illinois
4  Jane  Stone  Senior  Mrktg   Arizona
7  Jane  Jones   Year1  Mrktg  Illinois
```

Listing 3.28 displays the contents of `drop_duplicates.py` that illustrates how to drop duplicate rows in a `Pandas DataFrame`.

LISTING 3.28: drop_duplicates.py

```
import pandas as pd

df = pd.read_csv("duplicates.csv")
print("Contents of data frame:")
print(df)
print()

fname_filtered = df.drop_duplicates(['fname'])
print("Drop duplicate first names:")
print(fname_filtered)
print()

fname_lname_filtered = df.drop_duplicates(['fname','lname'])
print("Drop duplicate first and last names:")
print(fname_lname_filtered)
print()
```

Listing 3.28 initializes the `DataFrame df` with the contents of the `CSV` file `duplicates.csv`, and then displays the contents of the DataFrame. The next portion of Listing 3.28 deletes the rows that have duplicate `fname` values, followed by a code block that drops rows with duplicate `fname` and `lname` values. Launch the code in Listing 3.28 and you will see the following output:

```
Contents of data frame:
  fname  lname   level    dept       state
0  Jane  Smith  Senior   Sales  California
1  Dave  Smith  Senior   Devel  California
2  Jane  Jones   Year1   Mrktg    Illinois
3  Jane  Jones   Year1   Mrktg    Illinois
4  Jane  Stone  Senior   Mrktg     Arizona
5  Dave  Stone   Year2   Devel     Arizona
6  Mark  Aster   Year3  BizDev     Florida
7  Jane  Jones   Year1   Mrktg    Illinois


Drop duplicate first names:
  fname  lname   level    dept       state
0  Jane  Smith  Senior   Sales  California
```

```
1  Dave  Smith  Senior   Devel  California
6  Mark  Aster   Year3  BizDev     Florida

Drop duplicate first and last names:
  fname  lname   level    dept       state
0  Jane  Smith  Senior   Sales  California
1  Dave  Smith  Senior   Devel  California
2  Jane  Jones   Year1   Mrktg    Illinois
4  Jane  Stone  Senior   Mrktg     Arizona
5  Dave  Stone   Year2   Devel     Arizona
6  Mark  Aster   Year3  BizDev     Florida
```

FINDING MISSING VALUES IN PANDAS

Listing 3.29 displays the contents of `employees2.csv` and Listing 3.30 displays the contents of `missing_values.py` that illustrates how to display rows of a DataFrame that have missing values in a `Pandas DataFrame`.

LISTING 3.29: employees2.csv

```
name,year,month
Jane-Smith,2015,Aug
Jane-Smith,2015,Aug
Dave-Smith,2020,
Dave-Stone,Apr
Jane-Jones,2018,Dec
Jane-Stone,2017,Feb
Jane-Stone,2017,Feb
Mark-Aster,Oct
Jane-Jones,NaN,Jun
```

LISTING 3.30: missing_values.py

```
import pandas as pd
import matplotlib.pyplot as plt
import numpy as np

df = pd.read_csv("employees2.csv")

print("=> contents of CSV file:")
print(df)
print()

#NA:  Not Available (Pandas)
#NaN: Not a Number (Pandas)
#NB:  NumPy uses np.nan() to check for NaN values

df = pd.read_csv("employees2.csv")

print("=> contents of CSV file:")
print(df)
print()
```

```
print("=> any NULL values per column?")
print(df.isnull().any())
print()

print("=> count of NAN/MISSING values in each column:")
print(df.isnull().sum())
print()
print("=> count of NAN/MISSING values in each column:")
print(pd.isna(df).sum())
print()

print("=> count of NAN/MISSING values in each column
(sorted):")
print(df.isnull().sum().sort_values(ascending=False))
print()

nan_null = df.isnull().sum().sum()
miss_values = df.isnull().any().sum()

print("=> count of NaN/MISSING values:",nan_null)
print("=> count of MISSING values:",miss_values)
print("=> count of NaN values:",nan_null-miss_values)
```

Listing 3.30 initializes the `DataFrame` `df` with the contents of the `CSV` file `employees2.csv`, and then displays the contents of the DataFrame. The next portion of Listing 3.30 displays the number of null values that appear in any row or column. The next portion of Listing 3.30 displays the fields and the names of the fields that have null values.

The next portion of Listing 3.30 displays the number of duplicate rows, followed by the row numbers that are duplicates. Launch the code in Listing 3.30 and you will see the following output:

```
=> contents of CSV file:
         name    year month
0  Jane-Smith  2015.0   Aug
1  Jane-Smith  2015.0   Aug
2  Dave-Smith  2020.0   NaN
3  Dave-Stone     NaN   Apr
4  Jane-Jones  2018.0   Dec
5  Jane-Stone  2017.0   Feb
6  Jane-Stone  2017.0   Feb
7  Mark-Aster     NaN   Oct
8  Jane-Jones     NaN   Jun

=> any NULL values per column?
name     False
year      True
month     True
dtype: bool

=> count of NAN/MISSING values in each column:
name     0
year     3
```

```
month     1
dtype: int64

=> count of NAN/MISSING values in each column:
name      0
year      3
month     1
dtype: int64

=> count of NAN/MISSING values in each column (sorted):
year      3
month     1
name      0
dtype: int64

=> count of NaN/MISSING values: 4
=> count of MISSING values: 2
=> count of NaN values: 2
```

SORTING DATAFRAMES IN PANDAS

Listing 3.31 displays the contents of `sort_df.py` that illustrates how to sort the rows in a `Pandas DataFrame`.

LISTING 3.31: sort_df.py

```
import pandas as pd

df = pd.read_csv("duplicates.csv")
print("Contents of data frame:")
print(df)
print()

df.sort_values(by=['fname'], inplace=True)
print("Sorted (ascending) by first name:")
print(df)
print()

df.sort_values(by=['fname'], inplace=True,ascending=False)
print("Sorted (descending) by first name:")
print(df)
print()

df.sort_values(by=['fname','lname'], inplace=True)
print("Sorted (ascending) by first name and last name:")
print(df)
print()
```

Listing 3.31 initializes the `DataFrame df` with the contents of the `CSV` file `duplicates.csv`, and then displays the contents of the DataFrame. The next portion of Listing 3.31 displays the rows in *ascending* order based on the first name, and the next code block displays the rows in *descending* order based on the first name.

The final code block in Listing 3.31 displays the rows in ascending order based on the first name as well as the last name. Launch the code in Listing 3.31 and you will see the following output:

```
Contents of data frame:
  fname  lname   level    dept       state
0  Jane  Smith  Senior   Sales  California
1  Dave  Smith  Senior   Devel  California
2  Jane  Jones   Year1   Mrktg    Illinois
3  Jane  Jones   Year1   Mrktg    Illinois
4  Jane  Stone  Senior   Mrktg     Arizona
5  Dave  Stone   Year2   Devel     Arizona
6  Mark  Aster   Year3  BizDev     Florida
7  Jane  Jones   Year1   Mrktg    Illinois

Sorted (ascending) by first name:
  fname  lname   level    dept       state
1  Dave  Smith  Senior   Devel  California
5  Dave  Stone   Year2   Devel     Arizona
0  Jane  Smith  Senior   Sales  California
2  Jane  Jones   Year1   Mrktg    Illinois
3  Jane  Jones   Year1   Mrktg    Illinois
4  Jane  Stone  Senior   Mrktg     Arizona
7  Jane  Jones   Year1   Mrktg    Illinois
6  Mark  Aster   Year3  BizDev     Florida

Sorted (descending) by first name:
  fname  lname   level    dept       state
6  Mark  Aster   Year3  BizDev     Florida
0  Jane  Smith  Senior   Sales  California
2  Jane  Jones   Year1   Mrktg    Illinois
3  Jane  Jones   Year1   Mrktg    Illinois
4  Jane  Stone  Senior   Mrktg     Arizona
7  Jane  Jones   Year1   Mrktg    Illinois
1  Dave  Smith  Senior   Devel  California
5  Dave  Stone   Year2   Devel     Arizona

Sorted (ascending) by first name and last name:
  fname  lname   level    dept       state
1  Dave  Smith  Senior   Devel  California
5  Dave  Stone   Year2   Devel     Arizona
2  Jane  Jones   Year1   Mrktg    Illinois
3  Jane  Jones   Year1   Mrktg    Illinois
7  Jane  Jones   Year1   Mrktg    Illinois
0  Jane  Smith  Senior   Sales  California
4  Jane  Stone  Senior   Mrktg     Arizona
6  Mark  Aster   Year3  BizDev     Florida
```

WORKING WITH GROUPBY() IN PANDAS

Listing 3.32 displays the contents of `groupby1.py` that illustrates how to invoke the `Pandas groupby()` method in order to compute subtotals of feature values.

LISTING 3.32: groupby1.py

```
import pandas as pd

# colors and weights of balls:
data = {'color':['red','blue','blue','red','blue'],
        'weight':[40,50,20,30,90]}
df1 = pd.DataFrame(data)
print("df1:")
print(df1)
print()
print(df1.groupby('color').mean())
print()

red_filter = df1['color']=='red'
print(df1[red_filter])
print()
blue_filter = df1['color']=='blue'
print(df1[blue_filter])
print()

red_avg = df1[red_filter]['weight'].mean()
blue_avg = df1[blue_filter]['weight'].mean()
print("red_avg,blue_avg:")
print(red_avg,blue_avg)
print()

df2 = pd.DataFrame({'color':['blue','red'],'weight':
[red_avg,blue_avg]})
print("df2:")
print(df2)
print()
```

Listing 3.32 defines the variable `data` containing `color` and `weight` values, and then initializes the `DataFrame` `df` with the contents of the variable `data`. The next two code blocks define `red_filter` and `blue_filter` that match the rows whose colors are red and blue, respectively, and then prints the matching rows.

The next portion of Listing 3.32 defines the two filters `red_avg` and `blue_avg` that calculate the average weight of the red value and the blue values, respectively. The last code block in Listing 3.32 defines the `DataFrame` `df2` with a `color` column and a `weight` column, where the latter contains the average weight of the red values and the blue values. Launch the code in Listing 3.32 and you will see the following output:

```
initial data frame:
df1:
  color  weight
0   red      40
1  blue      50
2  blue      20
3   red      30
4  blue      90
```

```
color  weight
blue   53.333333
red    35.000000

  color  weight
0   red      40
3   red      30

  color  weight
1  blue      50
2  blue      20
4  blue      90

red_avg,blue_avg:
35.0 53.333333333333336

df2:
  color     weight
0  blue  35.000000
1   red  53.333333
```

AGGREGATE OPERATIONS WITH THE TITANIC.CSV DATASET

Listing 3.33 displays the contents of `aggregate2.py` that illustrates how to perform aggregate operations with columns in the `CSV` file `titanic.csv`.

LISTING 3.33: aggregate2.py

```
import pandas as pd

#Loading titanic.csv in Seaborn:
#df = sns.load_dataset('titanic')
df = pd.read_csv("titanic.csv")

# convert floating point values to integers:
df['survived'] = df['survived'].astype(int)

# specify column and aggregate functions:
aggregates1 = {'embark_town': ['count', 'nunique', 'size']}

# group by 'deck' value and apply aggregate functions:
result = df.groupby(['deck']).agg(aggregates1)
print("=> Grouped by deck:")
print(result)
print()

# some details regarding count() and nunique():
# count() excludes NaN values whereas size() includes them
# nunique() excludes NaN values in the unique counts

# group by 'age' value and apply aggregate functions:
result2 = df.groupby(['age']).agg(aggregates1)
```

```
print("=> Grouped by age (before):")
print(result2)
print()

# some "age" values are missing (so drop them):
df = df.dropna()

# convert floating point values to integers:
df['age'] = df['age'].astype(int)

# group by 'age' value and apply aggregate functions:
result3 = df.groupby(['age']).agg(aggregates1)
print("=> Grouped by age (after):")
print(result3)
print()
```

Listing 3.33 initializes the `DataFrame` `df` with the contents of the `CSV` file `titanic.csv`. The next code snippet converts floating point values to integer, followed by defining the variable `aggregates1` that specifies the functions `count()`, `nunique()`, and `size()` that will be invoked on the `embark_town` field.

The next code snippet initializes the variable `result` after invoking the `groupby()` method on the `deck` field, followed by invoking the `agg()` method.

The next code block performs the same computation to initialize the variable result2, except that the `groupby()` function is invoked on the `age` field instead of the `embark_town` field. Notice the comment section regarding the `count()` and `nunique()` functions: let's drop the rows with missing values via `df.dropna()` and investigate how that affects the calculations.

After dropping the rows with missing values, the final code block initializes the variable `result3` in exactly the same way that `result2` was initialized. Launch the code in Listing 3.33 and the output is shown here:

```
=> Grouped by deck:
      embark_town
            count nunique size
deck
A              15       2   15
B              45       2   47
C              59       3   59
D              33       2   33
E              32       3   32
F              13       3   13
G               4       1    4

=> Grouped by age (before):
        age
     count nunique size
age
0.42     1       1    1
0.67     1       1    1
0.75     2       1    2
0.83     2       1    2
0.92     1       1    1
...    ...     ...  ...
```

```
70.00      2        1    2
70.50      1        1    1
71.00      2        1    2
74.00      1        1    1
80.00      1        1    1

[88 rows x 3 columns]

=> Grouped by age (after):
     age
    count nunique size
age
0       1       1    1
1       1       1    1
2       3       1    3
3       1       1    1
4       3       1    3
6       1       1    1
11      1       1    1
14      1       1    1
15      1       1    1
// details omitted for brevity
60      2       1    2
61      2       1    2
62      1       1    1
63      1       1    1
64      1       1    1
65      2       1    2
70      1       1    1
71      1       1    1
80      1       1    1
```

WORKING WITH apply() AND mapapply() IN PANDAS

Earlier in this chapter you saw an example of the Pandas apply() method for modifying the categorical values of a feature in the CSV file shirts.csv. This section contains more examples of the apply() method, along with examples of the mapappy() method.

Listing 3.34 displays the contents of apply1.py that illustrates how to invoke the Pandas apply() method in order to compute the sum of a set of values.

LISTING 3.34: apply1.py

```
import pandas as pd

df = pd.DataFrame({'X1': [1,2,3], 'X2': [10,20,30]})

def cube(x):
  return x * x * x

df1 = df.apply(cube)
# same result:
```

```
# df1 = df.apply(lambda x: x * x * x)
print("initial data frame:")
print(df)
print("cubed values:")
print(df1)
```

Listing 3.34 initializes the DataFrame df with columns X1 and X2, where the values for X2 are 10 times the corresponding values in X1. Next, the Python function cube() returns the cube of its argument. Listing 3.34 then defines the variable df1 by invoking the apply() function, which specifies the user-defined Python function cube(), and then prints the values of df as well as df1. Launch the code in Listing 3.34 and you will see the following output:

```
initial data frame:
   X1  X2
0   1  10
1   2  20
2   3  30
cubed values:
   X1     X2
0   1   1000
1   8   8000
2  27  27000
```

Listing 3.35 displays the contents of apply2.py that illustrates how to invoke the Pandas apply() method in order to compute the sum of a set of values.

LISTING 3.35: apply2.py

```
import pandas as pd
import numpy as np

df = pd.DataFrame({'X1': [10,20,30], 'X2': [50,60,70]})

df1 = df.apply(np.sum, axis=0)
df2 = df.apply(np.sum, axis=1)

print("initial data frame:")
print(df)
print("add values (axis=0):")
print(df1)
print("add values (axis=1):")
print(df2)
```

Listing 3.35 is a variation of Listing 3.34: the variables df1 and df2 contain the column-wise sum and the row-wise sum, respectively, of the DataFrame df. Launch the code in Listing 3.35 and you will see the following output:

```
   X1  X2
0  10  50
1  20  60
```

```
2  30  70
add values (axis=0):
X1      60
X2     180
dtype: int64
add values (axis=1):
0      60
1      80
2     100
dtype: int64
```

Listing 3.36 displays the contents of `mapapply1.py` that illustrates how to invoke the `Pandas mapapply()` method in order to compute the sum of a set of values.

LISTING 3.36: mapapply1.py

```
import pandas as pd
import math

df = pd.DataFrame({'X1': [1,2,3], 'X2': [10,20,30]})
df1 = df.applymap(math.sqrt)

print("initial data frame:")
print(df)
print("square root values:")
print(df1)
```

Listing 3.36 is yet another variant of Listing 3.34: in this case, the variable `df1` is defined by invoking the `applymap()` method of the variable `df`, which in turn references (but does not execute) the `math.sqrt()` function. Next, a `print()` statement displays the contents of `df`, followed by a `print()` statement that displays the contents of `df1`: it is at this point that the built-in `math.sqrt()` function is invoked in order to calculate the square root of the values in `df`. Launch the code in Listing 3.36 and you will see the following output:

```
initial data frame:
   X1  X2
0   1  10
1   2  20
2   3  30

square root values:
         X1        X2
0  1.000000  3.162278
1  1.414214  4.472136
2  1.732051  5.477226
```

Listing 3.37 displays the contents of `mapapply2.py` that illustrates how to invoke the `Pandas mapapply()` method in order to convert strings to lowercase and uppercase.

LISTING 3.37: mapapply2.py

```
import pandas as pd

df = pd.DataFrame({'fname': ['Jane'], 'lname': ['Smith']},
                  {'fname': ['Dave'], 'lname': ['Jones']})

df1 = df.applymap(str.lower)
df2 = df.applymap(str.upper)

print("initial data frame:")
print(df)
print()
print("lowercase:")
print(df1)
print()
print("uppercase:")
print(df2)
print()
```

Listing 3.37 initializes the variable `df` with two first and last name pairs, and then defines the variables `df1` and `df2` by invoking the `applymap()` method to the variable `df`. The variable `df1` converts its input values to lowercase, whereas the variable `df2` converts its input values to uppercase. Launch the code in Listing 3.37 and you will see the following output:

```
initial data frame:
      fname  lname
fname  Jane  Smith
lname  Jane  Smith

lowercase:
      fname  lname
fname  jane  smith
lname  jane  smith

uppercase:
      fname  lname
fname  JANE  SMITH
lname  JANE  SMITH
```

USEFUL ONE-LINE COMMANDS IN PANDAS

This section contains an eclectic mix of one-line commands in `Pandas` (some of which you have already seen in this chapter) that are useful to know:

Save a `DataFrame` to a `CSV` file (comma separated and without indices):

```
df.to_csv("data.csv", sep=",", index=False)
```

List the column names of a DataFrame:

```
df.columns
```

Drop missing data from a DataFrame:

```
df.dropna(axis=0, how='any')
```

Replace missing data in a DataFrame:

```
df.replace(to_replace=None, value=None)
```

Check for NANs in a DataFrame:

```
pd.isnull(object)
```

Drop a feature in a DataFrame:

```
df.drop('feature_variable_name', axis=1)
```

Convert object type to float in a DataFrame:

```
pd.to_numeric(df["feature_name"], errors='coerce')
```

Convert data in a DataFrame to NumPy array:

```
df.as_matrix()
```

Display the first n rows of a DataFrame:

```
df.head(n)
```

Get data by feature name in a DataFrame:

```
df.loc[feature_name]
```

Apply a lambda function to a DataFrame, such as multiplying all values in the "height" column of the DataFrame by 3:

```
df["height"].apply(lambda height: 3 * height)
```

OR:

```
def multiply(x):
    return x * 3
df["height"].apply(multiply)
```

Rename the fourth column of the DataFrame as "height":

```
df.rename(columns = {df.columns[3]:'height'}, inplace=True)
```

Get the unique entries of the column "first" in a DataFrame:

```
df["first"].unique()
```

Create a DataFrame with columns `first` and `last` from an existing `DataFrame`:

```
new_df = df[["first", "last"]]
```

Sort the data in a DataFrame:

```
df.sort_values(ascending = False)
```

Filter the data column named "size" to display only values equal to 7:

```
df[df["size"] == 7]
```

Select the first row of the "height" column in a `DataFrame`:

```
df.loc([0], ['height'])
```

WHAT IS TEXTHERO?

`Texthero` is a `Python`-based open source toolkit that functions as a layer of abstraction over `Pandas`, and its home page is here:

https://github.com/jbesomi/texthero

`Texthero` leverages very useful `Python` libraries for `NLP`, such as `Gensim`, `NLTK`, `SpaCy`, and `Sklearn`. Moreover, `Texthero` supports the following functionality:

- NER and topic modeling (for NLP)
- TF-IDF, term frequency, and word-embeddings (for NLP)
- DBSCAN, Hierarchical, k-Means, and Meanshift algorithms
- various types of text visualization

Open a command shell and install texthero with the following command:

```
pip3 install texthero
```

`Texthero` supports various other algorithms, including dimensionality reduction algorithms for machine learning. Navigate to the following link for documentation and other information about `Texthero`:

https://texthero.org/docs/getting-started

DATA VISUALIZATION IN PANDAS

Although `Matplotlib` and `Seaborn` are often the "go to" Python libraries for data visualization, you can also use `Pandas` for such tasks.

Listing 3.38 displays the contents `pandas_viz1.py` that illustrates how to render various types of charts and graphs using `Pandas` and `Matplotlib`.

LISTING 3.38: pandas_viz1.py

```
import pandas as pd
import numpy as np
import matplotlib.pyplot as plt

df = pd.DataFrame(np.random.rand(16,3),
columns=['X1','X2','X3'])
print("First 5 rows:")
print(df.head())
print()

print("Diff of first 5 rows:")
print(df.diff().head())
print()

# bar chart:
#ax = df.plot.bar()

# horizontal stacked bar chart:
#ax = df.plot.barh(stacked=True)

# vertical stacked bar chart:
ax = df.plot.bar(stacked=True)

# stacked area graph:
#ax = df.plot.area()

# non-stacked area graph:
#ax = df.plot.area(stacked=False)

#plt.show(ax)
```

Listing 3.38 initializes the `DataFrame` `df` with a 16x3 matrix of random numbers, followed by the contents of `df`. The bulk of Listing 3.38 contains code snippets for generating a bar chart, a horizontal stacked bar chart, a vertical stacked bar chart, a stacked area graph, and a nonstacked area graph. You can uncomment the individual code snippet that displays the graph of your choice with the contents of `df`. Launch the code in Listing 3.38 and you will see the following output:

```
First 5 rows:
         X1        X2        X3
0  0.051089  0.357183  0.344414
1  0.800890  0.468372  0.800668
2  0.492981  0.505133  0.228399
3  0.461996  0.977895  0.471315
4  0.033209  0.411852  0.347165

Diff of first 5 rows:
         X1        X2        X3
0       NaN       NaN       NaN
1  0.749801  0.111189  0.456255
2 -0.307909  0.036760 -0.572269
3 -0.030984  0.472762  0.242916
4 -0.428787 -0.566043 -0.124150
```

SUMMARY

This chapter introduced you to Pandas for creating labeled DataFrames and displaying metadata of Pandas DataFrames. Then you learned how to create Pandas DataFrames from various sources of data, such as random numbers and hard-coded data values.

You also learned how to read Excel spreadsheets and perform numeric calculations on that data, such as the minimum, mean, and maximum values in numeric columns. Then you saw how to create Pandas DataFrames from data stored in CSV files. In addition, you learned how to generate a scatterplot from data in a Pandas DataFrame.

Then you got a brief introduction to JSON, along with an example of converting a Python dictionary to JSON-based data (and vice versa). Finally, you learned about Texthero, which is an open source Python-based toolkit that is a layer of abstraction over Pandas.

CHAPTER 4

PANDAS AND SQL

This chapter contains a variety of Python code samples that contain Pandas, SQL, and SQLite3. You will also see examples of working with XML documents and JSON data in Python code samples.

The first section contains code samples of data visualization in Pandas, such as bar charts, area charts, and line graphs.

The first section contains code samples of data visualization in Pandas, such as bar charts, area charts, and line graphs.

The second section contains code samples that show you how to write Python code that contains MySQL commands. You will also see code samples that contain Python and Pandas. In addition, you will learn how to export SQL data from Pandas to an Excel spreadsheet.

The third section briefly introduces XML and JSON, and how to read such data in a Pandas DataFrame. Moreover, there is section that discusses regular expressions.

The fourth section shows you how to combine Python and SQLite to perform database-related operations, such as creating a table in a sqlite3 database and then inserting data into such a table. You will then learn how to select data from that table and populate a Pandas DataFrame with that data.

The final section contains a brief introduction to Beautiful Soup, along with code samples that show you how to use Beautiful Soup in order to parse HTML Web pages.

PANDAS AND DATA VISUALIZATION

The following subsections contain Python-based code samples that use Pandas in order to render the following types of charts and graphs:

- bar chart
- horizontal stacked bar chart

- vertical stacked bar chart
- nonstacked area chart
- stacked area chart

Pandas and Bar Charts

Listing 4.1 displays the contents of `pandas_barchart.py` that shows you how to render a bar chart in `Pandas`.

LISTING 4.1: pandas_barchart.py

```
import pandas as pd
import numpy as np
import matplotlib.pyplot as plt

df = pd.DataFrame(np.random.rand(16,3),
columns=['X1','X2','X3'])
print("First 5 rows:")
print(df.head())
print()

print("Diff of first 5 rows:")
print(df.diff().head())
print()

# bar chart:
ax = df.plot.bar()
plt.show()
```

Listing 4.1 starts with `import` statements and then initializes the `Pandas DataFrame df1` with a set of data values. Launch the code in Listing 4.1 and you will see the following output:

```
First 5 rows:
         X1        X2        X3
0  0.752462  0.742749  0.950918
1  0.957054  0.836334  0.547507
2  0.022269  0.994618  0.861796
3  0.038466  0.911388  0.545711
4  0.483224  0.468873  0.412120

Diff of first 5 rows:
         X1        X2        X3
0       NaN       NaN       NaN
1  0.204591  0.093585 -0.403411
2 -0.934785  0.158284  0.314289
3  0.016197 -0.083230 -0.316085
4  0.444758 -0.442515 -0.133591
```

Figure 4.1 displays the bar chart that is generated by the code in Listing 4.1.

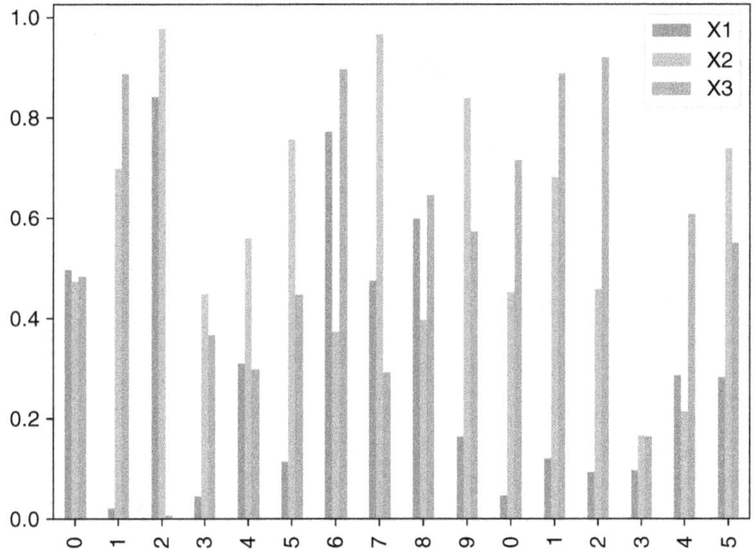

FIGURE 4.1 A bar chart in Pandas.

Pandas and Horizontally Stacked Bar Charts

Listing 4.2 displays the contents of `pandas_hstacked_bar1.py` that shows you how to render a horizontally stacked bar chart in `Pandas`.

LISTING 4.2: pandas_hstacked_bar1.py

```
import pandas as pd
import numpy as np
import matplotlib.pyplot as plt

df = pd.DataFrame(np.random.rand(16,3),
columns=['X1','X2','X3'])
print("First 5 rows:")
print(df.head())
print()

print("Diff of first 5 rows:")
print(df.diff().head())
print()

# horizontal stacked bar chart:
ax = df.plot.barh(stacked=True)
plt.show()
```

Listing 4.2 starts with `import` statements and then initializes the `Pandas DataFrame df1` with a set of data values. Launch the code in Listing 4.2 and you will see the following output:

```
First 5 rows:
         X1        X2        X3
0  0.272391  0.737949  0.617566
1  0.532135  0.234155  0.720543
2  0.500043  0.740288  0.930658
3  0.565021  0.846596  0.379988
4  0.340198  0.063606  0.841024

Diff of first 5 rows:
         X1        X2        X3
0       NaN       NaN       NaN
1  0.259743 -0.503794  0.102977
2 -0.032091  0.506133  0.210115
3  0.064977  0.106308 -0.550671
4 -0.224823 -0.782989  0.461036
```

Figure 4.2 displays the horizontally stacked bar chart that is generated by the code in Listing 4.2.

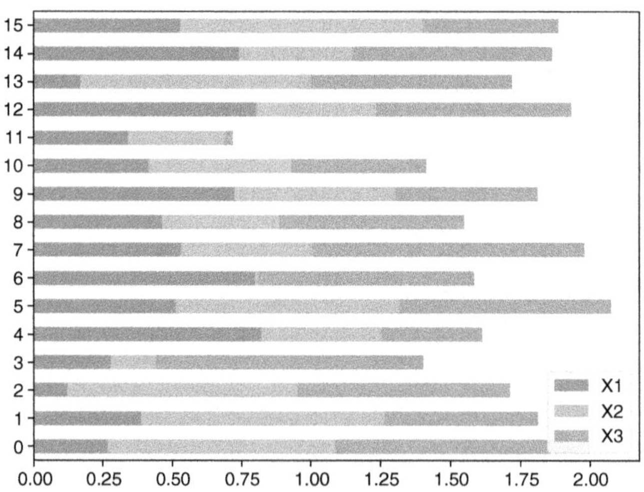

FIGURE 4.2 A horizontally stacked bar chart in Pandas.

Pandas and Vertically Stacked Bar Charts

Listing 4.3 displays the contents of `pandas_vstacked_bar1.py` that shows you how to render a vertically stacked bar chart in `Pandas`.

LISTING 4.3: pandas_vstacked_bar1.py

```
import pandas as pd
import numpy as np
import matplotlib.pyplot as plt

df = pd.DataFrame(np.random.rand(16,3),
columns=['X1','X2','X3'])
print("First 5 rows:")
print(df.head())
print()

print("Diff of first 5 rows:")
print(df.diff().head())
print()

# vertical stacked bar chart:
ax = df.plot.bar(stacked=True)
plt.show()
```

Listing 4.3 starts with `import` statements and then initializes the `Pandas DataFrame df1` with a set of data values. Launch the code in Listing 4.3 and you will see the following output:

```
First 5 rows:
         X1        X2        X3
0  0.529936  0.100616  0.683788
1  0.924753  0.320835  0.823198
2  0.925181  0.043236  0.349372
3  0.496390  0.739566  0.759168
4  0.168874  0.241563  0.320381

Diff of first 5 rows:
         X1        X2        X3
0       NaN       NaN       NaN
1  0.394817  0.220219  0.139410
2  0.000428 -0.277599 -0.473826
3 -0.428791  0.696330  0.409796
4 -0.327516 -0.498003 -0.438787
```

Figure 4.3 displays the vertically stacked bar chart that is generated by the code in Listing 4.3.

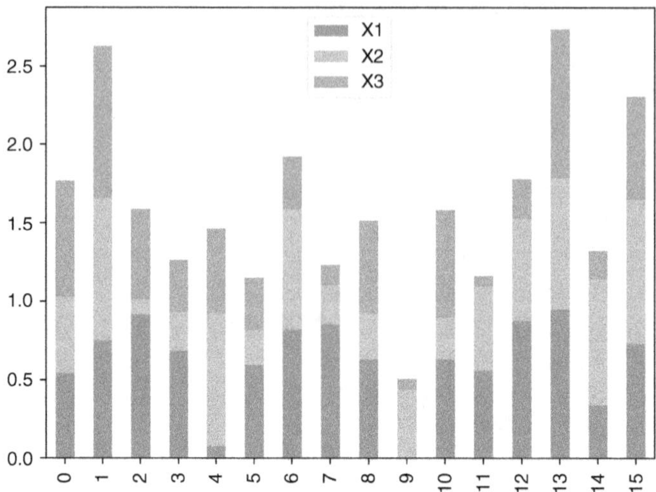

FIGURE 4.3 A vertically stacked bar chart in Pandas.

Pandas and Nonstacked Area Charts

Listing 4.4 displays the contents of `pandas_area_nonstacked.py` that shows you how to render a nonstacked area chart in `Pandas`.

LISTING 4.4: pandas_area_nonstacked.py

```
import pandas as pd
import numpy as np
import matplotlib.pyplot as plt

df = pd.DataFrame(np.random.rand(16,3),
columns=['X1','X2','X3'])
print("First 5 rows:")
print(df.head())
print()

print("Diff of first 5 rows:")
print(df.diff().head())
print()

# non-stacked area graph:
ax = df.plot.area(stacked=False)
plt.show()
```

Listing 4.4 starts with `import` statements and then initializes the `Pandas DataFrame df1` with a set of data values. Launch the code in Listing 4.4 and you will see the following output:

```
First 5 rows:
         X1        X2        X3
0  0.347024  0.887191  0.431096
1  0.201923  0.097674  0.521704
```

```
2  0.763501  0.516445  0.266348
3  0.055767  0.870355  0.679274
4  0.180045  0.621363  0.152446

Diff of first 5 rows:
         X1        X2        X3
0       NaN       NaN       NaN
1 -0.145101 -0.789517  0.090608
2  0.561577  0.418771 -0.255356
3 -0.707734  0.353910  0.412926
4  0.124278 -0.248992 -0.526828
```

Figure 4.4 displays the nonstacked area chart that is generated by the code in Listing 4.4.

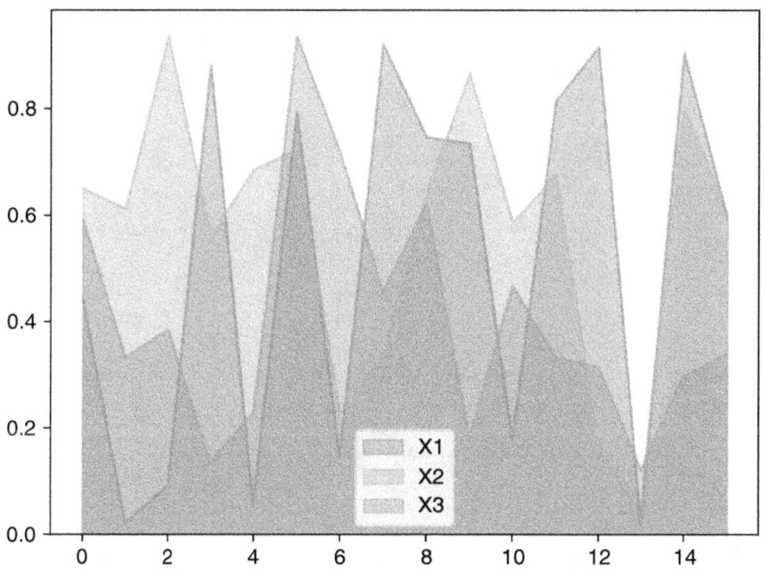

FIGURE 4.4 A Nonstacked area chart in Pandas.

Pandas and Stacked Area Charts

Listing 4.5 displays the contents of `pandas_area_stacked.py` that shows you how to render a stack area chart in `Pandas`.

LISTING 4.5: pandas_area_stacked.py

```
import pandas as pd
import numpy as np
import matplotlib.pyplot as plt

df = pd.DataFrame(np.random.rand(16,3),
columns=['X1','X2','X3'])
print("First 5 rows:")
print(df.head())
print()
```

```
print("Diff of first 5 rows:")
print(df.diff().head())
print()

# stacked area graph:
ax = df.plot.area()
plt.show()
```

Listing 4.5 starts with `import` statements and then initializes the `Pandas DataFrame df1` with a set of data values. Launch the code in Listing 4.5 and you will see the following output:

```
First 5 rows:
         X1        X2        X3
0  0.801187  0.635952  0.585165
1  0.776911  0.393118  0.887285
2  0.248293  0.785893  0.409110
3  0.557084  0.402462  0.180559
4  0.201810  0.456198  0.576540

Diff of first 5 rows:
         X1        X2        X3
0       NaN       NaN       NaN
1 -0.024276 -0.242834  0.302120
2 -0.528618  0.392775 -0.478175
3  0.308790 -0.383431 -0.228551
4 -0.355274  0.053737  0.395981
```

Figure 4.5 displays the stacked area chart that is generated by the code in Listing 4.5.

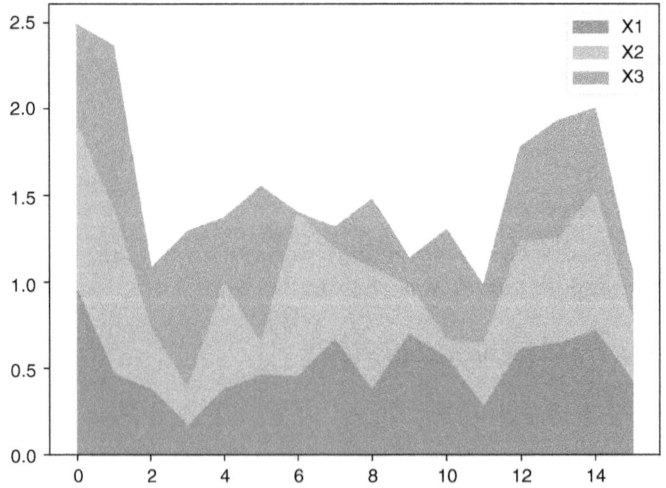

FIGURE 4.5 A stacked area chart in Pandas.

This concludes the portion of the chapter regarding `Pandas` and basic charts and graphs.

WHAT IS FUGUE?

Fugue a Python-based library that enables you to invoke SQL-like queries against Pandas DataFrames via FugueSQL. Install Fugue with the following command (specify a different version if you need to do so):

```
pip3.7 install fugue
```

Listing 4.6 displays the contents of fugue1.py that illustrates how to populate a Pandas DataFrame and then invoke various SQL commands to retrieve a subset of the data from the Pandas DataFrame.

LISTING 4.6: fugue1.py

```
import pandas as pd
from fugue_sql import fsql

df1 = pd.DataFrame({'fnames': ['john', 'dave', 'sara', 'eddy'],
                    'lnames': ['smith','stone','stein','bower'],
                    'ages':   [30,33,34,35],
                    'gender': ['m','m','f','m']})

print("=> DataFrame:")
print(df1)
print()

# Example #1: select users who are older than 33:
query_1 = """
SELECT fnames, lnames, ages, gender FROM df1
WHERE ages > 33
PRINT
"""

# display the extracted data:
fsql(query_1).run()
```

Listing 4.6 starts with import statements and then initializes the Pandas DataFrame df1 with a set of data values. The next portion of Listing 4.6 constructs a query that retrieves the data values of all users who are older than 33. Launch the code in Listing 4.6 and you will see the following output:

```
=> DataFrame:
  fnames lnames  ages gender
0   john  smith    30      m
1   dave  stone    33      m
2   sara  stein    34      f
3   eddy  bower    35      m

ANTLR runtime and generated code versions disagree: 4.8!=4.9
ANTLR runtime and generated code versions disagree: 4.8!=4.9
ANTLR runtime and generated code versions disagree: 4.8!=4.9
ANTLR runtime and generated code versions disagree: 4.8!=4.9
```

```
PandasDataFrame
fnames:str|lnames:str|ages:long|gender:str
----------+----------+---------+----------
sara      |stein     |34       |f
eddy      |bower     |35       |m
Total count: 2
```

MYSQL, SQLALCHEMY, AND PANDAS

There are several ways to interact with a MySQL database, one of which is via SQLAlchemy. The Python code samples in subsequent sections rely on SQLAlchemy (which is briefly described in the next section) and Pandas.

What Is SQLAlchemy?

SQLAlchemy is an ORM (Object Relational Mapping), which serves as a "bridge" between Python code and a database. Install SQLAlchemy with this command:

```
pip3 install sqlalchemy
```

SQLAlchemy handles the task of converting Python function invocations into the appropriate SQL statements, as well as providing support for custom SQL statements. In addition, SQLAlchemy supports multiple databases, including MySQL, Oracle, PostgreSQL, and SQLite.

Read MySQL Data via SQLAlchemy

The previous section showed you how to install SQLAlchemy, and install Pandas (if you haven't done so already) with this command:

```
pip3 install pandas
```

The Pandas functionality in the code samples involves the intuitively named read_sql() method and the related read_sql_query() method, both of which read the contents of a MySQL table.

Listing 4.7 displays the contents of read_sql_data.py that reads the contents of the people table.

LISTING 4.7: read_sql_table.py

```
from sqlalchemy import create_engine
import pymysql
import pandas as pd

engine = create_engine('mysql+pymysql://root:yourpassword@
127.0.0.1',pool_recycle=3600)
dbConn = engine.connect()
frame  = pd.read_sql("select * from mytools.people", dbConn);

pd.set_option('display.expand_frame_repr', False)
print(frame)
dbConn.close()
```

Listing 4.7 starts with several `import` statements that are required in order to access a `MySQL` database. The next portion of code initializes the variable `engine` as a reference to `MySQL`, followed by `dbConn` that is a database connection. Next, the variable `frame` is initialized with the rows in the `people` table. Launch the following command in a command shell:

```
python3 read_sql_table.py
```

You will see the following output generated by the preceding command:

```
  fname  lname age gender  country
0  john  smith  30      m      usa
1  jane  smith  31      f   france
2  jack  jones  32      m   france
3  dave  stone  33      m    italy
4  sara  stein  34      f  germany
5  eddy  bower  35      m    spain
```

Listing 4.8 displays the contents of `sql_query.py` that reads the contents of the `people` table.

LISTING 4.8: sql_query.py

```
from sqlalchemy import create_engine
import pymysql
import pandas as pd
engine = create_engine('mysql+pymysql://root:yourpassword@
127.0.0.1',pool_recycle=3600)

query_1 = '''
select * from mytools.people
'''

print("create dataframe from table:")
df_2 = pd.read_sql_query(query_1, engine)

print("dataframe:")
print(df_2)
```

Listing 4.8 starts with several `import` statements followed by initializing the variable `engine` as a reference to a `MySQL` instance. Next, the variable `query_1` is defined as a string variable that specifies a `SQL` statement that selects all the rows of the `people` table, followed by the variable `df_2` (a dataframe) that returns the result of executing the `SQL` statement specified in the variable `query_1`. The final code snippet displays the contents of the `people` table. Launch the following command in a command shell:

```
python3 sql_query.py
```

You will see the following output generated by the preceding command:

```
  fname  lname age gender  country
0  john  smith  30      m      usa
1  jane  smith  31      f   france
2  jack  jones  32      m   france
3  dave  stone  33      m    italy
4  sara  stein  34      f  germany
5  eddy  bower  35      m    spain
```

Launch the following `Python` script in a command shell:

```
python3 sql_query.py
```

You will see the following output generated by the preceding command:

```
  fname  lname age gender  country
0  john  smith  30      m      usa
1  jane  smith  31      f   france
2  jack  jones  32      m   france
3  dave  stone  33      m    italy
4  sara  stein  34      f  germany
5  eddy  bower  35      m    spain
```

EXPORT SQL DATA FROM PANDAS TO EXCEL

Listing 4.9 displays the contents of `sql_query_excel.py` that reads the contents of the `people` table into a `Pandas` DataFrame and then exports the latter to an `Excel` file.

LISTING 4.9: sql_query_excel.py

```
from sqlalchemy import create_engine
import pymysql
import pandas as pd

engine = create_engine('mysql+pymysql://root:yourpassword@
127.0.0.1/',pool_recycle=3600)

query_1 = '''
select * from mytools.people
'''

print("create dataframe from table:")
df_2 = pd.read_sql_query(query_1, engine)

print("Contents of Pandas dataframe:")
print(df_2)

import openpyxl
print("saving dataframe to people.xlsx")
df_2.to_excel('people.xlsx', index=False)
```

Listing 4.9 contains several `import` statements followed by the variable `engine` that is initialized to an "endpoint" from which a `MySQL` database can be accessed. The next code snippet initializes the variable `query_1` as a string that contains a simple `SQL SELECT` statement.

Next, the variable `df_2` is a `Pandas` DataFrame that initialized to the result of invoking the `SQL` statement defined in the variable `query_1`, after which the contents of `df_2` are displayed. The final portion of code in Listing 4.9 saves the contents of `df_2` to an `Excel` document called `people.xlsx`. Launch the following command in a command shell:

```
python3 sql_query_excel.py
```

The preceding command will generate the following output:

```
Creating dataframe from table people
Contents of Pandas dataframe:
   fname  lname age gender  country
0   john  smith  30      m      usa
1   jane  smith  31      f   france
2   jack  jones  32      m   france
3   dave  stone  33      m    italy
4   sara  stein  34      f  germany
..   ...    ...  ..    ...      ...
73  jane  smith  31      f   france
74  jack  jones  32      m   france
75  dave  stone  33      m    italy
76  sara  stein  34      f  germany
77  eddy  bower  35      m    spain

[78 rows x 5 columns]
saving dataframe to people.xlsx
```

NOTE *You might need to launch the earlier `Python` script using `Python 3.7` instead of `Python 3.8` or `Python 3.9`.*

The next section contains `Pandas`-related functionality that does not involve any database connectivity. Since the previous portion of this chapter contains `Pandas`-related functionality, it's a convenient a convenient location for this material. However, if you prefer, you can skip this section with no loss of continuity and proceed to the following section that discusses `SQLite`.

MYSQL AND CONNECTOR/PYTHON

`MySQL` provides a `connector/Python` API as another mechanism for connecting to a `MySQL` database. This section contains some simple `Python` code samples that rely on connector/`Python` to connect to a database and retrieve rows from a database table.

Before delving into the code samples, keep in mind that `MySQL` 8 uses `mysql_native_password` instead of `caching_sha2_password`. As a result, you need to specify a value for auth_plugin (which is not specified in various online code samples). Here is the error message:

```
mysql.connector.errors.NotSupportedError: Authentication
plugin 'caching_sha2_password' is not supported
```

The solution is highlighted in the Python code sample in the next section.

Establishing a Database Connection

Listing 4.10 displays the contents of mysql_conn1.py that illustrates how to establish a connector/Python database connection.

LISTING 4.10: mysql_conn1.py

```
import mysql.connector

cnx = mysql.connector.connect(user='root',
                              password='yourpassword',
                              host='localhost',
                              database='employees',
                              auth_plugin='mysql_native_password')
cnx.close()
```

Listing 4.10 contains an import statement in order to set the appropriate path for Python 3.9. If the code executes correctly on your system without these two lines of code, then you can safely delete them.

The next code snippet is an import statement, followed by initializing the variable cnx as a database connection. Note the snippet shown in bold, which is required for MySQL 8 in order to connect to a MySQL database, as described in the introductory portion of this section. Launch the code in Listing 4.10, and if you don't see any error messages, then the code worked correctly.

Reading Data From a Database Table

Listing 4.11 displays the contents of mysql_pandas.py that illustrates how to establish a database connection and retrieve the rows in a database table.

LISTING 4.11: mysql_pandas.py

```
import mysql.connector

mydb = mysql.connector.connect(user='root',
                               password='yourpassword',
                               host='localhost',
                               database='employees',
                               auth_plugin='mysql_native_password')

mycursor = mydb.cursor()

# select all rows from the employees table:
mycursor.execute('SELECT * FROM employees')
```

```
import pandas as pd

# populate a Pandas data frame with the data:
table_rows = mycursor.fetchall()
df = pd.DataFrame(table_rows)

print("data frame:")
print(df)

mydb.close()
```

Listing 4.11 starts with the same `import` statement as Listing 4.10 and for the same purpose. The next code snippet is an import statement, followed by initializing the variable `cnx` as a database connection. Note the snippet shown in bold, which is required for `MySQL` 8 in order to connect to a `MySQL` database. Launch the code in Listing 4.11 and if everything worked correctly you will see the following output:

```
=> Contents of data frame:
      0     1                   2
0  1000  2000           Developer
1  2000  3000        Project Lead
2  3000  4000         Dev Manager
3  4000  4000  Senior Dev Manager
```

Creating a Database Table

Listing 4.12 displays the contents of `create_fun_table.py` that illustrates how to establish a database connection and create a database table.

LISTING 4.12: create_fun_table.py

```
my_table = (
    "CREATE TABLE 'for_fun' ("
    "  'dept_no' char(4) NOT NULL,"
    "  'dept_name' varchar(40) NOT NULL,"
    "  PRIMARY KEY ('dept_no'), UNIQUE KEY 'dept_name' ('dept_name')"
    ") ENGINE=InnoDB")

DB_NAME = 'for_fun_db'

import mysql.connector
cnx = mysql.connector.connect(user='root',
                              password='yourpassword',
                              host='localhost',
                              database='mytools')
cursor = cnx.cursor()

try:
  print("Creating table {}: ".format(my_table), end='')
  cursor.execute(my_table)
except mysql.connector.Error as err:
  if err.errno == errorcode.ER_TABLE_EXISTS_ERROR:
    print("already exists.")
  else:
```

```
    print(err.msg)
else:
  print("Table created:",my_table)

cursor.close()

cnx.close()
```

Listing 4.12 starts by initializing the variable `my_table` as a string that contains a `SQL` statement for creating a `MySQL` table. The next portion of Listing 4.12 initializes the variable `cnx` as a connection to the `mytools` database, and then initializes the variable `cursor` as a database cursor.

The next portion of Listing 4.12 contains a `try/catch` block in order to create the table `for_fun` that is specified in the string variable `my_table`. The `except` block catches the connection-related error and displays an appropriate message if the error occurred because the specified table already exists, or for some other reason.

Launch the code in Listing 4.12 and if everything worked correctly you will see the following output:

```
Creating table CREATE TABLE 'for_fun' (  'dept_no' char(4)
NOT NULL,  'dept_name' varchar(40) NOT NULL,  PRIMARY
KEY ('dept_no'), UNIQUE KEY 'dept_name' ('dept_name'))
ENGINE=InnoDB: Table created: CREATE TABLE 'for_fun' (
'dept_no' char(4) NOT NULL,  'dept_name' varchar(40) NOT
NULL,  PRIMARY KEY ('dept_no'), UNIQUE KEY 'dept_name'
('dept_name')) ENGINE=InnoDB
```

Now open a command shell and from the `MySQL` prompt enter the following command:

```
MySQL [mytools]> desc for_fun;
+-----------+-------------+------+-----+---------+-------+
| Field     | Type        | Null | Key | Default | Extra |
+-----------+-------------+------+-----+---------+-------+
| dept_no   | char(4)     | NO   | PRI | NULL    |       |
| dept_name | varchar(40) | NO   | UNI | NULL    |       |
+-----------+-------------+------+-----+---------+-------+
2 rows in set (0.060 sec)
```

WRITING PANDAS DATA TO A MYSQL TABLE

Listing 4.13 displays the contents of `pandas_write_sql.py` that shows you how to write data from a `Pandas` DataFrame into a `MySQL` table.

LISTING 4.13: pandas_write_sql.py

```
import pandas as pd

data = pd.DataFrame({
```

```
    'book_id':[12345, 12346, 12347],
    'title':['Python Programming', 'Learn MySQL', 'Data
Science Cookbook'],
    'price':[29, 23, 27]
})

import mysql.connector

mydb = mysql.connector.connect (
        host="localhost",
        user="root",
        password="os1wald123",
        database = "mytools",
        auth_plugin='mysql_native_password'
       )

from sqlalchemy import create_engine

engine = create_engine('mysql+pymysql://
root:os1wald123@127.0.0.1:3306/mytools',pool_recycle=3600)
dbConn = engine.connect()

# The to_sql writes data into the book_details table:
data.to_sql('book_details', engine, if_exists='append',
index=False)

df = pd.read_sql("SELECT * FROM book_details", dbConn);
pd.set_option('display.expand_frame_repr', False)
print("Rows from book_details table:")
print(df)
dbConn.close()
```

Listing 4.13 starts by initializing the variable `data` as a `Pandas` DataFrame with data values, followed by the variable `mydb` that is initialized as an instance for a database connection.

The next portion of Listing 4.13 instantiates the variables engine and also the variable `dbConn` that will be invoked while writing data to the database. Next, the variable `data` invokes its `to_sql()` method that also specifies the table `book_details`, the `engine` variable, and also uses `append` mode to the database if the table already exists.

The final portion of Listing 4.13 populates the variable `df` with all the data in the `book_details` table and then displays its contents before closing the database connection. Now launch the code in Listing 4.13 and if everything worked correctly you will see the following output:

```
Rows from book_details table:
   book_id                 title  price
0    12345    Python Programming     29
1    12346           Learn MySQL     23
2    12347  Data Science Cookbook     27
```

Navigate to the `MySQL` prompt and enter the following statements:

```
mysql> use mytools;
Database changed
```

```
mysql> desc book_details;
+---------+--------+------+-----+---------+-------+
| Field   | Type   | Null | Key | Default | Extra |
+---------+--------+------+-----+---------+-------+
| book_id | bigint | YES  |     | NULL    |       |
| title   | text   | YES  |     | NULL    |       |
| price   | bigint | YES  |     | NULL    |       |
+---------+--------+------+-----+---------+-------+
3 rows in set (0.00 sec)

mysql> select * from book_details;
+---------+-----------------------+-------+
| book_id | title                 | price |
+---------+-----------------------+-------+
|   12345 | Python Programming    |    29 |
|   12346 | Learn MySQL           |    23 |
|   12347 | Data Science Cookbook |    27 |
+---------+-----------------------+-------+
3 rows in set (0.00 sec)
```

Now launch the code in Listing 4.13 again and then execute the preceding SQL statement again:

```
mysql> select * from book_details;
+---------+-----------------------+-------+
| book_id | title                 | price |
+---------+-----------------------+-------+
|   12345 | Python Programming    |    29 |
|   12346 | Learn MySQL           |    23 |
|   12347 | Data Science Cookbook |    27 |
|   12345 | Python Programming    |    29 |
|   12346 | Learn MySQL           |    23 |
|   12347 | Data Science Cookbook |    27 |
+---------+-----------------------+-------+
6 rows in set (0.00 sec)
```

As you can see, there are now 6 crows in the book_details table. The reason for the insertion of the same three rows of data is the append value in the following SQL statement:

```
data.to_sql('book_details', engine, if_exists='append',
index=False)
```

This concludes the portion of the chapter pertaining to Pandas and MySQL The next section introduces you to SQLite, which is an RDBMS that is available on multiple platforms.

READ XML DATA IN PANDAS

Listing 4.14 displays the contents of books.xml and Listing 4.15 displays the contents of pandas_read_xml.py that shows you how to read the contents of an XML document in Pandas.

LISTING 4.14: books.xml

```
<?xml version="1.0" encoding="UTF-8"?>
<books>
  <book>
   <name>SQL Fundamentals</name>
  </book>
  <book>
   <name>SVG Fundamentals</name>
  </book>
  <book>
   <name>Python and Machine Learning</name>
  </book>
</books>
```

LISTING 4.15: pandas_read_xml.py

```
# this code might require Python3.7
import pandas as pd

filename="books.xml"

df = pd.read_xml(filename)
print("XML data:")
print(df)
```

Listing 4.15 starts by initializing the variable with the name of an existing XML document and then invokes the Pandas read_xml() method in order to populate the variable df with data from the XML document, after which the contents of df are printed. Now launch the code in Listing 4.15 and if everything worked correctly you will see the following output:

```
Rows from book_details table:

XML data:
                  name
0  SQL Fundamentals
1  SVG Fundamentals
2  Python and Machine Learning
```

READ JSON DATA IN PANDAS

Listing 4.16 displays the contents of pandas_read_json.py that shows you how to read a JSON string in Pandas.

LISTING 4.16: pandas_read_json.py

```
from io import StringIO
import pandas as pd

books =  '{"name": "SQL Fundamentals"}\n{"name": "SQL
Fundamentals"}\n{"name": "Python and Machine Learning"}\n'
```

```
json = StringIO(books)
result = pd.read_json(json, lines=True)

print("json:",result)
```

Listing 4.16 starts with two `import` statements and then initializes the variable `books` with a string of name/value pairs. Next, the variable `json` is initialized as a `JSON` string based on the contents of `books`. Then the variable `result` is initialized by invoking the `Pandas read_json()` method with the variable `json`, after which its contents are printed. Now launch the code in Listing 4.16 and if everything worked correctly you will see the following output:

```
XML data:
                       name
0   SQL Fundamentals
1   SVG Fundamentals
2   Python and Machine Learning
```

Listing 4.17 displays the contents of `books.json` and Listing 4.18 displays the contents of `pandas_read_json.py` that shows you how to read the contents of a `JSON` file in `Pandas`.

LISTING 4.17: books.json

```
[
{"name": "SQL Fundamentals"},
{"name": "SQL Fundamentals"},
{"name": "Python and Machine Learning"}
]
```

LISTING 4.18: pandas_read_json2.py

```
import pandas as pd

filename="books.json"

df = pd.read_json(filename)
print("JSON data:")
print(df.to_string())
```

Listing 4.18 is similar to Listing 4.16, but this time without the use of the `StringIO`, and the contents of the DataFrame `df` are printed by invoking the `to_string()` method. Now launch the code in Listing 4.18 and if everything worked correctly you will see the following output:

```
JSON data:
                       name
0   SQL Fundamentals
1   SVG Fundamentals
2   Python and Machine Learning
```

WORKING WITHJSON-BASED DATA

A JSON object consists of data represented as colon-separated name/value pairs and data objects are separated by commas. An object is specified inside curly braces {}, and an array of objects is indicated by square brackets []. Note that character-valued data elements are inside a pair of double quotes "" (but no quotes for numeric data).

Here is a simple example of a JSON object:

```
{ "fname":"Jane", "lname":"Smith", "age":33, "city":"SF" }
```

Here is a simple example of an array of JSON objects (note the outer enclosing square brackets):

```
[
{ "fname":"Jane", "lname":"Smith", "age":33, "city":"SF" },
{ "fname":"John", "lname":"Jones", "age":34, "city":"LA" },
{ "fname":"Dave", "lname":"Stone", "age":35, "city":"NY" },
]
```

Python Dictionary and JSON

The Python json library enables you to work with JSON-based data in Python.

Listing 4.19 displays the contents of dict2json.py that illustrates how to convert a Python dictionary to a JSON string.

LISTING 4.19: dict2json.py

```
import json

dict1 = {}
dict1["fname"]  = "Jane"
dict1["lname"]  = "Smith"
dict1["age"]    = 33
dict1["city"]   = "SF"

print("Python dictionary to JSON data:")
print("dict1:",dict1)
json1 = json.dumps(dict1, ensure_ascii=False)
print("json1:",json1)
print("")

# convert JSON string to Python dictionary:
json2 = '{"fname":"Dave", "lname":"Stone", "age":35,
"city":"NY"}'
dict2 = json.loads(json2)
print("JSON data to Python dictionary:")
print("json2:",json2)
print("dict2:",dict2)
```

Listing 4.19 invokes the json.dumps() function to perform the conversion from a Python dictionary to a JSON string. Launch the code in Listing 4.19 and you will see the following output:

```
Python dictionary to JSON data:
dict1: {'fname': 'Jane', 'lname': 'Smith', 'age': 33,
'city': 'SF'}
json1: {"fname": "Jane", "lname": "Smith", "age": 33,
"city": "SF"}

JSON data to Python dictionary:
json2: {"fname":"Dave", "lname":"Stone", "age":35,
"city":"NY"}
dict2: {'fname': 'Dave', 'lname': 'Stone', 'age': 35,
'city': 'NY'}
```

Python, Pandas, and JSON

Listing 4.20 displays the contents of `pd_python_json.py` that illustrates how to convert a `Python` dictionary to a `Pandas DataFrame` and then convert the DataFrame to a `JSON` string.

LISTING 4.20: pd_python_json.py

```
import json
import pandas as pd

dict1 = {}
dict1["fname"]  = "Jane"
dict1["lname"]  = "Smith"
dict1["age"]    = 33
dict1["city"]   = "SF"

df1 = pd.DataFrame.from_dict(dict1, orient='index')
print("Pandas df1:")
print(df1)
print()

json1 = json.dumps(dict1, ensure_ascii=False)
print("Serialized to JSON1:")
print(json1)
print()

print("Data frame to JSON2:")
json2 = df1.to_json(orient='split')
print(json2)
```

Listing 4.20 initializes a `Python` dictionary `dict1` with multiple attributes for a user (first name, last name, and so forth). Next, the DataFrame `df1` is created from the `Python` dictionary `dict1`, and its contents are displayed.

The next portion of Listing 4.20 initializes the variable `json1` by serializing the contents of `dict1`, and its contents are displayed. The last code block in Listing 4.20 initializes the variable `json2` to the result of converting the DataFrame `df1` to a JSON string. Launch the code in Listing 4.20 and you will see the following output:

```
dict1: {'fname': 'Jane', 'lname': 'Smith', 'age': 33,
'city': 'SF'}
```

```
Pandas df1:
           0
fname   Jane
lname  Smith
age       33
city      SF

Serialized to JSON1:
{"fname": "Jane", "lname": "Smith", "age": 33, "city": "SF"}

Data frame to JSON2:
{"columns":[0],"index":["fname","lname","age","city"],
"data":[["Jane"],["Smith"],[33],["SF"]]}
json1: {"fname": "Jane", "lname": "Smith", "age": 33,
"city": "SF"}
```

PANDAS AND REGULAR EXPRESSIONS (OPTIONAL)

This section is marked "optional" because the code snippets require an understanding of regular expressions. If you are not ready to learn about regular expressions, you can skip this section with no loss of continuity.

Listing 4.21 displays the contents `pandas_regexs.py` that illustrates how to extract data from a `Pandas DataFrame` using regular expressions.

LISTING 4.21: pandas_regexs.py

```
import pandas as pd

schedule = ["Monday: Prepare lunch at 12:30pm for VIPs",
            "Tuesday: Yoga class from 10:00am to 11:00am",
            "Wednesday: PTA meeting at library at 3pm",
            "Thursday: Happy hour at 5:45 at Julie's house.",
            "Friday: Prepare pizza dough for lunch at 12:30pm.",
            "Saturday: Early shopping for the week at 8:30am.",
            "Sunday: Neighborhood bbq block party at 2:00pm."]
# create a Pandas DataFrame:
df = pd.DataFrame(schedule, columns = ['dow_of_week'])
# convert to lowercase:
df = df.applymap(lambda s:s.lower() if type(s) == str else s)
print("df:")
print(df)
print()

# character count for each string in df['dow_of_week']:
print("string lengths:")
print(df['dow_of_week'].str.len())
print()

# the number of tokens for each string in df['dow_of_week']
print("number of tokens in each string in df['dow_of_week']:")
```

```
print(df['dow_of_week'].str.split().str.len())
print()

# the number of occurrences of digits:
print("number of digits:")
print(df['dow_of_week'].str.count(r'\d'))
print()

# display all occurrences of digits:
print("show all digits:")
print(df['dow_of_week'].str.findall(r'\d'))
print()

# display hour and minute values:
print("display (hour, minute) pairs:")
print(df['dow_of_week'].str.findall(r'(\d?\d):(\d\d)'))
print()

# create new columns from hour:minute value:
print("hour and minute columns:")
print(df['dow_of_week'].str.extract(r'(\d?\d):(\d\d)'))
print()
```

Listing 4.21 initializes the variable `schedule` with a set of strings, each of which specifies a daily to-do item for an entire week. The format for each to-do item is of the form `day:task`, where is a day of the week and task is a string that specifies what needs to be done on that particular day.

Next, the DataFrame `df1` is initialized with the contents of `schedule`, followed by an example of defining a lambda expression that converts string-based values to lower case, as shown here:

```
df = df.applymap(lambda s:s.lower() if type(s) == str else s)
```

The preceding code snippet is useful because you do not need to specify individual columns of a DataFrame: the code ignores any nonstring values (such as integers and floating point values).

The next pair of code blocks involve various operations using the methods `applymap()`, `split()`, and `len()` that you have seen in previous examples. The next code block displays the number of digits in each to-do item by means of the regular expression in the following code snippet:

```
print(df['dow_of_week'].str.count(r'\d'))
```

The next code block displays the actual digits (instead of the number of digits) in each to-do item by means of the regular expression in the following code snippet:

```
print(df['dow_of_week'].str.findall(r'\d'))
```

The final code block displays the strings of the form `hour:minutes` by means of the regular expression in the following code snippet:

```
print(df['dow_of_week'].str.findall(r'(\d?\d):(\d\d)'))
```

As mentioned in the beginning of this section, you can learn more about regular expressions by reading one of the appendices of this book. Launch the code in Listing 4.21 and you will see the following output:

```
=> df:
                                      dow_of_week
0         monday: prepare lunch at 12:30pm for vips
1       tuesday: yoga class from 10:00am to 11:00am
2          wednesday: pta meeting at library at 3pm
3    thursday: happy hour at 5:45 at julie's house.
4  friday: prepare pizza dough for lunch at 12:30pm.
5   saturday: early shopping for the week at 8:30am.
6    sunday: neighborhood bbq block party at 2:00pm.

=> string lengths:
0    41
1    43
2    40
3    46
4    49
5    48
6    47
Name: dow_of_week, dtype: int64

=> number of tokens in each string in df['dow_of_week']:
0    7
1    7
2    7
3    8
4    8
5    8
6    7
Name: dow_of_week, dtype: int64
=> number of digits:
0    4
1    8
2    1
3    3
4    4
5    3
6    3
Name: dow_of_week, dtype: int64

=> show all digits:
0                [1, 2, 3, 0]
1    [1, 0, 0, 0, 1, 1, 0, 0]
2                         [3]
```

```
3                    [5, 4, 5]
4                 [1, 2, 3, 0]
5                    [8, 3, 0]
6                    [2, 0, 0]
Name: dow_of_week, dtype: object

=> display (hour, minute) pairs:
0               [(12, 30)]
1    [(10, 00), (11, 00)]
2                       []
3                [(5, 45)]
4               [(12, 30)]
5                [(8, 30)]
6                [(2, 00)]
Name: dow_of_week, dtype: object

=> hour and minute columns:

     0    1
0   12   30
1   10   00
2  NaN  NaN
3    5   45
4   12   30
5    8   30
6    2   00
```

WHAT IS SQLITE?

SQLite is a light weight, portable, and open source RDBMS that is available on Windows, Linux, and MacOS, as well as Android and iOS. The official website is here:

https://www.sqlite.org

Here is where you can find a tutorial for some of the most commonly used SQLite commands:

https://www.sqlitetutorial.net/sqlite-commands/

In addition, SQLite is ACID-compliant and also implements most SQL standards. Let's look at some features of SQLite and the installation process, both of which are discussed in two subsections.

SQLite Features

SQLite provides several useful features, some of which are listed below:

- doesn't require a separate server process or system to operate
- no system administration
- no external dependencies

- can operate in a serverless environment.
- available in multiple platforms (Unix, Linux, Mac, Windows)
- ACID transactions
- full support for all features in SQL92

SQLite Installation

Navigate to the following Web site and download the distribution for your operating system:

https://www.sqlite.org/download.html

The second step is to unzip the downloaded file in a convenient location, which we'll assume is the directory `$HOME/sqlite3_home`.

Note that if you have a MacBook then the directory that contains the `sqlite3` executable is automatically in the `PATH` variable. Just to be sure, type the following command to see if the `sqlite3` is accessible:

```
which sqlite3
```

If the preceding command returns a blank line, then you need to include the path to the `bin` directory where `sqlite3` is located. For example, if the preceding directory is `$HOME/sqlite3_home/bin`, then update the `PATH` environment variable as follows:

```
export PATH=/$HOME/sqlite_home/bin:$PATH
```

Create a Database and a Table

The following sequence of commands show you how to launch `sqlite` and create a database called `test.db`:

```
$ sqlite3 test.db
SQLite version 3.28.0 2019-04-15 14:49:49
Enter ".help" for usage hints.
sqlite>
sqlite> .help
.auth ON|OFF             Show authorizer callbacks
.backup ?DB? FILE        Backup DB (default "main") to FILE
.bail on|off             Stop after hitting an error.  Default OFF
.binary on|off           Turn binary output on or off.  Default OFF
.cd DIRECTORY            Change the working directory to DIRECTORY
.changes on|off          Show number of rows changed by SQL
// details omitted for brevity
.trace ?OPTIONS?         Output each SQL statement as it is run
.vfsinfo ?AUX?           Information about the top-level VFS
.vfslist                 List all available VFSes
.vfsname ?AUX?           Print the name of the VFS stack
.width NUM1 NUM2 ...     Set column widths for "column" mode
```

```
sqlite> .databases
databases
main: /tmp/test.db
sqlite> .quit
List the files in the current directory and you will see the following:
-rw-r--r--   1 oswaldcampesato  staff        0 Aug  5 10:36 test.db
```

Now create a table called `books` in `sqlite3` by executing the following sequence of commands:

```
$ sqlite3 test.db
SQLite version 3.28.0 2019-04-15 14:49:49
Enter ".help" for usage hints.
sqlite>
sqlite> CREATE TABLE books(author text, title text, year
integer, price real);
sqlite> .tables
books
sqlite> select * from books;
sqlite> # insert data later
sqlite>
sqlite> .quit
```

Insert, Select, and Delete Table Data

The following sequence of commands show you how perform data-related operations with the books table in the database called “test.db”:

```
$ sqlite3 test.db
SQLite version 3.28.0 2019-04-15 14:49:49
Enter ".help" for usage hints.
sqlite> INSERT INTO books(author, title, year, price)
VALUES ("John Doe", "Unix Tips", "2020", "34.95");
sqlite> select * from books;
John Doe|Unix Tips|2020|34.95
sqlite> delete from books;
sqlite> select * from books;
sqlite>
sqlite> .tables
books
sqlite> drop table books;
sqlite>
sqlite> .quit
```

Launch SQL Files

Listing 4.22 displays the contents of create_table.sql and Listing 4.23 displays the contents of insert_data.sql.

LISTING 4.22: create_table.sql

```
CREATE TABLE books2(author text, title text, year integer,
price real);
```

LISTING 4.23: insert_data.sql

```
INSERT INTO books2(author, title, year, price)
VALUES ("Oswald Campesato", "C Programming", "2018",
"35.95");
```

Launch the preceding SQL files as follows:

```
sqlite3 test.db < create_table.sql
sqlite3 test.db < insert_data.sql
```

Let's return to the sqlite3 prompt and check the structure of the table books2 and its contents:

```
$ sqlite3 test.db
SQLite version 3.28.0 2019-04-15 14:49:49
Enter ".help" for usage hints.
sqlite>
sqlite> .schema books2
CREATE TABLE books2(author text, title text, year integer,
price real);
sqlite> select * from books2;
Oswald Campesato|C Programming|2018|35.95
```

Drop Tables and Databases

```
$ sqlite3 test.db
SQLite version 3.28.0 2019-04-15 14:49:49
Enter ".help" for usage hints.
sqlite>
sqlite> drop table books2;
sqlite> .tables
sqlite>
$ sqlite3 test.db

SQLite version 3.28.0 2019-04-15 14:49:49
Enter ".help" for usage hints.
sqlite>
sqlite> .tables
sqlite>
sqlite> .quit
```

Now remove the database `test.db` by invoking the `bash rm` command, as shown here:

```
rm test.db
sqlite> .quit
```

Load CSV Data Into a sqlite Table

Listing 4.24 displays the contents of rainfall.csv that contains 65 rows of data and Listing 4.25 displays the contents of `load_rainfall.sql`.

LISTING 4.24: rainfall.csv

```
CREATE
2023-01-02,0
2023-01-03,1
2023-01-04,0
2023-01-05,2
2023-01-06,3
// details omitted for brevity
2023-03-27,60
2023-03-28,29
2023-03-29,26
2023-03-30,44
2023-03-31,8
```

LISTING 4.25: load_rainfall.sql

```
DROP TABLE IF EXISTS rainfall;
CREATE TABLE rainfall ( "day" TEXT, "centimeters" REAL);

.mode csv
.import rainfall.csv rainfall
```

Listing 4.25 drops the table `rainfall` if it already exists, and then creates the `rainfall` table with a text column and a real-valued column called `day` and `centimeters`, respectively. Now launch the code in Listing 4.25, and then navigate to the `sqlite3` prompt to check the number of rows in the `rainfall` table:

```
sqlite3 mytools.db
SQLite version 3.28.0 2019-04-15 14:49:49
Enter ".help" for usage hints.
sqlite> select count(*) from rainfall;
65
sqlite> .quit
```

In the next section, you will learn how to write `Python` code for managing data in `sqlite3` and also learn how to extract data from the `rainfall` table in order to generate a histogram using `Pandas`.

PYTHON AND SQLITE

This section contains an assortment of Python files that illustrate how to perform various operations in sqlite3, which are the counterpart to the examples that you learned how to perform from the sqlite3 prompt. Note that the Python code samples use the mytools.db database instead of the test.db database.

Connect to a sqlite3 Database

Listing 4.26 displays the contents of connect_db.py that shows you how to connect to a sqlite3 database in Python.

LISTING 4.26: connect_db.py

```
import sqlite3

con = sqlite3.connect("mytools.db")
cursor = con.cursor()
con.commit()
con.close()
```

Listing 4.26 is a "do nothing" Python code sample that simply connects to the mytools.db database.

Create a Table in a sqlite3 Database

Listing 4.27 displays the contents of connect_db.py that shows you how to connect to a sqlite3 database in Python.

LISTING 4.27: create_table.py

```
import sqlite3

con = sqlite3.connect("mytools.db")
cursor = con.cursor()

cursor.execute(
  CREATE TABLE books(author text, title text, year integer,
price real);
)

con.commit()
con.close()
```

Listing 4.27 creates a cursor and then executes the SQL create statement in order to create the table books in the mytools.db database.

Insert Data in a sqlite3 Table

Listing 4.28 displays the contents of insert_data.py that shows you how to insert data in a sqlite3 table in Python.

LISTING 4.28: insert_data.py

```
import sqlite3

con = sqlite3.connect("mytools.db")
cursor = con.cursor()

sql = """ INSERT INTO books(author, title, year, price)
          VALUES ("Tom Smith", "Intro to TypeScript",
"2022", "39.95") """

cursor.execute(sql)

con.commit()
con.close()
```

Listing 4.28 creates a cursor and then executes the SQL insert statement in order to insert data in the table books in the mytools.db database.

Select Data From a sqlite3 Table

Listing 4.29 displays the contents of select_data.py that shows you how to insert data in a sqlite3 table in Python.

LISTING 4.29: select_data.py

```
import sqlite3

con = sqlite3.connect("mytools.db")
cursor = con.cursor()

sql = """ SELECT * FROM books; """

cursor.execute(sql)

row_count = 0
all_rows = cursor.fetchall()

print("Contents of table books:")
for row in all_rows:
  row_count += 1
  print("row:",row)

con.commit()
con.close()

print("row count:",row_count)
print()
```

Listing 4.29 creates a cursor and then executes the SQL select statement in order to select data from the table books in the mytools.db database. The next portion of Listing 4.29 initializes the variable all_rows as a reference to the data in the books table, followed by a loop that iterates through the elements in all_rows and prints their contents. Notice that the final code snippet displays the numbers of rows in the books table.

Populate a Pandas Dataframe From a sqlite3 Table

Listing 4.30 displays the contents of `read_sqlite3_into_pandas.py` that shows you how to populate a `Pandas` DataFrame with data from a `sqlite3` table in `Python`.

LISTING 4.30: read_sqlite3_into_pandas.py

```
import sqlite3
import pandas as pd

con = sqlite3.connect("mytools.db")
df = pd.read_sql_query("SELECT * FROM books;", con)
con.close()

print("=> Contents of book table:")
print(df)
```

Listing 4.30 creates a cursor and then executes the `SQL` select statement in order to select data from the table `books` in the `mytools.db` database. The next portion of Listing 4.30 initializes the `df` with the contents of the `books` table by invoking the `Pandas` method `read_sql_query()`. The next code snippet in Listing 4.30 displays the contents of the `Pandas` DataFrame `df`. Launch the code in Listing 4.30 and you will see the following output:

```
=> Contents of book table:
      author                title  year  price
0   John Doe           Unix Tips  2020  34.95
1   Oswald C       C Programming  2018  35.95
2  Tom Smith  Intro to TypeScript  2022  39.95
```

Although you can perform `SQL` operations from the command line, just like you can with `MySQL`, it's probably easier to work with `SQLite` in an IDE. In fact, a very robust IDE is `SQLiteStudio`, which is discussed in the next section.

Histogram With Data From a sqlite3 Table (1)

Listing 4.31 displays the contents of `rainfall_hist1.py` that shows you how to define a simple `SQL` query in order to create a histogram based on the data from the `rainfall` table.

LISTING 4.31: rainfall_hist1.py

```
import sqlite3
import pandas as pd

sql = """
  SELECT
  cast(centimeters/10.00 as int)*10 as cent_floor,
  count(*) as count
```

```
FROM rainfall
GROUP by 1
ORDER by 1;
"""

con = sqlite3.connect("mytools.db")
df = pd.read_sql_query(sql, con)
con.close()

print("=> Histogram of Rainfall:")
print(df)
```

Listing 4.31 starts with two `import` statements and then initializes the string variable `sql` with a `SQL` statement involving the table `rainfall`. Next, the variable `con` is initialized as a database connection to the database `mytools.db`.

The next portion of Listing 4.31 invokes the `read_sql_query()` method to read the contents of the `rainfall` table and populate the `DataFrame df` with that data. Finally, the connection is closed and the contents of `df` are printed. Now launch the code in Listing 4.31 and you will see the following output:

```
=> Histogram of Rainfall:
   cent_floor  count
0           0     27
1          10     14
2          20      9
3          30      9
4          40      3
5          50      2
6          60      1
```

If you want to replace the value 10.00 with a variable, you can use the following code snippet:

```
factor = 10.00
sql = "SELECT cast(centimeters/"+str(factor)+" as
int)*"+str(factor)+" as cent_floor, count(*) as count FROM
rainfall GROUP by 1 ORDER by 1;"
```

However, the preceding style can quickly become cumbersome for longer and more complex `SQL` statements.

Histogram With Data From a sqlite3 Table (2)

Listing 4.32 displays the contents of `rainfall_hist2.py` that shows you how to define a simple `SQL` query in order to create a histogram based on the data from the `rainfall` table.

LISTING 4.32: rainfall_hist2.py

```
import sqlite3
import pandas as pd

sql = """
select
  bucket_floor,
  'FROM ' || bucket_floor || ' TO ' || bucket_ceiling as
bucket_name,
  count(*) as count
from (
  select
    cast(centimeters/10.00 as int)*10 as bucket_floor,
    cast(centimeters/10.00 as int)*10 + 10 as bucket_
ceiling
  from rainfall
) x
group by 1, 2
order by 1;
"""

con = sqlite3.connect("mytools.db")
df = pd.read_sql_query(sql, con)
con.close()

print("=> Histogram of Rainfall:")
print(df)
```

Listing 4.32 is similar to the previous example, along with some fine tuning in order to print a more detailed version of the data. Now launch the code in Listing 4.32 and you will see the following output:

```
=> Histogram of Rainfall:
   bucket_floor     bucket_name  count
0             0    FROM 0 TO 10     27
1            10   FROM 10 TO 20     14
2            20   FROM 20 TO 30      9
3            30   FROM 30 TO 40      9
4            40   FROM 40 TO 50      3
5            50   FROM 50 TO 60      2
6            60   FROM 60 TO 70      1
```

WORKING WITH SQLITE3 TOOLS

The previous two sections showed you how to work directly with `sqlite3`, either through the `sqlite3` prompt or from the command line. The following subsections briefly discuss the following useful tools for working with `sqlite3`:

- SQLiteStudio
- DB Browser
- SQLiteDict

SQLiteStudio Installation

`SQLiteStudio` is an open source IDE for `SQLite` that enables you to perform many database operations, such as creating, updating, and dropping tables and views. Navigate to the following Web site, download the distribution for your operating system, and perform the specified installation steps:

https://sqlitestudio.pl/

https://mac.softpedia.com/get/Developer-Tools/SQLiteStudio.shtml

Figure 4.6 displays the structure of the `employees` table whose definition is the same as the `employees` table in the `mytools` database in `MySQL`.

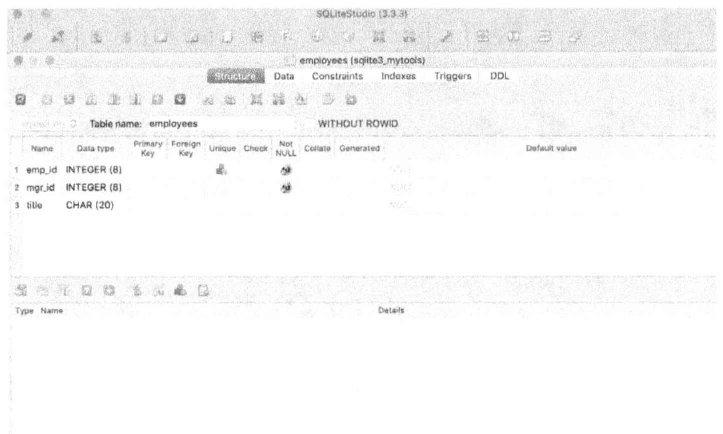

FIGURE 4.6 The employees table.

Figure 4.7 displays a screenshot of three rows in the `employees` table, where you can insert a fourth row of data in the top row that is pre-populated with `NULL` values.

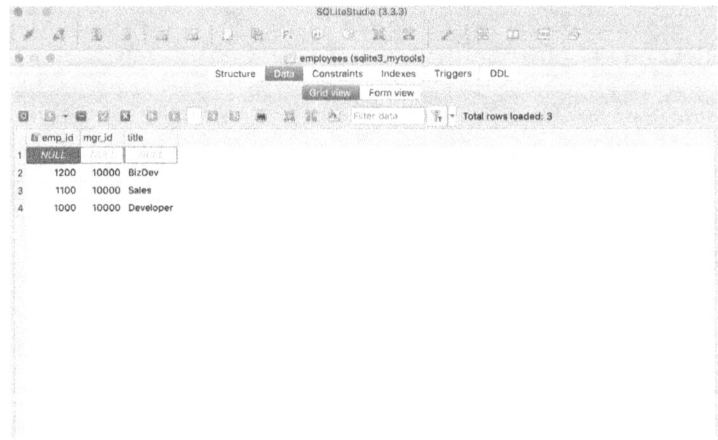

FIGURE 4.7 Three rows in the `employees` table.

DB Browser for SQLite Installation

`DB Browser` is an open source and visual-oriented tool for `SQLite` that that enables you to perform various database-related operations, such as creating and updating files. Moreover, this tool enables you to manage data through an interface that resembles a spreadsheet.

Navigate to the following Web site, download the distribution for your operating system, and perform the specified installation steps:

https://www.macupdate.com/app/mac/38584/db-browser-for-sqlite/download/secure

The following Web site contains a multitude of URLs that provide details regarding the features of `DB Browser`:

https://sqlitebrowser.org

SQLiteDict (Optional)

`SQLiteDict` is an open source tool that is a wrapper around `sqlite3`, and it's downloadable here:

https://pypi.org/project/sqlitedict/

`SQLiteDict` enables you to persist dictionaries to a file on the file system, as illustrated by the code in Listing 4.33.

LISTING 4.33: sqlitesavedict1.py

```
# pip3 install sqlitedict

from sqlitedict import SqliteDict

mydict = SqliteDict('./my_db.sqlite', autocommit=True)
mydict['pasta'] = 'pasta'
mydict['pizza'] = 'pizza'

for key, value in mydict.iteritems():
  print("key:",key," value:",value)

# dictionary functions work:
print("length:",len(mydict))
mydict.close()

# a client instance:
myclient = MongoClient("localhost",27017)
```

Listing 4.33 contains an `import` statement followed by the variable `mydict` that is initialized as a dictionary that includes the two strings `pasta` and `pizza`. The next code snippet contains a look that displays the key/value pairs of `mydict`, followed by the length of the `mydict` dictionary. The next close snippet closes the dictionary and then launches a MongoDB client at the default port. Now launch the code in Listing 4.33 and you will see the following output:

```
key: pasta  value: pasta
key: pizza  value: pizza
number of items: 2
```

Listing 4.34 illustrates how to read the contents of the file that was saved in Listing 4.33.

LISTING 4.34: sqlitereaddict1.py

```
# pip3 install sqlitedict

# read the contents of my_db.sqlite
# and note no autocommit=True
with SqliteDict('./my_db.sqlite') as mydict:
  print("old:", mydict['pasta'])
  mydict['pasta'] = u"more pasta"
  print("new:", mydict['pasta'])
  mydict['pizza'] = range(10)
  mydict.commit()
  # this is not persisted to disk:
  mydict['dish'] = u"deep dish"

# open the same file again:
with SqliteDict('./my_db.sqlite') as mydict:
  print("pasta:",mydict['pasta'])
  # this line will cause an error:
  #print("dish  value:",mydict['dish'])
```

Listing 4.34 contains a block of code that reads the existing value of past from mydict, then updates its value, and then saves its new value. The final code block in Listing 4.34 reads the stored contents and displays the key/value pairs. Now launch the code in Listing 4.34 and you will see the following output:

```
old: pasta
new: more pasta
pasta: more pasta
```

Check the online documentation for information regarding other functionality that is available through sqlitedict.

WORKING WITH BEAUTIFUL SOUP

Beautiful Soup is a Python library that enables you to parse data from HTML Web pages and XML documents. If you are familiar with XPath, then you already understand what you can do with Beautiful Soup (which supports a subset of XPath functionality).

Beautiful Soup can traverse the tree-like structure of HTML Web pages and XML documents (which include SVG documents) in order to extract the desired data or text.

Moreover, Beautiful Soup works with documents on the file system of your laptop as well as data that has been "scraped" from a live HTML Web page. Just to give you an idea, Beautiful Soup can easily extract the data from each row in the following Web page:

```
<html>
<body>
  <table>
   <tr><td>50</td><td>80</td></tr>
   <tr><td>150</td><td>180</td></tr>
  </table>
</body>
</html>
```

Parsing an HTML Web Page

Listing 4.35 displays of `sample.html` and Listing 4.36 displays the contents of `bsoup1.py` that extracts data from `sample.html` and then uses `Pandas` to render a bar chart.

LISTING 4.35: sample.html

```
<html>
<body>
  <table>
   <tr>
     <td>50</td>
     <td>80</td>
     <td>72</td>
     <td>68</td>
   </tr>
   <tr>
     <td>150</td>
     <td>180</td>
     <td>172</td>
     <td>168</td>
   </tr>
  </table>
</body>
</html>
```

LISTING 4.36: bsoup1.py

```
import pandas as pd

# pip3 install BeautifulSoup4
from bs4 import BeautifulSoup

# read file and parse HTML:
filename="sample.html"
```

```
with open(filename) as f:
  content = f.read()
  soup = BeautifulSoup(content, 'html.parser')

print("=> table data:")
#table = soup.table
table = soup.find("table")
print(table)
print()

print("=> table rows:")
rows = soup.find_all('tr')
for row in rows:
  print ("=> found row:",row)
print()

"""
# scraping a live HTML Web page:
# pip3 install requests
import requests
URL = "https://www.yahoo.com"
page = requests.get(URL)
soup = BeautifulSoup(page.content, 'html.parser')
"""
```

Listing 4.36 starts with `import` statements and then initializes the variable `content` with the contents of the `HTML` Web page `sample.html`. After the contents of the variable `content` are printed, the next code block populates the variable `table` with the set of tables that are in `sample.html` via the variable `content`, and a simple look displays the set of tables.

The next portion of Listing 4.36 finds all the `<tr>` elements and populates the variable `rows` with that data. A simple loop iterates through the contents of the variable `rows` and prints each data row. Now launch the code in Listing 4.36 and you will see the following output:

```
=> table data:
<table>
<tr>
<td>50</td>
<td>80</td>
<td>72</td>
<td>68</td>
</tr>
<tr>
<td>150</td>
<td>180</td>
<td>172</td>
<td>168</td>
</tr>
</table>
```

```
=> table rows:
=> found row: <tr>
<td>50</td>
<td>80</td>
<td>72</td>
<td>68</td>
</tr>
=> found row: <tr>
<td>150</td>
<td>180</td>
<td>172</td>
<td>168</td>
</tr>
```

BEAUTIFUL SOUP AND PANDAS

The code sample in this section uses Beautiful Soup to extract data values from an HTML table in the Web page sample.html that you saw in the previous section. That data is used to populate a `Pandas DataFrame`, after which a bar chart is displayed using a `Pandas` API and `Matplotlib` API, both of which are displayed in bold at the end of Listing 4.38. Although `Matplotlib` is not discussed until Chapter 5, the code snippet is very intuitive and does not require any substantive knowledge of `Matplotlib`.

Listing 4.37 displays the contents of `bsoup2.py` that shows you how to render a bar chart in `Pandas`.

LISTING 4.37: bsoup2.py

```
from bs4 import BeautifulSoup
import numpy as np
import pandas as pd

# read file and parse HTML:
filename="sample.html"
with open(filename) as f:
  content = f.read()
  soup = BeautifulSoup(content, 'html.parser')

rows = soup.find_all('tr')
all_data = []
for row in rows:
  row_items = row.find_all('td')
  print("row_items:",row_items)
  # create an array of <td> for each row:
  values = [td.get_text() for td in row_items]
  print("values:",values)
  # convert to integers:
  values = np.asarray(values)
  values = values.astype(int)
  print("values:",values)
  # append to matrix:
  all_data.append(values)
```

```
  print()
print("all_data:",all_data)

df = pd.DataFrame(all_data)
print("df:")
print(df)

# bar chart:
ax = df.plot.bar()
plt.show()
```

Listing 4.37 starts with import statements and then. Now launch the code in Listing 4.37 and you will see the following output:

```
row_items: [<td>50</td>, <td>80</td>, <td>72</td>,
<td>68</td>]
values: ['50', '80', '72', '68']
values: [50 80 72 68]

row_items: [<td>150</td>, <td>180</td>, <td>172</td>,
<td>168</td>]
values: ['150', '180', '172', '168']
values: [150 180 172 168]

all_data: [array([50, 80, 72, 68]), array([150, 180, 172,
168])]
df:
     0    1    2    3
0   50   80   72   68
1  150  180  172  168
```

Figure 4.8 displays the bar chart that is populated with data from the `HTML` Web page `sample.html`.

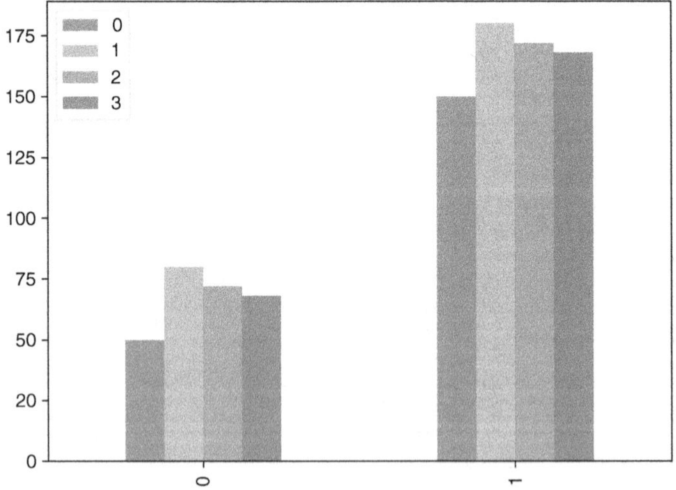

FIGURE 4.8 A bar chart from an HTML Web page.

BEAUTIFUL SOUP AND LIVE HTML WEB PAGES

The code sample in this section uses Beautiful Soup to parse the contents of a live HTML Web page. The key difference in this section is the inclusion of a code snippet for scraping the contents of an online HTML Web page.

Listing 4.38 displays the contents of bsoup3.py that shows you how to render a bar chart in Pandas.

LISTING 4.38: bsoup3.py

```
from bs4 import BeautifulSoup

import re
import requests

URL = "https://www.yahoo.com"
page = requests.get(URL)
soup = BeautifulSoup(page.content, 'html.parser')

print("------------------------")
print("page before:")
print(page.text)
print("------------------------")
print()

divs = soup.find('div')
print("------------------------")
print("<div> elements:")
print(divs)
print("------------------------")
print()

tables = soup.find('tables')
print("------------------------")
print("table elements:")
print(tables)
print("------------------------")
print()

#links = soup.find('html/head/links')
links = soup.find('links')
print("------------------------")
print("link elements:")
print(links)
print("------------------------")
print()
```

Listing 4.38 starts with import statements and then initializes the variable content with the contents of the HTML Web page located at the specified URL. After the text in the variable page are printed, the next code block populates the variable divs with the set of <div> elementals in that are in Web page. In a similar fashion, the next two code blocks display the tables and the link elements in the Web page. Now launch the code in Listing 4.38 and you will see the following output:

```
row_items:
------------------------
page before:
<!DOCTYPE html>
<html id="atomic" lang="en-US" class="atomic   l-out Pos-r
https fp fp-default dt-default mini-uh-on uh-topbar-on ltr
desktop Desktop bkt201">
<head>
    <meta http-equiv="X-UA-Compatible" content="IE=edge">

    <title>Yahoo | Mail, Weather, Search, Politics, News,
Finance, Sports & Videos</title><meta http-equiv="x-
dns-prefetch-control" content="on"><link rel="dns-
prefetch" href="//s.yimg.com"><link rel="preconnect"
href="//s.yimg.com"><link rel="dns-prefetch" href="//
search.yahoo.com"><link rel="preconnect" href="//
search.yahoo.com"><link rel="dns-prefetch"
href="//11.at.atwola.com"><link rel="preconnect"
href="//11.at.atwola.com"><link rel="dns-prefetch"
href="//geo.yahoo.com"><link rel="preconnect" href="//
geo.yahoo.com"><link rel="dns-prefetch" href="//
video-api.yql.yahoo.com"><link rel="preconnect" href="//
video-api.yql.yahoo.com">
// detail omitted for brevity
</div>
------------------------

------------------------
table elements:
None
------------------------

------------------------
link elements:
None
------------------------
```

This concludes the brief section regarding Beautiful Soup. The following Web page contains documentation and code snippets that show you how to use various features of Beautiful Soup:

https://beautiful-soup-4.readthedocs.io/en/latest/

SUMMARY

This chapter started with some code samples that showed you how to perform data visualization in `Pandas`, such as bar charts, area charts, and line graphs. Next, you saw how to write Python code that contains `MySQL` commands.

Next, you learned about XML documents and JSON data, and how to read such data in a Pandas DataFrame.

In addition, you learned how to combine Python and SQLite to perform database-related operations, such as creating a table in a sqlite3 database and then inserting data into such a table. Moreover, you saw how to select data from that table and populate a Pandas DataFrame with that data.

Finally, you learned about Beautiful Soup, along with code samples that showed you how to use Beautiful Soup in order to parse HTML Web pages.

CHAPTER 5

MATPLOTLIB AND VISUALIZATION

This chapter introduces data visualization, along with a collection of Python-based code samples that use Matplotlib to render charts and graphs. In addition, this chapter contains visualization code samples that combine Pandas and Matplotlib.

The first part of this chapter briefly discusses data visualization, with a short list of some data visualization tools, and a list of various types of visualizations (bar graphs, pie charts, and so forth). Some introductory information can be found online:

https://medium.datadriveninvestor.com/dont-beat-the-bush-use-chatgpt-to-visualize-your-data-94cee442cc29

https://medium.datadriveninvestor.com/stop-wasting-times-to-learn-machine-learning-read-this-instead-5abfab230279

The first part of this chapter contains a short introduction to Matplotlib, followed by code samples that display the available colors in Matplotlib.

The second part of this chapter contains an assortment of Python code samples that render horizontal lines, slanted lines, and parallel lines. This section also contains a set of code samples that show you how to render a grid of points in several ways.

The third part of this chapter shows you how to load images, display a checkerboard pattern, and plot a trigonometric function in Matplotlib. The fourth section contains examples of rendering charts and graphs in Matplotlib, which includes histograms, bar charts, pie charts, and heat maps.

The final section contains code samples for rendering 3D charts, financial data, and data from a sqlite3 database.

WHAT IS DATA VISUALIZATION?

Data visualization refers to presenting data in a graphical manner, such as bar charts, line graphs, and heat maps. As you probably know, Big Data comprises massive amounts of data, which leverages data visualization tools to assist in making better decisions.

Data visualization is a crucial aspect of data analysis, providing an intuitive understanding of the underlying patterns and relationships. With tools like Matplotlib and Seaborn, Python has become an efficient platform for crafting compelling visuals. As always, the key lies in practice and exploration.

Visual representation of data enables viewers to quickly grasp complex data insights. Python, with its rich ecosystem of visualization libraries, provides tools to render data in meaningful ways. This chapter focuses on various visualization tasks using libraries such as Matplotlib and Seaborn.

Python is a versatile and powerful programming language that can be used for various applications ranging from Web development to data analysis. In this chapter, we will explore solutions to common programming tasks using Python. Each task will have a detailed explanation and solution.

Advanced visualization techniques offer deeper insights and more comprehensive narratives from data. Tools like Matplotlib and Seaborn make these tasks more accessible. While these visuals are powerful, it is essential to ensure clarity and avoid misrepresentation. Continue experimenting and refining your visualization skills to tell more compelling data stories.

In the realm of data visualization, the journey from novice to expert is marked by the adoption of advanced techniques that can extract and depict deeper insights from data. In this chapter, we will explore some of these advanced visualization techniques and understand how they can be applied to various data scenarios.

Effective data visualization is about conveying complex data narratives in an intuitive manner. As we continue our exploration, this chapter unfolds more advanced visualization techniques, enabling us to represent data in a multitude of insightful ways.

Good data visualization tells a meaningful story, focusing on useful information that resides in datasets that can contain many data points (i.e., billions of rows of data). Another aspect of data visualization is its effectiveness: how well does it convey the trends that might exist in the dataset?

There are many open source data visualization tools available, some of which are listed here (many others are available):

- Matplotlib
- Seaborn
- Bokeh
- YellowBrick
- Tableau
- D3.js (JavaScript and SVG)

In case you have not already done so, it would be helpful to install the following Python libraries (using `pip3`) on your computer so that you can launch the code samples in this chapter:

```
pip3 install matplotlib
pip3 install seaborn
pip3 install bokeh
```

Types of Data Visualization

Bar graphs, line graphs, and pie charts are common ways to present data, and yet many other types exist, some of which are listed here:

- 2D/3D Area Chart
- Bar Chart
- Gantt Chart
- Heat Map
- Histogram
- Polar Area
- Scatterplot (2D or 3D)
- Timeline

The Python code samples in the next several sections illustrate how to perform visualization via rudimentary APIs from Matplotlib.

WHAT IS MATPLOTLIB?

Matplotlib is a plotting library that supports NumPy, SciPy, and toolkits such as wxPython (among others). Matplotlib supports only version 3 of Python: support for version 2 of Python was available only through 2020. Matplotlib is a multi-platform library that is built on NumPy arrays.

The plotting-related code samples in this chapter use pyplot, which is a Matplotlib module that provides a MATLAB-like interface. Here is an example of using pyplot to plot a smooth curve based on negative powers of Euler's constant e:

```
import matplotlib.pyplot as plt
import numpy as np

a = np.linspace(0, 10, 100)
b = np.exp(-a)
plt.plot(a, b)
plt.show()
```

Keep in mind that the code samples that plot line segments assume that you are familiar with the equation of a (non-vertical) line in the plane: `y = m*x + b`, where `m` is the slope and `b` is the y-intercept.

Furthermore, some code samples use NumPy APIs, such as `np.linspace()`, `np.array()`, `np.random.rand()`, and `np.ones()`, which are discussed in Chapter 3, so you can refresh your memory regarding these APIs.

MATPLOTLIB STYLES

Listing 5.1 displays the content of `mpl_styles.py` that illustrates how to plot a pie chart in Matplotlib.

LISTING 5.1: mpl_styles.py

```
import matplotlib.pyplot as plt

print("plt.style.available:")
styles = plt.style.available

for style in styles:
  print("style:",style)
```

Listing 5.1 contains an `import` statement, followed by the variable `styles`, which is initialized with the set of available styles in Matplotlib. The final portion of Listing 5.1 contains a loop that iterates through the values in the `styles` variable. Launch the code in Listing 5.1, and you will see the following output:

```
plt.style.available:
style: Solarize_Light2
style: _classic_test_patch
style: bmh
style: classic
style: dark_background
style: fast
style: fivethirtyeight
style: ggplot
style: grayscale
style: seaborn
style: seaborn-bright
style: seaborn-colorblind
style: seaborn-dark
style: seaborn-dark-palette
style: seaborn-darkgrid
style: seaborn-deep
style: seaborn-muted
style: seaborn-notebook
style: seaborn-paper
style: seaborn-pastel
style: seaborn-poster
style: seaborn-talk
style: seaborn-ticks
style: sea born-white
style: seaborn-whitegrid
style: tableau-colorblind10
```

DISPLAY ATTRIBUTE VALUES

Listing 5.2 displays the content of `mat_attrib_values.py` that shows the attribute values of an object in Matplotlib (subplots are discussed later in this chapter).

LISTING 5.2: mat_attrib_values.py

```
import matplotlib.pyplot as plt

fig, ax = plt.subplots()

print("=> attribute values:")
print(plt.getp(fig))
```

Listing 5.2 contains an `import` statement, followed by the variables `fig` and `ax`, which are initialized by invoking the `subplots()` method of the `plt` class. The next block of code prints the attribute values in `fig` by invoking the `plt.getp()` method. Launch the code in Listing 5.2, and you will see the following output:

```
=> attribute values:
    agg_filter = None
    alpha = None
    animated = False
    axes = [<AxesSubplot:>]
    children = [<matplotlib.patches.Rectangle object at
0x11c34f0...
    clip_box = None
    clip_on = True
    clip_path = None
    constrained_layout = False
    constrained_layout_pads = (0.04167, 0.04167, 0.02, 0.02)
    contains = None
    default_bbox_extra_artists = [<AxesSubplot:>,
<matplotlib.spines.Spine object a...
    dpi = 100.0
    edgecolor = (1.0, 1.0, 1.0, 1.0)
    facecolor = (1.0, 1.0, 1.0, 1.0)
    figheight = 4.8
    figure = None
    figwidth = 6.4
    frameon = True
    gid = None
    in_layout = True
    label =
    path_effects = []
    picker = None
    rasterized = None
    size_inches = [6.4 4.8]
    sketch_params = None
    snap = None
    tight_layout = False
    transform = IdentityTransform()
    transformed_clip_path_and_affine = (None, None)
```

```
    url = None
    visible = True
    window_extent = TransformedBbox(      Bbox(x0=0.0,
y0=0.0, x1=6.4, ...
    zorder = 0
None
```

COLOR VALUES IN MATPLOTLIB

Listing 5.3 displays the content of `mat_colors.py` that shows the colors that are available in Matplotlib.

LISTING 5.3: heatmap1.py

```
import matplotlib
import matplotlib.pyplot as plt

colors = plt.colormaps()

col_count=5
idx=0
for color in colors:
  if(color.endswith("_r") == False):
    print(color," ",end="")
    idx += 1
    if(idx % col_count == 0):
      print()
print()
print("=> color count:",idx)
```

Listing 5.3 contains two `import` statements, after which the variable `colors` are initialized with the list of available colors. The next portion of Listing 5.3 contains a loop that iterates through the `colors` variable, and prints the value of each color, provided that it does not have the suffix "_r" in its name. A new line is printed each time that five colors have been printed. Launch the code in Listing 5.3, and you will see the following output:

```
Accent  Blues  BrBG  BuGn  BuPu
CMRmap  Dark2  GnBu  Greens  Greys
OrRd  Oranges  PRGn  Paired  Pastel1
Pastel2  PiYG  PuBu  PuBuGn  PuOr
PuRd  Purples  RdBu  RdGy  RdPu
RdYlBu  RdYlGn  Reds  Set1  Set2
Set3  Spectral  Wistia  YlGn  YlGnBu
YlOrBr  YlOrRd  afmhot  autumn  binary
bone  brg  bwr  cividis  cool
coolwarm  copper  cubehelix  flag  gist_earth
gist_gray  gist_heat  gist_ncar  gist_rainbow  gist_stern
gist_yarg  gnuplot  gnuplot2  gray  hot
hsv  inferno  jet  magma  nipy_spectral
ocean  pink  plasma  prism  rainbow
seismic  spring  summer  tab10  tab20
tab20b  tab20c  terrain  turbo  twilight
twilight_shifted  viridis  winter
=> color count: 83
```

Now let's proceed to the next section that contains a fast-paced set of basic code samples that display various types of line segments.

CUBED NUMBERS IN MATPLOTLIB

Listing 5.4 displays the content of `cubed_numbers.py` that illustrates how to plot a set of points using Matplotlib.

LISTING 5.4: cubed_numbers.py

```
import matplotlib.pyplot as plt

plt.plot([1, 2, 3, 4], [1, 8, 27, 64])
plt.axis([0, 5, 0, 70])
plt.xlabel("Integers (1-4)")
plt.ylabel("Cubed Integers")
plt.show()
```

Listing 5.4 plots a set of integer-valued points whose x-coordinate is between 1 and 4, inclusive, and whose y-coordinate is the cube of the corresponding x-coordinate. The code sample also labels the horizontal axis and the vertical axis. Figure 5.1 displays these points in Listing 5.4.

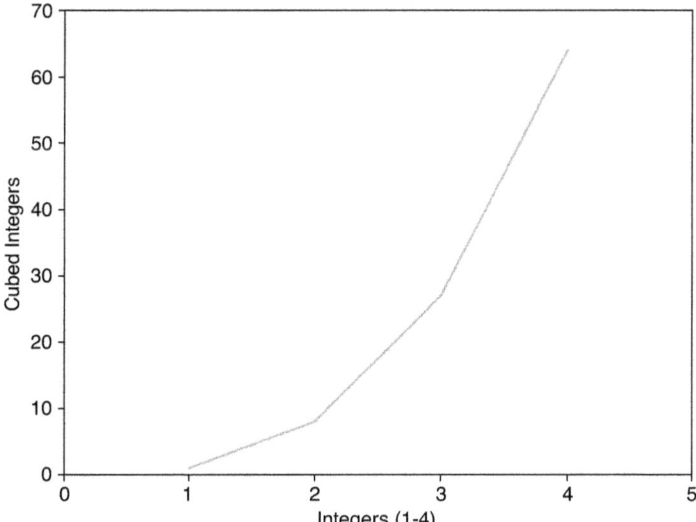

FIGURE 5.1 A graph of cubed numbers

HORIZONTAL LINES IN MATPLOTLIB

Listing 5.5 displays the content of `hlines1.py` that illustrates how to plot horizontal lines using Matplotlib. Recall that the equation of a non-vertical line in the 2D plane is `y = m*x + b`, where `m` is the slope of the line and `b` is the y-intercept of the line.

LISTING 5.5: hlines1.py

```
import numpy as np
import matplotlib.pyplot as plt

# top line
x1 = np.linspace(-5,5,num=200)
y1 = 4 + 0*x1

# middle line
x2 = np.linspace(-5,5,num=200)
y2 = 0 + 0*x2

# bottom line
x3 = np.linspace(-5,5,num=200)
y3 = -3 + 0*x3

plt.axis([-5, 5, -5, 5])
plt.plot(x1,y1)
plt.plot(x2,y2)
plt.plot(x3,y3)
plt.show()
```

Listing 5.5 uses the `np.linspace()` API to generate a list of 200 equally-spaced numbers for the horizontal axis, all of which are between -5 and 5. The three lines defined via the variables `y1`, `y2`, and `y3`, are defined in terms of the variables `x1`, `x2`, and `x3`, respectively.

Figure 5.2 displays three horizontal line segments whose equations are contained in Listing 5.5.

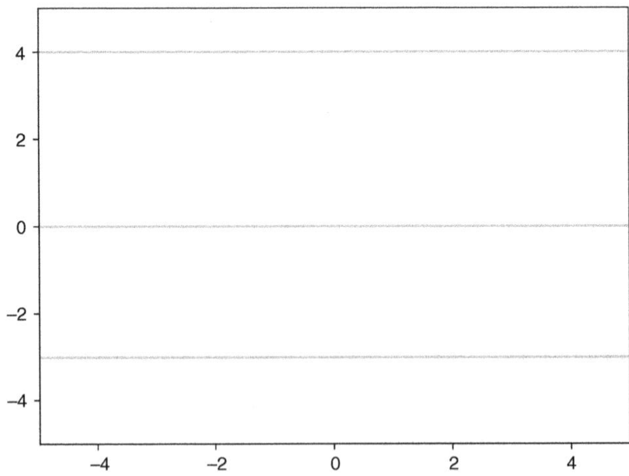

FIGURE 5.2 A graph of three horizontal line segments

SLANTED LINES IN MATPLOTLIB

Listing 5.6 displays the content of `diagonallines.py` that illustrates how to plot slanted lines.

LISTING 5.6: diagonallines.py

```
import matplotlib.pyplot as plt
import numpy as np

x1 = np.linspace(-5,5,num=200)
y1 = x1

x2 = np.linspace(-5,5,num=200)
y2 = -x2

plt.axis([-5, 5, -5, 5])
plt.plot(x1,y1)
plt.plot(x2,y2)
plt.show()
```

Listing 5.6 defines two lines using the technique that you saw in Listing 5.5, except that these two lines define `y1 = x1` and `y2 = -x2`, which produces slanted lines instead of horizontal lines.

Figure 5.3 displays two slanted line segments whose equations are defined in Listing 5.6.

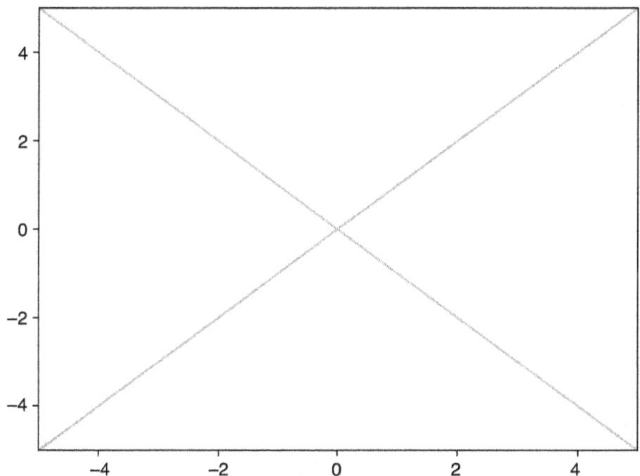

FIGURE 5.3 A graph of two slanted line segments

PARALLEL SLANTED LINES IN MATPLOTLIB

If two lines in the Euclidean plane have the same slope, then they are parallel. Listing 5.7 displays the content of `parallellines1.py` that illustrates how to plot parallel slanted lines.

LISTING 5.7: parallellines1.py

```
import matplotlib.pyplot as plt
import numpy as np

# lower line
x1 = np.linspace(-5,5,num=200)
y1 = 2*x1
```

```
# upper line
x2 = np.linspace(-5,5,num=200)
y2 = 2*x2 + 3

# horizontal axis
x3 = np.linspace(-5,5,num=200)
y3 = 0*x3 + 0

# vertical axis
plt.axvline(x=0.0)

plt.axis([-5, 5, -10, 10])
plt.plot(x1,y1)
plt.plot(x2,y2)
plt.plot(x3,y3)
plt.show()
```

Listing 5.7 defines three lines using the technique that you saw in Listing 5.6, where two lines are slanted and parallel, and the third line is horizontal. Launch the code in Listing 5.7, and you will see the result displayed in Figure 5.4.

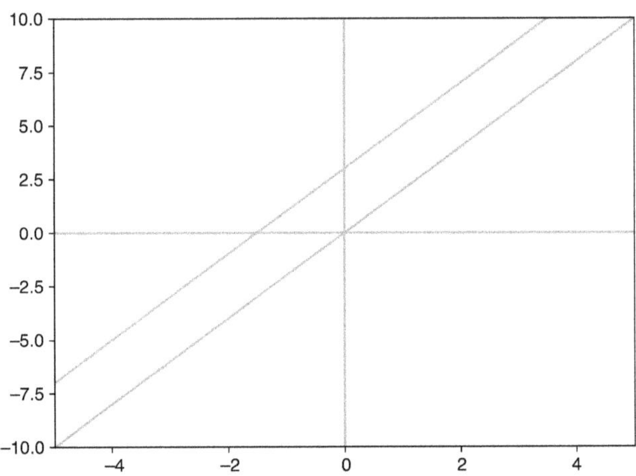

FIGURE 5.4 A graph of two slanted parallel line segments

A GRID OF POINTS IN MATPLOTLIB

Listing 5.8 displays the content of `plotgrid.py` that illustrates how to plot a simple grid.

LISTING 5.8: multi_lines.py

```
import matplotlib.pyplot as plt

x_coord = [ 50, 300, 175, 50]
y_coord = [ 50, 50,  150, 50]
plt.plot(x_coord,y_coord)
plt.scatter(x_coord,y_coord)
```

```
for x,y in zip(x_coord,y_coord):
  plt.text(x,y,'Coord ({x},{y})'.format(x=x,y=y))

x_coord = [ 175, 300,  50, 175]
y_coord = [  50, 150, 150, 50]
plt.plot(x_coord,y_coord)
plt.scatter(x_coord,y_coord)

for x,y in zip(x_coord,y_coord):
  plt.text(x,y,'Coord ({x},{y})'.format(x=x,y=y))
plt.show()
```

Listing 5.8 defines the NumPy variable `points` that defines a 2D list of points with three rows and four columns. The Pyplot API `plot()` uses the `points` variable to display a grid-like pattern. Figure 5.5 displays a grid of points, as defined in Listing 5.8.

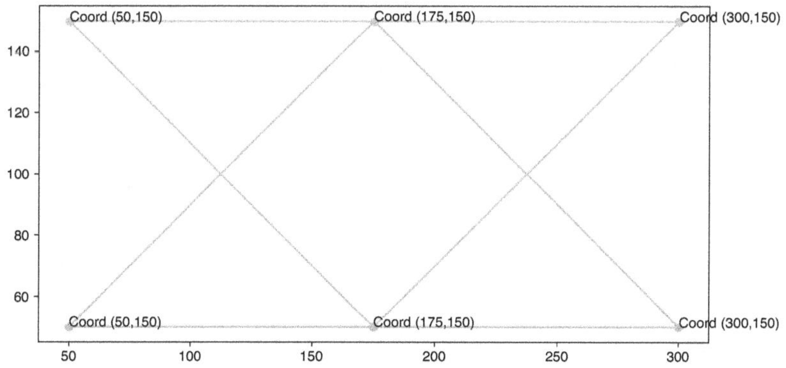

FIGURE 5.5 A grid of points generated by the code in Listing 5.8

A DOTTED GRID IN MATPLOTLIB

Listing 5.9 displays the content of `plotdottedgrid1.py` that illustrates how to plot a "dotted" grid pattern.

LISTING 5.9: plotdottedgrid1.py

```
import numpy as np
import pylab
from itertools import product
import matplotlib.pyplot as plt

fig = pylab.figure()
ax = fig.add_subplot(1,1,1)

ax.grid(which='major', axis='both', linestyle='--')

[line.set zorder(3) for line in ax.lines]
fig.show() # to update

plt.gca().xaxis.grid(True)
plt.show()
```

Listing 5.9 is similar to the code in Listing 5.8 in that both of them plot a grid-like pattern; however, the former renders a "dotted" grid pattern whereas the latter renders a "dotted" grid pattern by specifying the value `'--'` for the `linestyle` parameter.

The next portion of Listing 5.9 invokes the `set_zorder()` method, that controls which items are displayed on top of other items, such as dots on top of lines, or vice versa. The final portion of Listing 5.9 invokes the `gca().xaxis.grid(True)` chained methods to display the vertical grid lines.

You can also use the `plt.style` directive to specify a style for figures. The following code snippet specifies the classic style of Matplotlib:

```
plt.style.use('classic')
```

Figure 5.6 displays a "dashed" grid pattern based on the code in Listing 5.9.

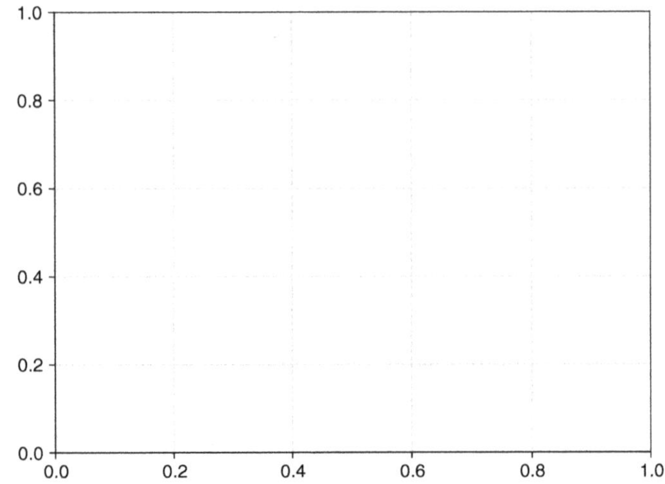

FIGURE 5.6 A "dashed" grid pattern generated using the code from Listing 5.9

TWO LINES AND A LEGEND IN MATPLOTLIB

Listing 5.10 displays the content of `plotgrid2.py` that illustrates how to display a colored grid.

LISTING 5.10: two_lines_legend.py

```
import matplotlib.pyplot as plt

# FIRST PLOT:
vals_x =  [91,93,95,96,97,98,99,99,104,115]
vals_y =  [1500,2000,3000,2500,1200,1500,2900,3200,5200,6500]
plt.plot(vals_x, vals_y) # alternate style
#plt.plot(vals_x, vals_y, label='First List')

# SECOND PLOT:
vals_x2 = [91,93,95,96,97,98,99,99,104,115]
```

```
vals_y2 = [1005,1006,1007,1008,1009,2031,3100,2033,3034,4035]
plt.plot(vals_x2, vals_y2)
#plt.plot(vals_x2, vals_y2, label='Second List') #
alternate style

# generate line plot:
plt.plot(vals_x, vals_y)
plt.title("Random Pairs of Numbers")
plt.xlabel("Random X Values")
plt.ylabel("Random Y Values")
plt.legend(['First List','Second List'])
#plt.legend() # alternate style
plt.show()
```

Listing 5.10 defines the NumPy variable data that defines a 2D set of points with ten rows and ten columns. The Pyplot API plot() uses the data variable to display two line graphs, as shown in Figure 5.7.

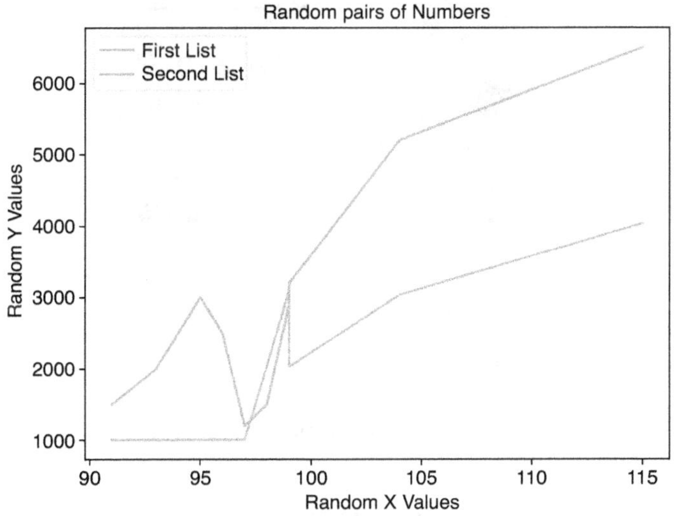

FIGURE 5.7 A pair of line segments

LOADING IMAGES IN MATPLOTLIB

Listing 5.11 displays the content of `load_images2.py` that illustrates how to display an image.

LISTING 5.11: load_images2.py

```
from sklearn.datasets import load_digits
from matplotlib import pyplot as plt

digits = load_digits()
```

```
#set interpolation='none'

fig = plt.figure(figsize=(3, 3))
plt.imshow(digits['images'][66], cmap="gray",
interpolation='none')
plt.show()
```

Listing 5.11 starts with two `import` statements, and then the `digits` variable is initialized with the contents of the `digits` dataset. The next portion of Listing 5.11 displays the contents of one of the images in the `digits` dataset. Launch the code in Listing 5.11, and you will see the image in Figure 5.8.

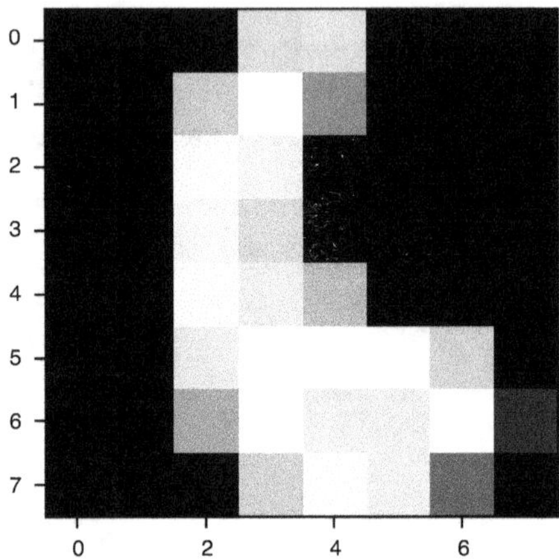

FIGURE 5.8 Loading an image in Matplotlib

A CHECKERBOARD IN MATPLOTLIB

Listing 5.12 displays the content of `checkerboard1.py` that illustrates how to display a checkerboard.

LISTING 5.12: checkerboard1.py

```
import matplotlib.pyplot as plt
from matplotlib import colors
import numpy as np

data = np.random.rand(10, 10) * 20

# create discrete colormap
cmap = colors.ListedColormap(['red', 'blue'])
bounds = [0,10,20]
norm = colors.BoundaryNorm(bounds, cmap.N)

fig, ax = plt.subplots()
ax.imshow(data, cmap=cmap, norm=norm)

# draw gridlines
```

```
ax.grid(which='major', axis='both', linestyle='-',
color='k', linewidth=2)
ax.set_xticks(np.arange(-.5, 10, 1));
ax.set_yticks(np.arange(-.5, 10, 1));

plt.show()
```

Listing 5.12 defines the NumPy variable `data` that defines a 2D set of points with ten rows and ten columns. The Pyplot API `plot()` uses the `data` variable to display a colored grid-like pattern. Figure 5.9 displays a colored grid whose equations are contained in Listing 5.12.

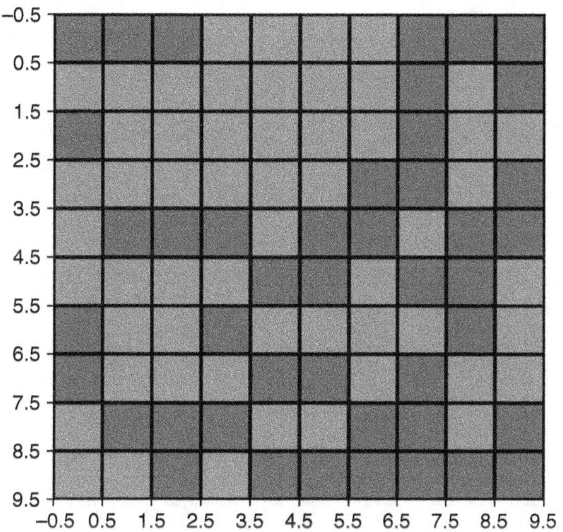

FIGURE 5.9 A checkerboard generated by Matplotlib

RANDOMIZED DATA POINTS IN MATPLOTLIB

Listing 5.13 displays the content of `lin_reg_plot.py` that illustrates how to plot a graph of random points.

LISTING 5.13: lin_plot_reg.py

```
import numpy as np
import matplotlib.pyplot as plt

trX = np.linspace(-1, 1, 101) # Linear space of 101 and [-1,1]

#Create the y function based on the x axis
trY = 2*trX + np.random.randn(*trX.shape)*0.4+0.2

#create figure and scatter plot of the random points
plt.figure()
plt.scatter(trX,trY)

# Draw one line with the line function
```

```
plt.plot (trX, .2 + 2 * trX)
plt.show()
```

Listing 5.13 defines the NumPy variable `trX` that contains 101 equally spaced numbers that are between -1 and 1 (inclusive). The variable `trY` is defined in two parts: the first part is `2*trX` and the second part is a random value that is partially based on the length of the one-dimensional array `trX`. The variable `trY` is the sum of these two "parts," which creates a "fuzzy" line segment.

The next portion of Listing 5.13 creates a scatterplot based on the values in `trX` and `trY`, followed by the Pyplot API `plot()` that renders a line segment. Figure 5.10 displays a random set of points based on the code in Listing 5.13.

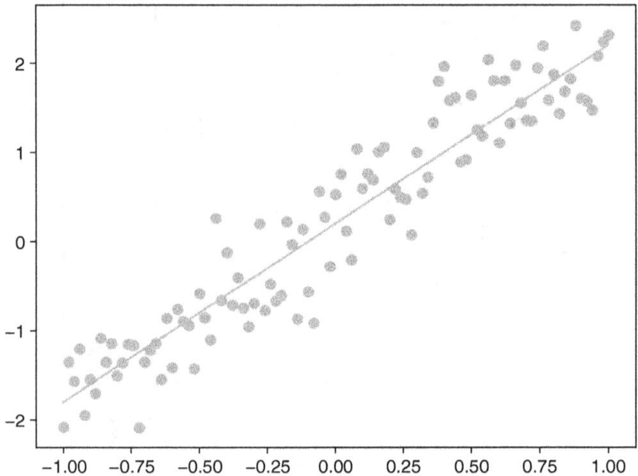

FIGURE 5.10 A random set of points based on the code in Listing 5.13

A SET OF LINE SEGMENTS IN MATPLOTLIB

Listing 5.14 displays the content of `line_segments.py` that illustrates how to plot a set of connected line segments in Matplotlib.

LISTING 5.14: line_segments.py

```
import numpy as np
import matplotlib.pyplot as plt

x = [7,11,13,15,17,19,23,29,31,37]

plt.plot(x) # OR: plt.plot(x, 'ro-') or bo
plt.ylabel('Height')
plt.xlabel('Weight')
plt.show()
```

Listing 5.14 defines the array `x` that contains a hard-coded set of values. The Pyplot API `plot()` uses the variable `x` to display a set of connected line segments. Figure 5.11 displays the result of launching the code in Listing 5.14.

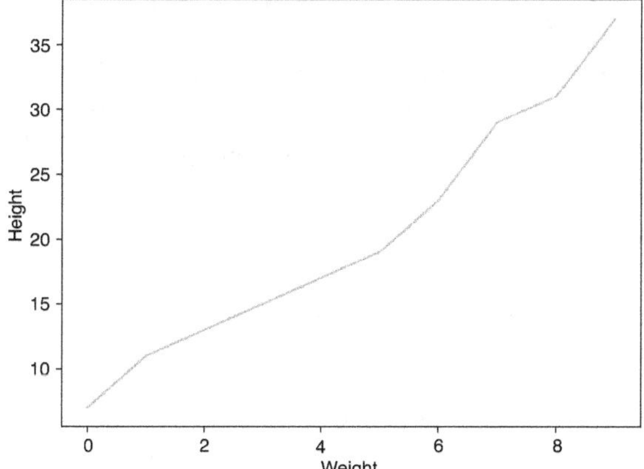

FIGURE 5.11 A set of connected line segments

PLOTTING MULTIPLE LINES IN MATPLOTLIB

Listing 5.15 displays the content of `plt_array2.py` that illustrates the ease with which you can plot multiple lines in Matplotlib.

LISTING 5.15: plt_array2.py

```
import matplotlib.pyplot as plt

x = [7,11,13,15,17,19,23,29,31,37]
data = [[8, 4, 1], [5, 3, 3], [6, 0, 2], [1, 7, 9]]
plt.plot(data, 'd-')
plt.show()
```

Listing 5.15 defines the array `data` that contains a hard-coded set of values. The Pyplot API `plot()` uses the variable `data` to display a line segment. Figure 5.12 displays multiple lines based on the code in Listing 5.15.

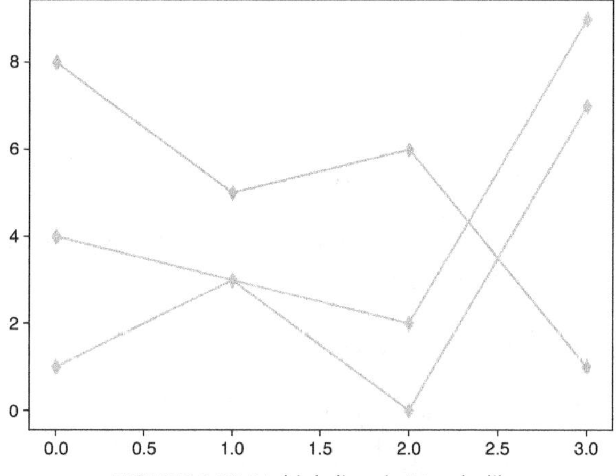

FIGURE 5.12 Multiple lines in Matplotlib

TRIGONOMETRIC FUNCTIONS IN MATPLOTLIB

You can display the graph of trigonometric functions as easily as you can render "regular" graphs using Matplotlib. Listing 5.16 displays the content of `sincos.py` that illustrates how to plot a sine function and a cosine function in Matplotlib.

LISTING 5.16: sincos.py

```
import numpy as np
import math

x = np.linspace(0, 2*math.pi, 101)
s = np.sin(x)
c = np.cos(x)

import matplotlib.pyplot as plt
plt.plot (s)
plt.plot (c)
plt.show()
```

Listing 5.16 defines the NumPy variables `x`, `s`, and `c` using the NumPy APIs `linspace()`, `sin()`, and `cos()`, respectively. Next, the Pyplot API `plot()` uses these variables to display a sine function and a cosine function.

Figure 5.13 displays a graph of two trigonometric functions based on the code in Listing 5.16.

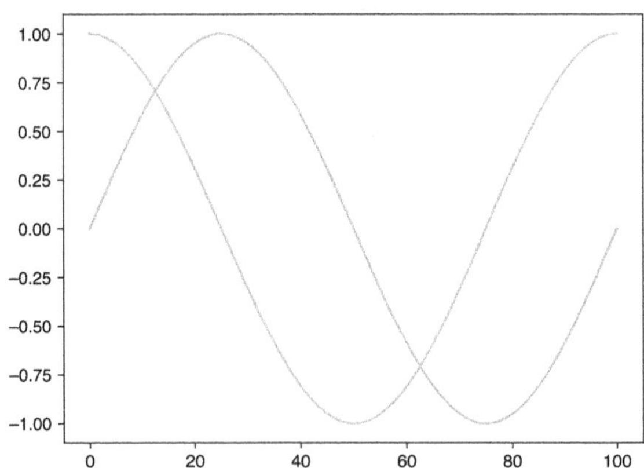

FIGURE 5.13 Sine and cosine trigonometric functions

Now let's look at a simple dataset consisting of discrete data points, which is the topic of the next section.

A HISTOGRAM IN MATPLOTLIB

Listing 5.17 displays the content of `histogram1.py` that illustrates how to plot a histogram using Matplotlib.

LISTING 5.17: histogram1.py

```
import matplotlib.pyplot as plt

x = [1, 2, 3, 4, 5, 6, 7, 4]

plt.hist(x, bins = [1, 2, 3, 4, 5, 6, 7])
plt.title("Histogram")
plt.legend(["bar"])
plt.show()
```

Listing 5.17 is straightforward: the variable `x` is initialized as a set of numbers, followed by a block of code that renders a histogram based on the data in the variable `x`. Launch the code in Listing 5.17, and you will see the histogram that is shown in Figure 5.14.

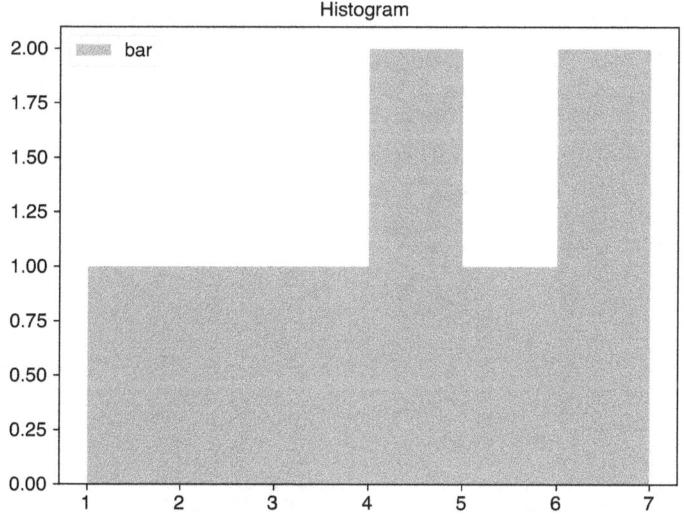

FIGURE 5.14 A histogram based on random values

HISTOGRAM WITH DATA FROM A SQLITE3 TABLE

Listing 5.18 displays the content of `rainfall_hist2.py` that shows you how to define a simple SQL query to create a histogram based on the data from the rainfall table.

LISTING 5.18: rainfall_hist3.py

```
import sqlite3
import pandas as pd
import matplotlib.pyplot as plt

sql = """
  SELECT
  cast(centimeters/5.00 as int)*5 as cent_floor,
  count(*) as count
```

```
FROM rainfall
GROUP by 1
ORDER by 1;
"""

con = sqlite3.connect("mytools.db")
df = pd.read_sql_query(sql, con)
con.close()

print("=> Histogram of Rainfall:")
print(df)

#df.hist(column='count', bins=7, grid=False, rwidth=1.0,
color='red')
df.hist(column='count', bins=14, grid=False, rwidth=.8,
color='red')
plt.show()
```

Listing 5.18 starts with several `import` statements and then initializes the variable `sql` with a SQL statement that selects data from the `rainfall` table. The next portion of Listing 5.18 initializes the variable `con` for accessing the `mytools.db` database, and then populates the Pandas data frame `df` with the result of executing the SQL statement contained in the variable `sql`. Now launch the code in Listing 5.18, and you will see the following output:

```
=> Histogram of Rainfall:
   bucket_floor      bucket_name  count
0             0     FROM 0 TO 10     27
1            10    FROM 10 TO 20     14
2            20    FROM 20 TO 30      9
3            30    FROM 30 TO 40      9
4            40    FROM 40 TO 50      3
5            50    FROM 50 TO 60      2
6            60    FROM 60 TO 70      1
```

The histogram that is shown in Figure 5.15 was created from this data.

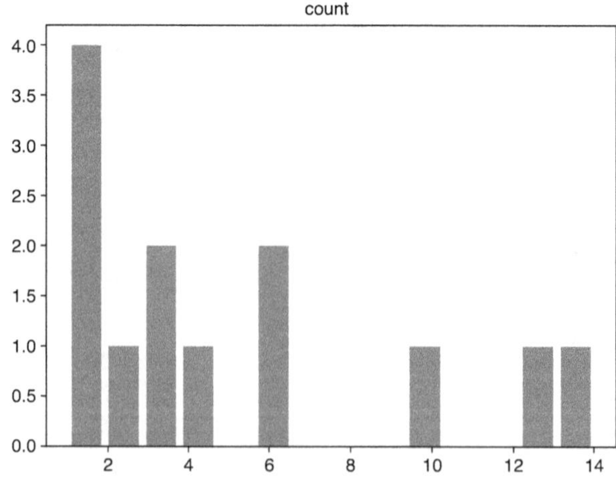

FIGURE 5.15 A histogram based on rainfall data

PLOT BAR CHARTS IN MATPLOTLIB

Listing 5.19 displays the content of `barchart1.py` that illustrates how to plot a bar chart in Matplotlib.

LISTING 5.19: barchart1.py

```
import matplotlib.pyplot as plt

x = [3, 1, 3, 12, 2, 4, 4]
y = [3, 2, 1, 4, 5, 6, 7]

plt.bar(x, y)

plt.title("Bar Chart")
plt.legend(["bar"])
plt.show()
```

Listing 5.19 contains an `import` statement followed by the variables `x` and `y` that are initialized as a list of numbers. Next, the bar chart is generated by invoking the `bar()` method of the `plt` class. The final block of code sets the title and legend for the bar chart and then displays the bar chart. Launch the code in Listing 5.19, and you will see the pie chart displayed in Figure 5.16.

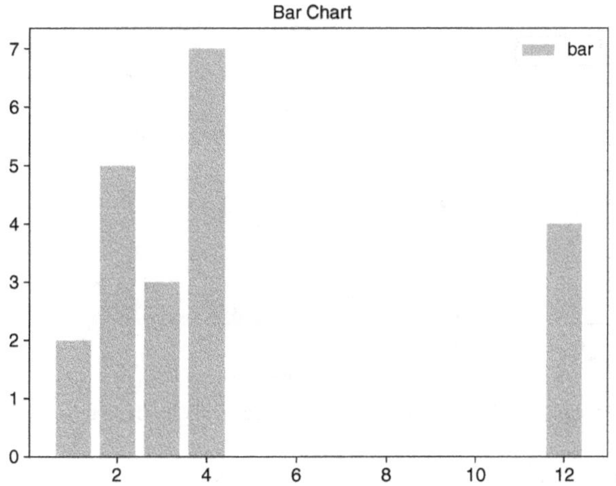

FIGURE 5.16 A bar chart using Matplotlib

Listing 5.20 displays the content of `barchart2.py` that illustrates how to plot a bar chart in Matplotlib.

LISTING 5.20: barchart2.py

```
import matplotlib.pyplot as plt

plt.bar([0.25,1.25,2.25,3.25,4.25],
        [50,40,70,80,20],
        label="GDP1",width=.5)
```

```
plt.bar([.75,1.75,2.75,3.75,4.75],
        [80,20,20,50,60],
        label="GDP2", color='r',width=.5)

plt.legend()
plt.xlabel('Months')
plt.ylabel('GDP (Billion Euross)')
plt.title('Bar Chart Comparison')
```

Listing 5.20 contains an `import` statement followed by the definition of two bar charts that are displayed in a side-by-side manner. Notice that the definition of each bar chart involves specifying the `x` and `y` (even though they are not explicitly included), followed by a value for the `label` and `width` arguments. The final block of code sets the legend and labels for the horizontal and vertical axes. Launch the code in Listing 5.20, and you will see the bar charts shown in Figure 5.17.

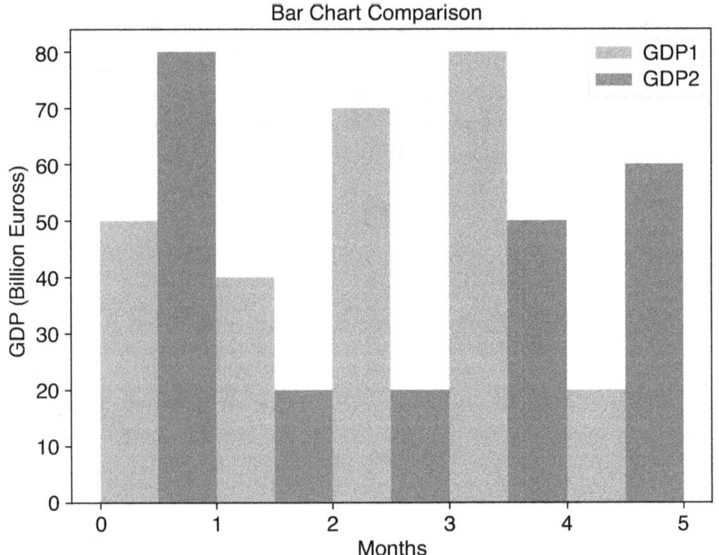

FIGURE 5.17 Two bar charts generated by the code in Listing 5.20

PLOT A PIE CHART IN MATPLOTLIB

Listing 5.21 displays the content of `piechart1.py` that illustrates how to plot a pie chart in Matplotlib.

LISTING 5.21: piechart1.py

```
import numpy as np

# data to display on plots
x = [1, 2, 3, 4]

# explode the first wedge:
e =(0.1, 0, 0, 0)
```

```
plt.pie(x, explode = e)
plt.title("Pie chart")
plt.show()
```

Listing 5.21 contains an `import` statement followed by the variables `x` and `e` that are initialized as a list of numbers. The values for `x` are used to calculate the relative size of each "slice" of the pie chart, and the values for the variable `e` indicate that the first pie slice is "exploded" slightly (indicated by the value 0.1 in `e`). Launch the code in Listing 5.21, and you will see the pie chart displayed in Figure 5.18.

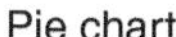

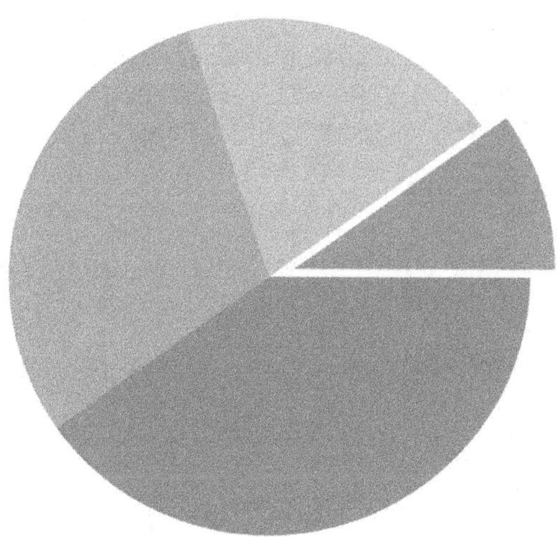

FIGURE 5.18 A pie chart generated by the code in Listing 5.21

HEAT MAPS IN MATPLOTLIB

Listing 5.22 displays the content of `heatmap1.py` that illustrates how to render a heat map in Matplotlib.

LISTING 5.22: heatmap1.py

```
import numpy as np

data = np.random.random((16, 16))
plt.imshow(data, cmap='tab20_r', interpolation='nearest')
plt.show()
```

Listing 5.22 contains an `import` statement, followed by the variable `data` that is initialized as a 16x16 matrix of random values. The next code snippet renders the heat map, and the final code snippet displays the heatmap. Launch the code in Listing 5.22, and you will see the image that is shown in Figure 5.19.

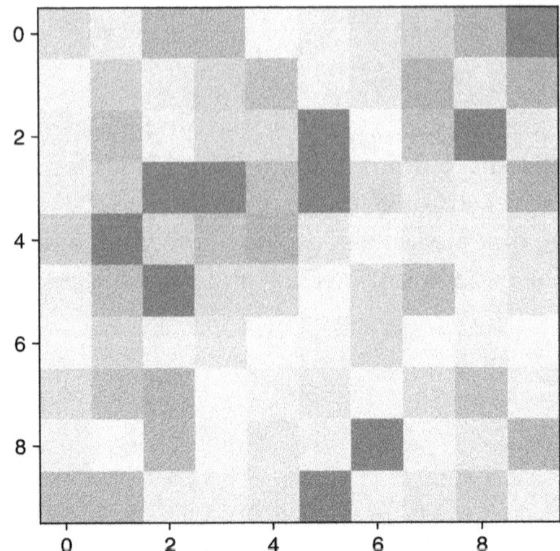

FIGURE 5.19 A heat map generated by the code in Listing 5.22

SAVE PLOT AS A PNG FILE

Listing 5.23 displays the content of `matplot2png.py` that shows you how to save a graphics image as a PNG file.

LISTING 5.23: matplot2png.py

```
import matplotlib.pyplot as plt
import numpy as np

outfile="graph1.png"

plt.figure()
plt.plot(range(6))

fig, ax = plt.subplots()

ax.plot([2, 3, 4, 5, 5, 6, 6],
        [5, 7, 1, 3, 4, 6 ,8])

ax.plot([1, 2, 3, 4, 5],
        [2, 3, 4, 5, 6])

x = np.linspace(0, 12, 100)
plt.plot(np.sin(x))
plt.plot(np.linspace(-4,4,50))

plt.savefig(outfile, dpi=300)
```

Listing 5.23 contains `import` statements, followed by the variable `outfile`, which is initialized with the name of the PNG file that will be saved to the file system. The contents of the PNG file consist of a sine wave and a set of line segments. Launch the code in Listing 5.23, and you will see the image that is shown in Figure 5.20.

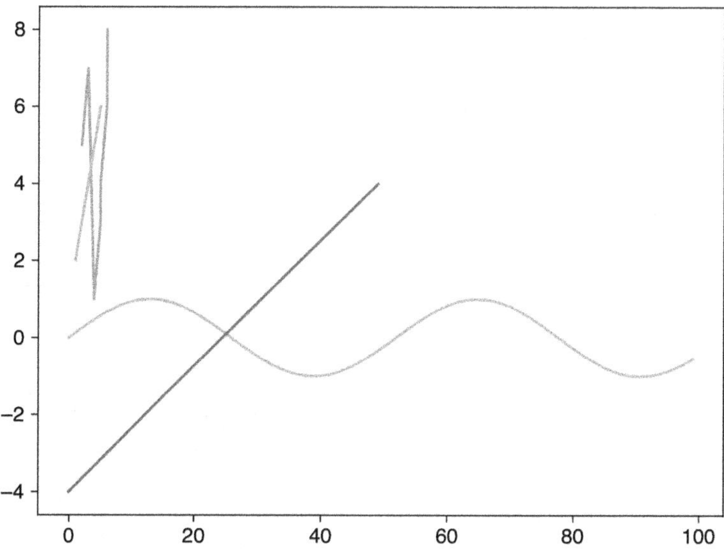

FIGURE 5.20 A heat map generated with the code from Listing 5.23

WORKING WITH SWEETVIZ

`SweetViz` is an open source Python module that generates remarkably detailed visualizations in the form of HTML Web pages based on five lines of Python code.

As a simple illustration, Listing 5.24 shows the content of `sweetviz1.py` that generates a visualization of various aspects of the `Iris` dataset that is available in Scikit-learn.

LISTING 5.24: sweetviz1.py

```
import sweetviz as sv
import seaborn as sns

df = sns.load_dataset('iris')
report = sv.analyze(df)
report.show_html()
```

Listing 5.24 starts with two `import` statements, followed by an initialization of the variable `df` with the contents of the `Iris` dataset. The next code snippet initializes the variable report as the result of invoking the `analyze()` method in `SweetViz`, followed by a code snippet that generates an HTML Web page with the result of the analysis.

Launch the code from the command line, and you will see a new HTML Web page called `SWEETVIZ_REPORT.html` in the same directory. Figure 5.21 displays the contents of the Web page `SWEETVIZ_REPORT.html`.

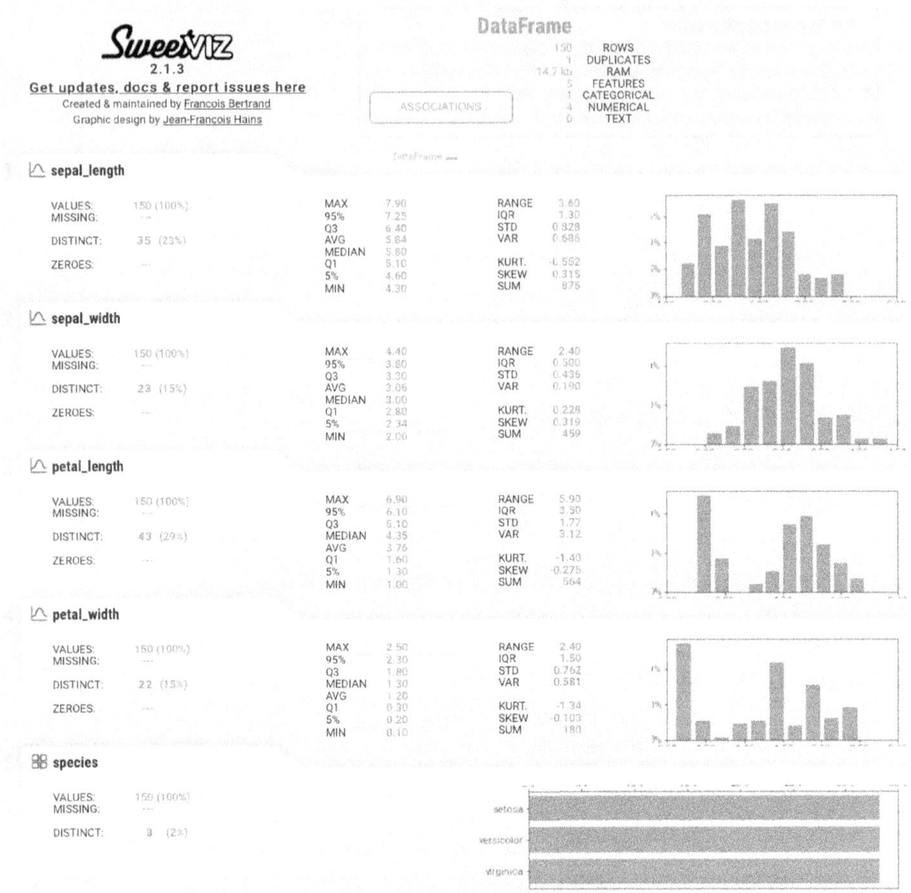

FIGURE 5.21 An analysis of the Iris dataset

WORKING WITH SKIMPY

`Skimpy` is an open-source Python module that generates an analysis of a dataset directly from the command line: no Python code is required. Install `Skimpy` with the following command:

```
pip3 install skimpy
```

Launch the following command to analyze the `Titanic` dataset (or a dataset of your own choice) and redirects the output to a text file (the latter is optional):

```
skimpy titanic.csv >titanic_out.txt
```

Figure 5.22 displays the contents of the generated output from the preceding command.

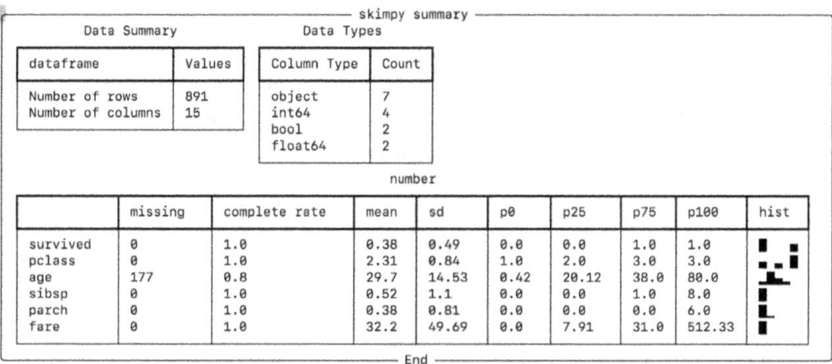

skimpy summary

Data Summary

dataframe	Values
Number of rows	891
Number of columns	15

Data Types

Column Type	Count
object	7
int64	4
bool	2
float64	2

number

	missing	complete rate	mean	sd	p0	p25	p75	p100	hist
survived	0	1.0	0.38	0.49	0.0	0.0	1.0	1.0	
pclass	0	1.0	2.31	0.84	1.0	2.0	3.0	3.0	
age	177	0.8	29.7	14.53	0.42	20.12	38.0	80.0	
sibsp	0	1.0	0.52	1.1	0.0	0.0	1.0	8.0	
parch	0	1.0	0.38	0.81	0.0	0.0	0.0	6.0	
fare	0	1.0	32.2	49.69	0.0	7.91	31.0	512.33	

End

FIGURE 5.22 An analysis of the Titanic dataset

3D CHARTS IN MATPLOTLIB

Listing 5.25 displays the content of `matplot_3d.py` that illustrates how to render a 3D plot in Matplotlib.

LISTING 5.25: matplot_3d.py

```
import matplotlib.pyplot as plt
import numpy as np

zline = np.linspace(0,40,1000)
xline = 2*np.sin(2*zline)
yline = 3*np.cos(3*zline)

ax = plt.axes(projection="3d")
ax.plot3D(xline,yline,zline,'red',linewidth=4)
plt.show()
```

Listing 5.25 contains `import` statements, followed by the variables `zline`, `xline`, and `yline` that are initialized via the NumPy methods `linspace()`, `sin()`, and `cos()`, respectively. The next portion of Listing 5.25 initializes the variable `ax` in order to display a 3D effort, which is rendered by the final code snippet. Launch the code in Listing 5.25, and you will see the image that is shown in Figure 5.23.

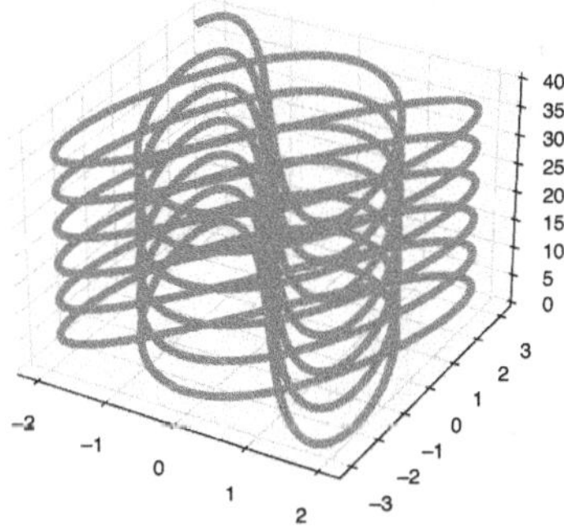

FIGURE 5.23 A 3D plot

PLOTTING FINANCIAL DATA WITH MPLFINANCE

The section contains a Python-based code sample that shows you how to plot financial data for a given stock. First, make sure that you have the necessary Python library installed, as shown here:

```
pip3 install mplfinance
```

Listing 5.26 displays the content of `financial_mpl.py` that illustrates how to plot financial data in Matplotlib.

LISTING 5.26: financial_mpl.py

```
#optional:
import sys
sys.path.append('/usr/local/lib/python3.9/site-packages')

import matplotlib.pyplot as plt
import pandas as pd

csvfile="aapl.csv"
daily = pd.read_csv(csvfile,index_col=0,parse_dates=True)
daily.index.name = 'Date'

print("daily.head():")
print(daily.head())
print()

print("daily.tail():")
print(daily.tail())

import mplfinance as mpf
mpf.plot(daily)

#Plot types: ohlc, candle, line, renko, and pnf
```

Listing 5.26 contains `import` statements, followed by the variable `csvfile` that contains AAPL data for the years 2017 and 2018. Next, the variable `daily` is initialized with the contents of `aapl.csv`, followed by a block of code that prints the first 5 lines and the final 5 lines of data in `aapl.csv`.

The final code snippet invokes the `plot()` method of the class `mpf` (which is imported from `mplfinance`) in order to render a chart. Launch the code in Listing 5.26, and you will see the following output:

```
daily.head():
                 Open        High  ...   Adj Close    Volume
Date                               ...
2017-01-03  115.800003  116.330002  ...  114.311760  28781900
2017-01-04  115.849998  116.510002  ...  114.183815  21118100
2017-01-05  115.919998  116.860001  ...  114.764473  22193600
2017-01-06  116.779999  118.160004  ...  116.043915  31751900
2017-01-09  117.949997  119.430000  ...  117.106812  33561900

[5 rows x 6 columns]
```

```
daily.tail():
                  Open        High  ...   Adj Close    Volume
Date                                ...
2018-01-12  176.179993  177.360001  ...  177.089996  25418100
2018-01-16  177.899994  179.389999  ...  176.190002  29565900
2018-01-17  176.149994  179.250000  ...  179.100006  34386800
2018-01-18  179.369995  180.100006  ...  179.259995  31193400
2018-01-19  178.610001  179.580002  ...  178.460007  31269600

[5 rows x 6 columns]
```

Figure 5.24 displays a plot of financial data based on the code in Listing 5.29.

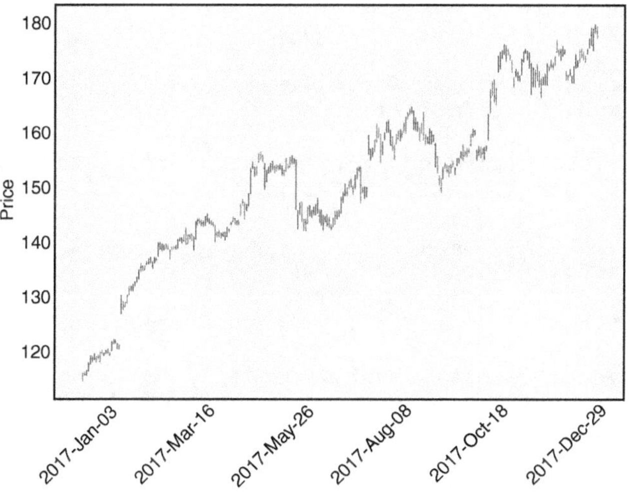

FIGURE 5.24 Plot of financial data for years 2017 and 2018

CHARTS AND GRAPHS WITH DATA FROM SQLITE3

Listing 5.27 displays the content of `rainfall_multiple.py` that shows you how to generate multiple charts and graphs from data that is extracted from a `sqlite3` database.

LISTING 5.27: rainfall_multiple.py

```
import sqlite3
import pandas as pd
import matplotlib.pyplot as plt

sql = """
  SELECT
  cast(centimeters/5.00 as int)*5 as cent_floor,
  count(*) as count
FROM rainfall
GROUP by 1
ORDER by 1;
```

```
"""

con = sqlite3.connect("mytools.db")
df = pd.read_sql_query(sql, con)
con.close()

####################################
# generate 7 types of charts/graphs
# and save them as PNG or TIFF files
####################################
df.hist(column='count', bins=14, grid=False, rwidth=.8,
color='red')
plt.savefig("rainfall_histogram.tiff")

df.plot.pie(y='count',figsize=(8,6))
plt.savefig("rainfall_pie.png")

df.plot.line(y='count',figsize=(8,6))
plt.savefig("rainfall_line.png")

df.plot.scatter(y='count',x='cent_floor',figsize=(8,6))
plt.savefig("rainfall_scatter.png")

df.plot.box(figsize=(8,6))
plt.savefig("rainfall_box.png")

df.plot.hexbin(x='count', y='cent_floor',gridsize=30,
figsize=(8,6))
plt.savefig("rainfall_hexbin.png")
df["cent_floor"].plot.kde()
plt.savefig("rainfall_kde.png")

df["count"].hist()
df.plot.line(x='count', y='cent_floor', figsize=(8,6))
df.plot.scatter(x='count', y='cent_floor', figsize=(8,6))
df.plot.box(figsize=(8,6))
df.plot.hexbin(x='count', y='cent_floor',gridsize=30,
figsize=(8,6))
df.plot.pie(y='cost', figsize=(8, 6))
df["cent_floor"].plot.kde()
```

Listing 5.27 contains several `import` statements and then initializes the variable `sql` with a SQL statement that selects data from the `rainfall` table. The next portion of Listing 5.27 initializes the variable `con` for accessing the `mytools.db` database, and then populates the Pandas data frame `df` with the result of executing the SQL statement contained in the variable `sql`.

The next portion of Listing 5.27 contains pairs of code snippets for rendering charts and graphs of various types (histogram, pie, line, scatter, box, hexbin, and kde). Launch the code in Listing 5.27, and you will see the following output:

```
=> Histogram of Rainfall:
    cent_floor  count
```

```
0              0     14
1              5     13
2             10      4
3             15     10
4             20      3
5             25      6
6             30      3
7             35      6
8             40      2
9             45      1
10            50      1
11            55      1
12            60      1
```

In addition to the preceding output, you will also see the following files in the same directory where you launched the code in Listing 5.27:

```
rainfall_histogram.tiff
rainfall_pie.png
rainfall_line.png
rainfall_scatter.png
rainfall_box.png
rainfall_hexbin.png
rainfall_kde.png
```

SUMMARY

This chapter started with a very short introduction to Matplotlib, along with code samples that displayed the available colors in Matplotlib.

Then you learned how to render horizontal lines, slanted lines, parallel lines, and a grid of points. In addition, you learned how to load images, display checkerboard patterns, and plot trigonometric functions. You also saw how to render histograms, bar charts, pie charts, and heat maps.

Next, you saw how to create a 3D plot, as well as how to render financial data and a chart with data from a sqlite3 database.

CHAPTER 6

SEABORN FOR DATA VISUALIZATION

This chapter introduces several tools for data visualization, including `Seaborn`, `Bokeh`, and `YellowBrick`. This chapter also contains a gentle introduction to `Scikit-learn` (which is typically imported as `sklearn`).

The first part of the chapter introduces you to `Seaborn` for data visualization, which is a layer above `Matplotlib`. Although `Seaborn` does not have all of the features that are available in `Matplotlib`, `Seaborn` provides an easier set of APIs for rendering charts and graphs.

The second portion of this chapter contains a very short introduction to `Bokeh`, along with a code sample that illustrates how to create a more artistic graphics effect with relative ease in `Bokeh`.

The third part of the chapter introduces you to `Scikit-learn`, which is a very powerful `Python` library that supports many machine learning algorithms and also supports visualization. If you are new to machine learning, fear not: *this section does not require a background in machine learning in order to understand the Python code samples.*

WORKING WITH SEABORN

`Seaborn` is a `Python` library for data visualization that also provides a high-level interface to `Matplotlib`. `Seaborn` is easier to work with than `Matplotlib`, and actually extends `Matplotlib`, but keep in mind that `Seaborn` is not as powerful as `Matplotlib`.

`Seaborn` addresses two challenges of `Matplotlib`. The first involves the default `Matplotlib` parameters. `Seaborn` works with different parameters, which provides greater flexibility than the default rendering of `Matplotlib` plots. `Seaborn` addresses the limitations of the `Matplotlib` default values for features such as colors, tick marks on the upper and right axes, and the style (among others).

In addition, Seaborn makes it easier to plot entire data frames (somewhat like Pandas) than doing so in Matplotlib. Nevertheless, since Seaborn extends Matplotlib, knowledge of the latter is advantageous and will simplify your learning curve.

Features of Seaborn

Seaborn provides a nice set of features and useful methods to control the display of data, some of which are listed here:

- scale Seaborn plots
- set the plot style
- set the figure size
- rotate label text
- set xlim or ylim
- set log scale
- add titles

Some useful Seaborn methods are listed here:

- plt.xlabel()
- plt.ylabel()
- plt.annotate()
- plt.legend()
- plt.ylim()
- plt.savefig()

Seaborn supports various built-in datasets, just like NumPy and Pandas, including the Iris dataset and the Titanic dataset, both of which you will see in subsequent sections. As a starting point, the next section contains the code that displays all the available built-in datasets in Seaborn.

SEABORN DATASET NAMES

Listing 6.1 displays the contents dataset_names.py that displays the Seaborn built-in datasets, one of which we will use in a subsequent section in order to render a heat map in Seaborn.

LISTING 6.1: dataset_names.py

```
import seaborn as sns

names = sns.get_dataset_names()
for name in names:
  print("name:",name)
```

Listing 6.1 contains an `import` statement and then the variable `names` that is initialized with the set of built-in dataset names in `Seaborn`. The next portion contains a loop that iterates through the dataset names in the variable `names` and displays their values. Launch the code in Listing 6.1 and you will see the following output:

```
name: anagrams
name: anscombe
name: attention
name: brain_networks
name: car_crashes
name: diamonds
name: dots
name: exercise
name: flights
name: fmri
name: gammas
name: geyser
name: iris
name: mpg
name: penguins
name: planets
name: taxis
name: tips
name: titanic
```

The three-line code sample in the next section shows you how to display the rows in the built-in "tips" dataset.

SEABORN BUILT-IN DATASETS

Listing 6.2 displays the contents of `seaborn_tips.py` that illustrates how to read the `tips` dataset into a data frame and display the first five rows of the dataset.

LISTING 6.2: seaborn_tips.py

```
import seaborn as sns

df = sns.load_dataset("tips")
print(df.head())
```

Listing 6.2 is very simple: after importing `seaborn`, the variable `df` is initialized with the data in the built-in dataset `tips`, and the `print()` statement displays the first five rows of `df`. Note that the `load_dataset()` API searches for online or built-in datasets. The output from Listing 6.2 is here:

```
   total_bill   tip     sex smoker  day    time  size
0       16.99  1.01  Female     No  Sun  Dinner     2
1       10.34  1.66    Male     No  Sun  Dinner     3
```

```
2        21.01  3.50    Male     No   Sun  Dinner     3
3        23.68  3.31    Male     No   Sun  Dinner     2
4        24.59  3.61  Female     No   Sun  Dinner     4
```

THE IRIS DATASET IN SEABORN

Listing 6.3 displays the contents of `seaborn_iris.py` that illustrates how to plot the `Iris` dataset.

LISTING 6.2: seaborn_iris.py

```
import seaborn as sns
import matplotlib.pyplot as plt

# Load iris data
iris = sns.load_dataset("iris")

# Construct iris plot
sns.swarmplot(x="species", y="petal_length", data=iris)

# Show plot
plt.show()
```

Listing 6.3 imports `Seaborn` and `matplotlib.pyplot` and then initializes the variable `iris` with the contents of the built-in `Iris` dataset. Next, the `swamplot()` API displays a graph with the horizontal axis labeled `species`, the vertical axis labeled `petal_length`, and the displayed points are from the `Iris` dataset.

Figure 6.1 displays the images in the `Iris` dataset based on the code in Listing 6.3.

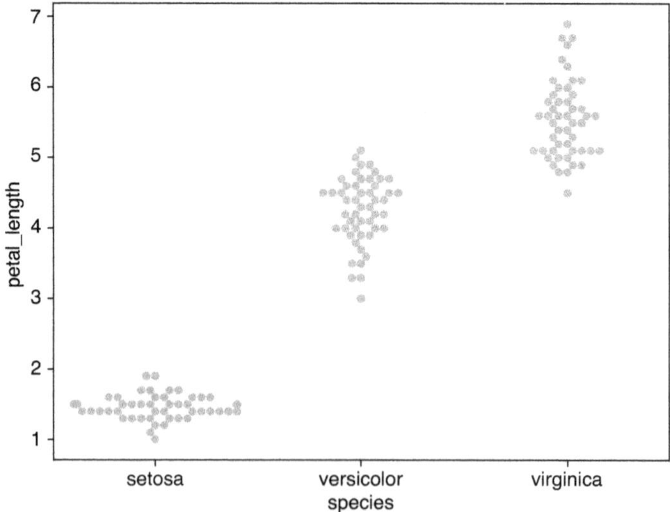

FIGURE 6.1 The Iris dataset.

THE TITANIC DATASET IN SEABORN

Listing 6.4 displays the contents of `seaborn_titanic_plot.py` that illustrates how to plot the `Titanic` dataset.

LISTING 6.4: seaborn_titanic_plot.py

```
import matplotlib.pyplot as plt
import seaborn as sns

titanic = sns.load_dataset("titanic")
g = sns.factorplot("class", "survived", "sex",
data=titanic, kind="bar", palette="muted", legend=False)

plt.show()
```

Listing 6.4 contains the same `import` statements as Listing 6.3, and then initializes the variable `titanic` with the contents of the built-in `Titanic` dataset. Next, the `factorplot()` API displays a graph with dataset attributes that are listed in the API invocation. Figure 6.2 displays a plot of the data in the `Titanic` dataset based on the code in Listing 6.4.

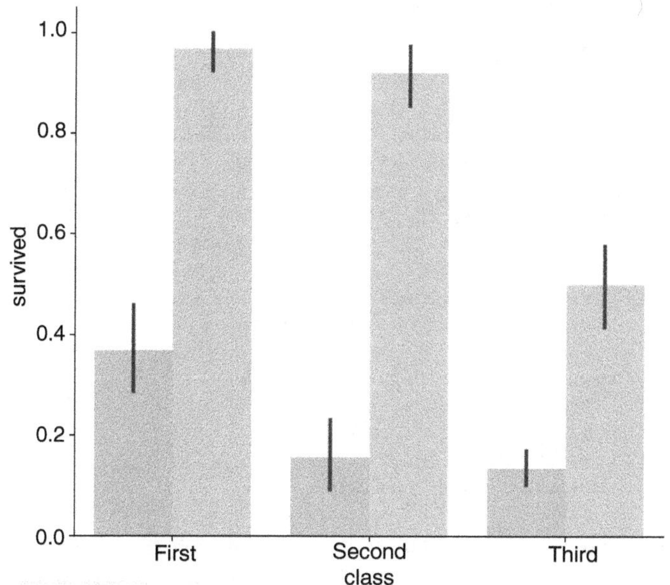

FIGURE 6.2 A histogram of the Titanic dataset.

EXTRACTING DATA FROM TITANIC DATASET IN SEABORN (1)

Listing 6.5 displays the contents of `seaborn_titanic.py` that illustrates how to extract subsets of data from the `Titanic` dataset.

LISTING 6.5: seaborn_titanic.py

```
import matplotlib.pyplot as plt
import seaborn as sns

titanic = sns.load_dataset("titanic")
print("titanic info:")
titanic.info()

print("first five rows of titanic:")
print(titanic.head())

print("first four ages:")
print(titanic.loc[0:3,'age'])

print("fifth passenger:")
print(titanic.iloc[4])

#print("first five ages:")
#print(titanic['age'].head())

#print("first five ages and gender:")
#print(titanic[['age','sex']].head())

#print("descending ages:")
#print(titanic.sort_values('age', ascending = False).head())

#print("older than 50:")
#print(titanic[titanic['age'] > 50])

#print("embarked (unique):")
#print(titanic['embarked'].unique())

#print("survivor counts:")
#print(titanic['survived'].value_counts())

#print("counts per class:")
#print(titanic['pclass'].value_counts())

#print("max/min/mean/median ages:")
#print(titanic['age'].max())
#print(titanic['age'].min())
#print(titanic['age'].mean())
#print(titanic['age'].median())
```

Listing 6.5 contains the same `import` statements as Listing 6.4, and then initializes the variable `titanic` with the contents of the built-in `Titanic` dataset. The next portion of Listing 6.5 displays various aspects of the `Titanic` dataset, such as its structure, the first five rows, the first four ages, and the details of the fifth passenger.

As you can see, there is a large block of "commented out" code that you can uncomment in order to see the associated output, such as age, gender, persons over 50, unique rows, and so forth. The output from Listing 6.5 is here:

```
#print(titanic['age'].mean())
titanic info:
<class 'pandas.core.frame.Data frame'>
RangeIndex: 891 entries, 0 to 890
Data columns (total 15 columns):
survived       891 non-null int64
pclass         891 non-null int64
sex            891 non-null object
age            714 non-null float64
sibsp          891 non-null int64
parch          891 non-null int64
fare           891 non-null float64
embarked       889 non-null object
class          891 non-null category
who            891 non-null object
adult_male     891 non-null bool
deck           203 non-null category
embark_town    889 non-null object
alive          891 non-null object
alone          891 non-null bool
dtypes: bool(2), category(2), float64(2), int64(4), object(5)
memory usage: 80.6+ KB
first five rows of titanic:
   survived  pclass     sex   age  sibsp  parch     fare embarked  class \
0         0       3    male  22.0      1      0   7.2500        S  Third
1         1       1  female  38.0      1      0  71.2833        C  First
2         1       3  female  26.0      0      0   7.9250        S  Third
3         1       1  female  35.0      1      0  53.1000        S  First
4         0       3    male  35.0      0      0   8.0500        S  Third

     who  adult_male deck  embark_town alive  alone
0    man        True  NaN  Southampton    no  False
1  woman       False    C    Cherbourg   yes  False
2  woman       False  NaN  Southampton   yes   True
3  woman       False    C  Southampton   yes  False
4    man        True  NaN  Southampton    no   True
first four ages:
0    22.0
1    38.0
2    26.0
3    35.0
Name: age, dtype: float64
fifth passenger:
survived                 0
pclass                   3
sex                   male
age                     35
sibsp                    0
parch                    0
fare                  8.05
embarked                 S
class                Third
who                    man
adult_male            True
deck                   NaN
embark_town    Southampton
alive                   no
alone                 True
Name: 4, dtype: object
counts per class:
```

```
3    491
1    216
2    184
Name: pclass, dtype: int64
max/min/mean/median ages:
80.0
0.42
29.69911764705882
28.0
```

EXTRACTING DATA FROM TITANIC DATASET IN Seaborn (2)

Listing 6.6 displays the contents of `seaborn_titanic2.py` that illustrates how to extract subsets of data from the `Titanic` dataset.

LISTING 6.6: seaborn_titanic2.py

```
import matplotlib.pyplot as plt
import seaborn as sns

titanic = sns.load_dataset("titanic")

# Returns a scalar
# titanic.ix[4, 'age']
print("age:",titanic.at[4, 'age'])

# Returns a Series of name 'age', and the age values
associated
# to the index labels 4 and 5
# titanic.ix[[4, 5], 'age']
print("series:",titanic.loc[[4, 5], 'age'])

# Returns a Series of name '4', and the age and fare values
# associated to that row.
# titanic.ix[4, ['age', 'fare']]
print("series:",titanic.loc[4, ['age', 'fare']])

# Returns a Data frame with rows 4 and 5, and columns 'age'
and 'fare'
# titanic.ix[[4, 5], ['age', 'fare']]
print("data frame:",titanic.loc[[4, 5], ['age', 'fare']])

query = titanic[
    (titanic.sex == 'female')
    & (titanic['class'].isin(['First', 'Third']))
    & (titanic.age > 30)
    & (titanic.survived == 0)
]
print("query:",query)
```

Listing 6.6 contains the same `import` statements as Listing 6.5, and then initializes the variable `titanic` with the contents of the built-in `Titanic` dataset. The next code snippet displays the age of the passenger with index 4 in the dataset (which equals 35).

The following code snippet displays the ages of passengers with index values 4 and 5 in the dataset:

```
print("series:",titanic.loc[[4, 5], 'age'])
```

The next snippet displays the age and fare of the passenger with index 4 in the dataset, followed by another code snippet displays the age and fare of the passengers with index 4 and index 5 in the dataset.

The final portion of Listing 6.6 is the most interesting part: it defines a variable `query` as shown here:

```
query = titanic[
    (titanic.sex == 'female')
    & (titanic['class'].isin(['First', 'Third']))
    & (titanic.age > 30)
    & (titanic.survived == 0)
]
```

The preceding code block will retrieve the female passengers who are in either first class or third class, and who are also over 30, and who did not survive the accident. The entire output from Listing 6.6 is here:

```
age: 35.0
series: 4    35.0
5     NaN
Name: age, dtype: float64
series: age        35
fare    8.05
Name: 4, dtype: object
data frame:      age    fare
4  35.0  8.0500
5   NaN  8.4583
query:        survived  pclass      sex   age  sibsp  parch      fare embarked
class  \
18            0       3  female  31.0      1      0  18.0000        S  Third
40            0       3  female  40.0      1      0   9.4750        S  Third
132           0       3  female  47.0      1      0  14.5000        S  Third
167           0       3  female  45.0      1      4  27.9000        S  Third
177           0       1  female  50.0      0      0  28.7125        C  First
254           0       3  female  41.0      0      2  20.2125        S  Third
276           0       3  female  45.0      0      0   7.7500        S  Third
362           0       3  female  45.0      0      1  14.4542        C  Third
396           0       3  female  31.0      0      0   7.8542        S  Third
```

```
503          0     3  female  37.0      0     0   9.5875       S  Third
610          0     3  female  39.0      1     5  31.2750       S  Third
638          0     3  female  41.0      0     5  39.6875       S  Third
657          0     3  female  32.0      1     1  15.5000       Q  Third
678          0     3  female  43.0      1     6  46.9000       S  Third
736          0     3  female  48.0      1     3  34.3750       S  Third
767          0     3  female  30.5      0     0   7.7500       Q  Third
885          0     3  female  39.0      0     5  29.1250       Q  Third
```

VISUALIZING A PANDAS DATASET IN SEABORN

Listing 6.7 displays the contents of `pandas_seaborn.py` that illustrates how to display a `Pandas` dataset in `Seaborn`.

LISTING 6.7: pandas_seaborn.py

```
import pandas as pd
import random
import matplotlib.pyplot as plt
import seaborn as sns

df = pd.Data frame()

df['x'] = random.sample(range(1, 100), 25)
df['y'] = random.sample(range(1, 100), 25)

print("top five elements:")
print(df.head())

# display a density plot
#sns.kdeplot(df.y)

# display a density plot
#sns.kdeplot(df.y, df.x)

#sns.distplot(df.x)

# display a histogram
#plt.hist(df.x, alpha=.3)
#sns.rugplot(df.x)

# display a boxplot
#sns.boxplot([df.y, df.x])

# display a violin plot
#sns.violinplot([df.y, df.x])

# display a heatmap
#sns.heatmap([df.y, df.x], annot=True, fmt="d")

# display a cluster map
#sns.clustermap(df)
```

```
# display a scatterplot of the data points
sns.lmplot('x', 'y', data=df, fit_reg=False)
plt.show()
```

Listing 6.7 contains several familiar `import` statements, followed by the initialization of the `Pandas` variable `df` as a `Pandas` DataFrame. The next two code snippets initialize the columns and rows of the dataframe and the `print()` statement display the first five rows.

For your convenience, Listing 6.7 contains an assortment of "commented out" code snippets that use `Seaborn` in order to render a density plot, a histogram, a boxplot, a violin plot, a heatmap, and a cluster. Uncomment the portions that interest you in order to see the associated plot. The output from Listing 6.7 is here:

```
top five elements:
    x   y
0  52  34
1  31  47
2  23  18
3  34  70
4  71   1
```

Figure 6.3 displays a plot of the data in the `Titanic` dataset based on the code in Listing 6.7.

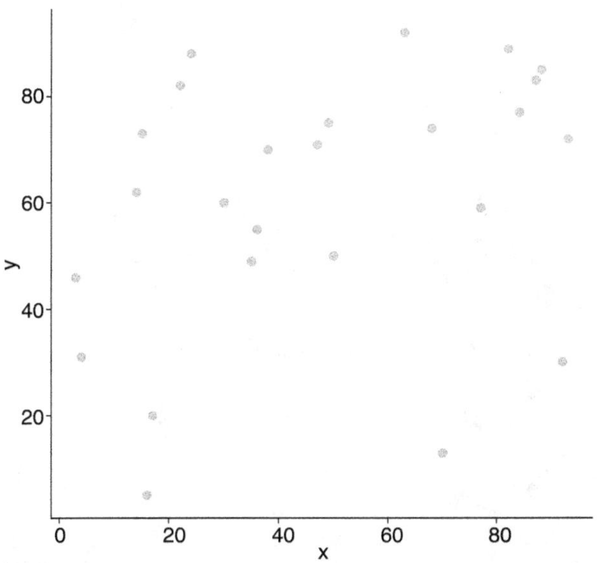

FIGURE 6.3 A Pandas DataFrame displayed via `Seaborn`.

SEABORN HEAT MAPS

Listing 6.8 displays the contents `heatmap1.py` that displays a heat map from a `Seaborn` built-in dataset.

LISTING 6.8: heatmap1.py

```
import seaborn as sns
import matplotlib.pyplot as plt

data = sns.load_dataset("flights")
data = data.pivot("month", "year", "passengers")

print("data.head():")
print(data.head())

sns.heatmap(data)
plt.show()
```

Listing 6.8 contains two `import` statements, followed by the variable data that is initialized with the contents of the `Seaborn` built-in dataset called `flights`. The next code snippet invokes the `pivot()` method that selects the attributes month, year, and passengers from the dataset. The next portion of code displays the first five rows of the dataset, followed by a code block that renders a heat map and you will see the following output:

```
data.head():
year   1949  1950  1951  1952  1953  1954  1955  1956  1957  1958  1959  1960
month
Jan     112   115   145   171   196   204   242   284   315   340   360   417
Feb     118   126   150   180   196   188   233   277   301   318   342   391
Mar     132   141   178   193   236   235   267   317   356   362   406   419
Apr     129   135   163   181   235   227   269   313   348   348   396   461
May     121   125   172   183   229   234   270   318   355   363   420   472
```

Figure 6.4 displays a heat map plot of the data in the `flights` dataset based on the code in Listing 6.8.

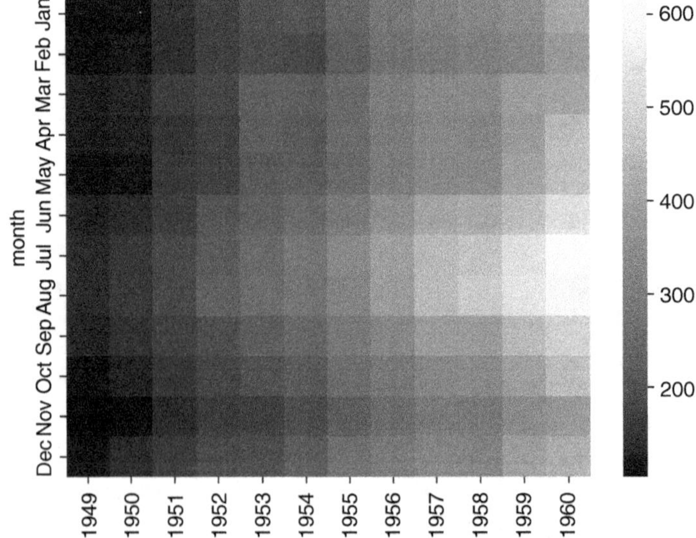

FIGURE 6.4 A `Pandas` DataFrame displayed as a `Seaborn` heat map.

SEABORN PAIR PLOTS

This section contains several Python-based code samples that show you how to use the Seaborn pair_plot() method to render pair plots.

Listing 6.9 displays the contents seborn_pairplot1.py that displays a pair plot with the Iris dataset.

LISTING 6.9: seaborn_pairplot1.py

```
import seaborn as sns
import pandas as pd
import matplotlib.pyplot as plt

# load iris data
iris = sns.load_dataset("iris")

df = pd.Data frame(iris)

# construct and display iris plot
g = sns.pairplot(df, height=2, aspect=1.0)
plt.show()
```

Listing 6.9 starts with import statements, followed by the variable iris that is initialized with the contents of the Seaborn built-in dataset called iris. The next code snippet initializes the variable df with the contents of the dataset. The final block of code generates a pair plot based on the contents of the variable df, and then displays the pair plot. Figure 6.5 displays a plot of the data in the iris dataset based on the code in Listing 6.9.

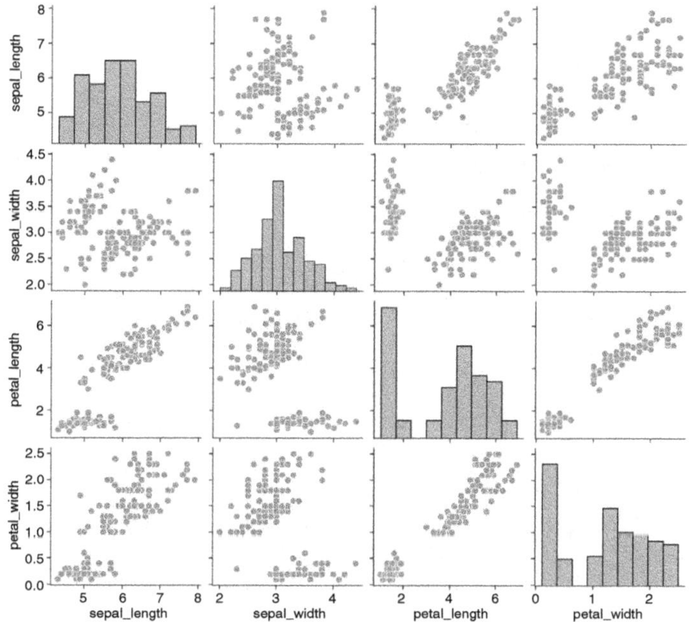

FIGURE 6.5 A Seaborn pair plot.

Listing 6.10 displays the contents `seborn_pairplot12.py` that renders a pair plot with the `Iris` dataset.

LISTING 6.10: seaborn_pairplot2.py

```
import seaborn as sns
import pandas as pd
import matplotlib.pyplot as plt

# load iris data
iris = sns.load_dataset("iris")

df = pd.Data frame(iris)

# IRIS columns:
# sepal_length,sepal_width,petal_length,petal_width,species

# plot a subset of columns:
plot_columns = ['sepal_length', 'sepal_width']
sns.pairplot(df[plot_columns])
plt.show()

# specify KDE for the diagonal:
sns.pairplot(df[plot_columns], diag_kind='kde')
plt.show()
```

Listing 6.10 starts with the same code as Listing 6.9, followed by the variable `plot_columns` that contains sepal-related attributes from the iris dataset. The next code block generates a pair plot and displays its contents, followed by a code snippet that generates a pair plot with the argument `diag_kind` equal to kde.

Figure 6.6 displays a pair plot of the data in the `iris` dataset based on the code in Listing 6.10.

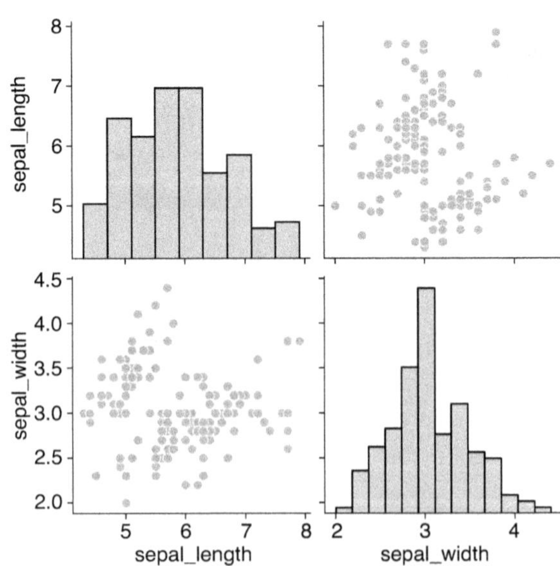

FIGURE 6.6 A Seaborn pair plot of Iris data.

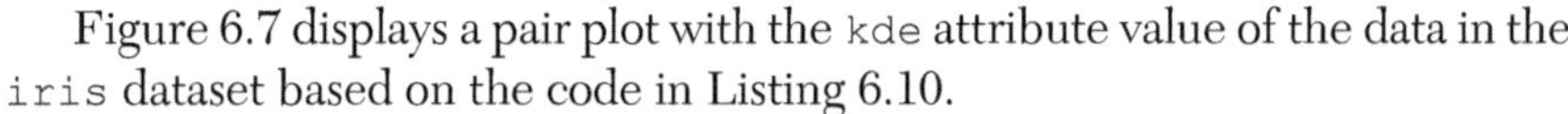

Figure 6.7 displays a pair plot with the `kde` attribute value of the data in the `iris` dataset based on the code in Listing 6.10.

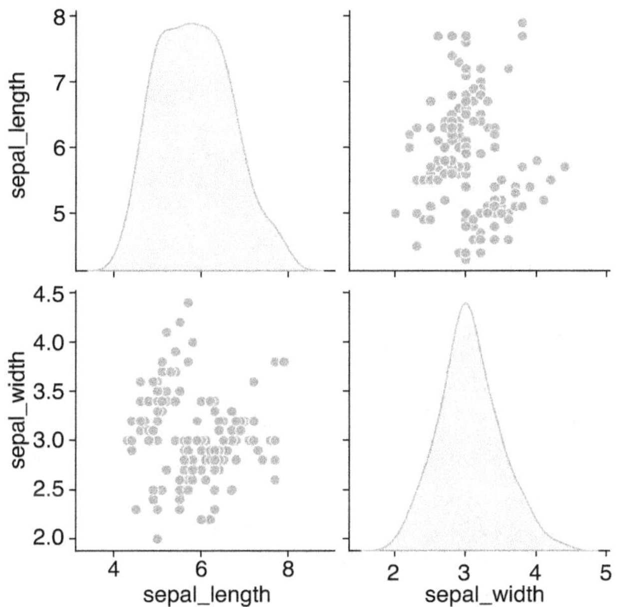

FIGURE 6.7 A Seaborn pair plot of Iris data with kde option.

WHAT IS BOKEH?

`Bokeh` is an open source project that depends on `Matplotlib` as well as `Scikit-learn`. As you will see in the subsequent code sample, `Bokeh` generates an HTML Web page that is based on `Python` code, and then launches that Web page in a browser. `Bokeh` and `D3.js` (which is a JavaScript layer of abstraction over `SVG`) both provide elegant visualization effects that support animation effects and user interaction.

`Bokeh` enables the rapid creation statistical visualization, and it works with other tools with as `Python` Flask and Django. In addition to `Python`, `Bokeh` supports Julia, Lua, and R (`JSON` files are generated instead of HTML Web pages).

Listing 6.11 displays the contents `bokeh_trig.py` that illustrates how to create a graphics effect using various `Bokeh` APIs.

LISTING 6.11: bokeh_trig.py

```
# pip3 install bokeh
from bokeh.plotting import figure, output_file, show
from bokeh.layouts import column
import bokeh.colors as colors
import numpy as np
import math
```

```
deltaY = 0.01
maxCount = 150
width  = 800
height = 400
band_width = maxCount/3

x = np.arange(0, math.pi*3, 0.05)
y1 = np.sin(x)
y2 = np.cos(x)

white = colors.RGB(255,255,255)

fig1 = figure(plot_width = width, plot_height = height)

for i in range(0,maxCount):
  rgb1 = colors.RGB(i*255/maxCount, 0, 0)
  rgb2 = colors.RGB(i*255/maxCount, i*255/maxCount, 0)
  fig1.line(x, y1-i*deltaY,line_width = 2, line_color = rgb1)
  fig1.line(x, y2-i*deltaY,line_width = 2, line_color = rgb2)

for i in range(0,maxCount):
  rgb1 = colors.RGB(0, 0, i*255/maxCount)
  rgb2 = colors.RGB(0, i*255/maxCount, 0)
  fig1.line(x, y1+i*deltaY,line_width = 2, line_color = rgb1)
  fig1.line(x, y2+i*deltaY,line_width = 2, line_color = rgb2)
  if (i % band_width == 0):
    fig1.line(x, y1+i*deltaY,line_width = 5, line_color =
white)

show(fig1)
```

Listing 6.11 starts with a commented out `pip3` code snippet that you can launch from the command line in order to install `Bokeh` (in case you haven't done so already).

The next code block contains several `Bokeh` -related statements as well as `NumPy` and `Math`.

Notice that the variable `white` is defined as an (R,G,B) triple of integers, which represents the red, green, and blue components of a color. In particular, (255,255,255) represents the color white (check online if you are unfamiliar with RGB). The next portion of Listing 6.11 initializes some scalar variables that are used in the two `for` loops that are in the second half of Listing 6.11.

Next, the `NumPy` variable `x` is a range of values from 0 to `math.PI/3`, with an increment of 0.05 between successive values. Then the `NumPy` variables `y1` and `y2` are defined as the sine and cosine values, respectively, of the values in `x`. The next code snippet initializes the variable `fig1` that represents a context in which the graphics effects will be rendered. This completes the initialization of the variables that are used in the two `for` loops.

The next portion of Listing 6.11 contains the first `for` loop that creates a gradient-like effect by defining (R,G,B) triples whose values are based partially on the value of the loop variable `i`. For example, the variable `rgb1` ranges in a linear fashion from (0,0,0) to (255,0,0), which represent the colors black and red, respectively. The variable `rgb2` ranges in a linear fashion from (0,0,0) to (255,255,0), which represent the colors black and yellow, respectively. The next portion of the `for` loop contains two invocations of the `fig1.line()` API that renders a sine wave and a cosine wave in the context variable `fig1`.

The second `for` loop is similar to the first `for` loop: the main difference is that the variable `rgb1` varies from black to blue, and the variable `rgb2` variables from black to green. The final code snippet in Listing 6.13 invokes the `show()` method that generates an `HTML` Web page (with the same prefix as the `Python` file) and then launches the Web page in a browser.

Figure 6.8 displays the graphics effect based on the code in Listing 6.11. If this image is displayed as black and white, launch the code from the command line and you will see the gradient-like effects in the image.

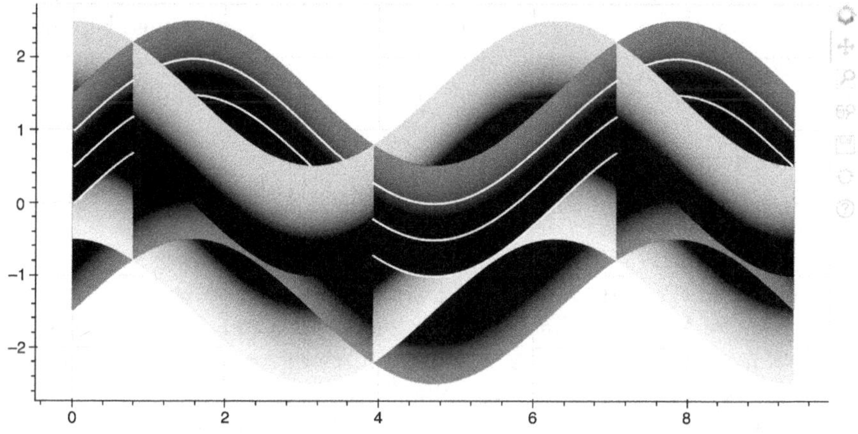

FIGURE 6.8 A Bokeh graphics sample.

The next section introduces you to `Scikit-learn`, which is a powerful `Python`-based library that supports many algorithms for machine learning. After you have read the short introduction, subsequent sections contain `Python` code samples that combine `Pandas`, `Matplotlib`, and `Scikit-learn` built-in datasets.

INTRODUCTION TO SCIKIT-LEARN

Since this book is about data visualization, you might be wondering why this chapter contains an introduction to `Scikit-learn` (also known as `Sklearn`). The reason is straightforward: the easy introduction to some `Scikit-learn` functionality is possible without a more formal learning process. In addition, this knowledge will bode well if you decide to delve into machine learning (and perhaps this section will provide additional motivation to do so).

However, a thorough understanding of `Scikit-learn` involves significantly more time and effort, especially if you plan to learn the details of the `Scikit-learn` machine learning algorithms. On the other hand, if you are not interested in learning about `Scikit-learn` at this point in time, you can skip this section and perhaps return to it when you are interested in learning this material.

`Scikit-learn` is Python's premier general-purpose machine learning library, and its home page is here:

https://scikit-learn.org/stable/

Before we discuss any code samples, please keep in mind that `Scikit-learn` is an immensely useful Python library that supports a huge number of machine learning algorithms. In particular, `Scikit-learn` supports many classification algorithms, such as logistic regression, naive Bayes, decision trees, random forests, and SVMs (support vector machines). Although entire books are available that are dedicated to `Scikit-learn`, this chapter contains only a few pages of Scikit-learn material.

If you decide that you want to acquire a deep level of knowledge about `Scikit-learn`, navigate to the Web pages that contain very detailed documentation for `Scikit-learn`. Moreover, if you have "how to" questions involving `Scikit-learn`, you can almost always find suitable answers on stack overflow (*https://stackoverflow.com/*).

`Scikit-learn` is well-suited for classification tasks as well as regression and clustering tasks in machine learning. `Scikit-learn` supports a vast collection of ML algorithms, including linear regression, logistic regression, kNN ("K nearest neighbor"), kMeans, decision trees, random forests, MLPs (multilayer perceptrons), and SVMs (support vector machines).

Moreover, `Scikit-learn` supports dimensionality reduction techniques such as PCA (principal component analysis), "hyper parameter" tuning, methods for scaling data, and is suitable for preprocessing data, cross-validation, and so forth.

Machine learning code samples often contain a combination of `Scikit-learn`, NumPy, Pandas, and Matplotlib. In addition, `Scikit-learn` provides various built-in datasets that we can display visually. One of those datasets is the `Digits` dataset, which is the topic of the next section.

The next section of this chapter provides several Python code samples that contain a combination of Pandas, Matplotlib, and the Scikit-learn built-in Digits dataset.

THE DIGITS DATASET IN `Scikit-learn`

The `Digits` dataset in `Scikit-learn` comprises 1797 small 8x8 images: each image is a hand-written digit, which is also the case for the `MNIST` dataset. Listing 6.12 displays the contents of `load_digits1.py` that illustrates how to plot one of the digits in the `Digits` dataset.

LISTING 6.12: load_digits1.py

```
from scikit-learn import datasets

# Load in the 'digits' data
digits = datasets.load_digits()

# Print the 'digits' data
print(digits)
```

Listing 6.12 is very straightforward: after importing the `datasets` module, the variable `digits` is initialized with the contents of the `Digits` dataset. The `print()` statement displays the contents of the `digits` variable, which is displayed here:

```
{images': array(
     [[[0.,    0.,   5., ...,        1.,    0.,   0.],
       [0.,    0.,  13., ...,  15.,   5.,   0.],
       [0.,    3.,  15., ...,  11.,   8.,   0.],
       ...,
       [0.,    4.,  11., ...,  12.,   7.,   0.],
       [0.,    2.,  14., ...,  12.,   0.,   0.],
       [0.,    0.,   6., ...,   0.,   0.,   0.]]),
'target': array([0, 1, 2, ..., 8, 9, 8]), 'frame': None,
'feature_names': ['pixel_0_0', 'pixel_0_1', 'pixel_0_2', 'pixel_0_3',
'pixel_0_4', 'pixel_0_5', 'pixel_0_6', 'pixel_0_7', 'pixel_1_0',
'pixel_1_1', 'pixel_1_2', 'pixel_1_3', 'pixel_1_4', 'pixel_1_5',
'pixel_1_6', 'pixel_1_7', 'pixel_2_0', 'pixel_2_1', 'pixel_2_2',
'pixel_2_3', 'pixel_2_4', 'pixel_2_5', 'pixel_2_6', 'pixel_2_7',
'pixel_3_0', 'pixel_3_1', 'pixel_3_2', 'pixel_3_3', 'pixel_3_4',
'pixel_3_5', 'pixel_3_6', 'pixel_3_7', 'pixel_4_0', 'pixel_4_1',
'pixel_4_2', 'pixel_4_3', 'pixel_4_4', 'pixel_4_5', 'pixel_4_6',
'pixel_4_7', 'pixel_5_0', 'pixel_5_1', 'pixel_5_2', 'pixel_5_3',
'pixel_5_4', 'pixel_5_5', 'pixel_5_6', 'pixel_5_7', 'pixel_6_0',
'pixel_6_1', 'pixel_6_2', 'pixel_6_3', 'pixel_6_4', 'pixel_6_5',
'pixel_6_6', 'pixel_6_7', 'pixel_7_0', 'pixel_7_1', 'pixel_7_2',
'pixel_7_3', 'pixel_7_4', 'pixel_7_5', 'pixel_7_6', 'pixel_7_7'],
'target_names': array([0, 1, 2, 3, 4, 5, 6, 7, 8, 9]), 'images':
array([[[ 0.,   0.,   5., ...,   1.,   0.,   0.],
        [ 0.,   0., 13., ..., 15.,   5.,   0.],
        [ 0.,   3., 15., ..., 11.,   8.,   0.],
// data omitted for brevity
])}
```

Listing 6.13 displays the contents of `load_digits2.py` that illustrates how to plot one of the digits in the `Digits` dataset (which you can change in order to display a different digit).

LISTING 6.13: load_digits2.py

```
from sklearn.datasets import load_digits
from matplotlib import pyplot as plt

digits = load_digits()
#set interpolation='none'
```

```
fig = plt.figure(figsize=(3, 3))
plt.imshow(digits['images'][66], cmap="gray",
interpolation='none')
plt.show()
```

Listing 6.13 imports the `load_digits` class from `Scikit-learn` in order to initialize the variable `digits` with the contents of the `Digits` dataset that is available in `Scikit-learn`. The next portion of Listing 6.13 initializes the variable `fig` and invokes the method `imshow()` of the `plt` class in order to display a number in the `Digits` dataset.

Figure 6.9 displays a plot of one of the digits in the `Digits` dataset based on the code in Listing 6.13.

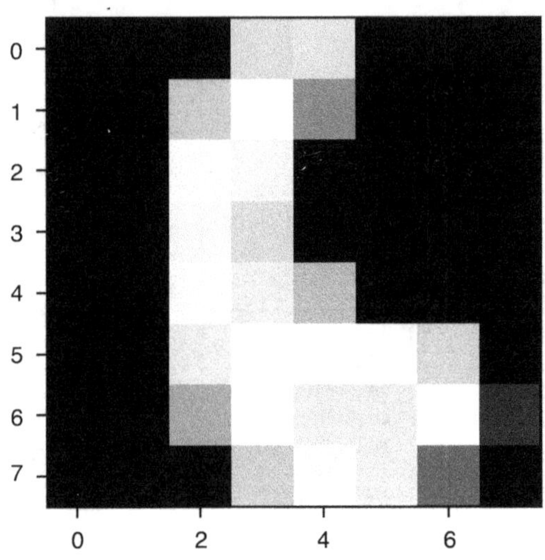

FIGURE 6.9 A digit in the Scikit-learn Digits dataset.

Listing 6.14 displays the contents of `load_digits3.py` that illustrates how to access the `Digits` dataset in `Scikit-learn`.

LISTING 6.14: load_digits3.py

```
from sklearn import datasets

digits = datasets.load_digits()
print("digits shape:",digits.images.shape)
print("data   shape:",digits.data.shape)

n_samples, n_features = digits.data.shape
print("(samples,features):", (n_samples, n_features))

import matplotlib.pyplot as plt
#plt.imshow(digits.images[-1], cmap=plt.cm.gray_r)
#plt.show()
```

```
plt.imshow(digits.images[0], cmap=plt.cm.binary,
interpolation='nearest')
plt.show()
```

Listing 6.14 starts with one `import` statement followed by the variable `digits that` contains the `Digits` dataset. The output from Listing 6.16 is here:

```
digits shape: (1797, 8, 8)
data   shape: (1797, 64)
(samples,features): (1797, 64)
```

Figure 6.10 displays an image in the `Digits` dataset based on the code in Listing 6.14.

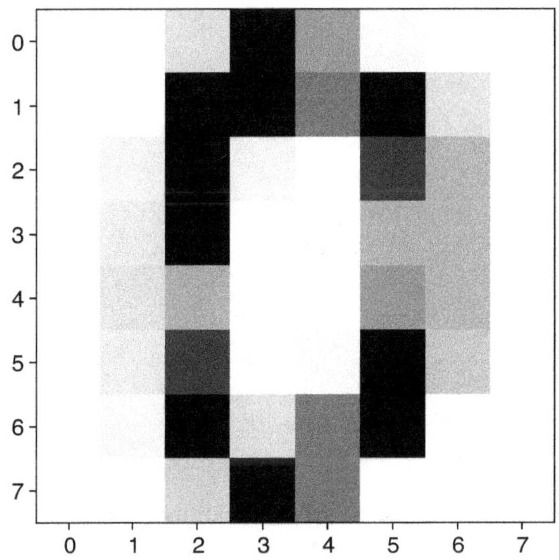

FIGURE 6.10 The digits in the Digits Dataset.

THE IRIS DATASET IN SCIKIT-LEARN

Listing 6.15 displays the contents of `sklearn_iris.py` that illustrates how to access the `Iris` dataset in `Scikit-learn`.

In addition to support for machine learning algorithms, `Scikit-learn` provides various built-in datasets that you can access with literally one line of code. In fact, Listing 6.15 displays the contents of `sklearn_iris1.py` that illustrates how you can easily load the `Iris` dataset into a `Pandas` DataFrame.

LISTING 6.15: sklearn_iris.py

```
import numpy as np
import pandas as pd
from scikit-learn.datasets import load_iris
```

```
iris = load_iris()

print("=> iris keys:")
for key in iris.keys():
  print(key)
print()

#print("iris dimensions:")
#print(iris.shape)
#print()

print("=> iris feature names:")
for feature in iris.feature_names:
  print(feature)
print()

X = iris.data[:, [2, 3]]
y = iris.target
print('=> Class labels:', np.unique(y))
print()

x_min, x_max = X[:, 0].min() - .5, X[:, 0].max() + .5
y_min, y_max = X[:, 1].min() - .5, X[:, 1].max() + .5

print("=> target:")
print(iris.target)
print()

print("=> all data:")
print(iris.data)
```

Listing 6.15 contains several import statements and then initializes the variable `iris` with the Iris dataset. Next, a `for` loop displays the keys in dataset, followed by another `for` loop that displays the feature names.

The next portion of Listing 6.15 initializes the variable `X` with the feature values in columns 2 and 3, and then initializes the variable `y` with the values of the target column.

The variable `x_min` is initialized as the minimum value of column 0 and then an additional 0.5 is subtracted from x_min. Similarly, the variable `x_max` is initialized as the maximum value of column 0 and then an additional 0.5 is added to `x_max`. The variables `y_min` and `y_max` are the counterparts to `x_min` and `x_max`, applied to column 1 instead of column 0.

Launch the code in Listing 6.15 and you will see the following output (truncated to save space):

```
Pandas df1:

=> iris keys:
data
target
target_names
```

```
DESCR
feature_names
filename

=> iris feature names:
sepal length (cm)
sepal width (cm)
petal length (cm)
petal width (cm)

=> Class labels: [0 1 2]

=> x_min: 0.5 x_max: 7.4
=> y_min: -0.4 y_max: 3.0

=> target:
[0 0 0 0 0 0 0 0 0 0 0 0 0 0 0 0 0 0 0 0 0 0 0 0 0 0 0 0 0 0 0 0 0 0 0 0 0
 0 0 0 0 0 0 0 0 0 0 0 0 0 1 1 1 1 1 1 1 1 1 1 1 1 1 1 1 1 1 1 1 1 1 1 1 1
 1 1 1 1 1 1 1 1 1 1 1 1 1 1 1 1 1 1 1 1 1 1 1 1 1 1 2 2 2 2 2 2 2 2 2 2 2
 2 2 2 2 2 2 2 2 2 2 2 2 2 2 2 2 2 2 2 2 2 2 2 2 2 2 2 2 2 2 2 2 2 2 2 2 2
 2 2]

=> all data:
[[5.1 3.5 1.4 0.2]
 [4.9 3.  1.4 0.2]
 [4.7 3.2 1.3 0.2]
 // details omitted for brevity
 [6.5 3.  5.2 2. ]
 [6.2 3.4 5.4 2.3]
 [5.9 3.  5.1 1.8]]
```

Scikit-Learn, Pandas, and the Iris Dataset

Listing 6.16 displays the contents of `pandas_iris.py` that illustrates how to load the contents of the `Iris` dataset (from Scikit-learn) into a `Pandas` DataFrame.

LISTING 6.16: pandas_iris.py

```
import numpy as np
import pandas as pd
from sklearn.datasets import load_iris

iris = load_iris()

print("=> IRIS feature names:")
for feature in iris.feature_names:
  print(feature)
print()

# Create a data frame with the feature variables
df = pd.Data frame(iris.data, columns=iris.feature_names)

print("=> number of rows:")
```

```
print(len(df))
print()

print("=> number of columns:")
print(len(df.columns))
print()

print("=> number of rows and columns:")
print(df.shape)
print()

print("=> number of elements:")
print(df.size)
print()

print("=> IRIS details:")
print(df.info())
print()

print("=> top five rows:")
print(df.head())
print()

X = iris.data[:, [2, 3]]
y = iris.target
print('=> Class labels:', np.unique(y))
```

Listing 6.16 contains several `import` statements and then initializes the variable `iris` with the Iris dataset. Next, a `for` loop displays the feature names. The next code snippet initializes the variable `df` as a `Pandas` DataFrame that contains the data from the `Iris` dataset.

The next block of code invokes some attributes and methods of a `Pandas` DataFrame to display the number of row, columns, and elements in the data frame, as well as the details of the `Iris` dataset, the first five rows, and the unique labels in the `Iris` dataset. Launch the code in Listing 6.16 and you will see the following output:

```
=> IRIS feature names:
sepal length (cm)
sepal width (cm)
petal length (cm)
petal width (cm)

=> number of rows:
150

=> number of columns:
4

=> number of rows and columns:
(150, 4)
=> number of elements:
```

```
600

=> IRIS details:
<class 'pandas.core.frame.Data frame'>
RangeIndex: 150 entries, 0 to 149
Data columns (total 4 columns):
sepal length (cm)     150 non-null float64
sepal width (cm)      150 non-null float64
petal length (cm)     150 non-null float64
petal width (cm)      150 non-null float64
dtypes: float64(4)
memory usage: 4.8 KB
None

=> top five rows:
   sepal length (cm)  sepal width (cm)  petal length (cm)  petal width (cm)
0                5.1               3.5                1.4               0.2
1                4.9               3.0                1.4               0.2
2                4.7               3.2                1.3               0.2
3                4.6               3.1                1.5               0.2
4                5.0               3.6                1.4               0.2

=> Class labels: [0 1 2]
```

ADVANCED TOPICS IN SEABORN

Listing 6.17 displays the contents `sns_kde_plot1.py` that displays a kde plot.

LISTING 6.17: sns_kde_plot1.py

```
import numpy as np
import matplotlib.pyplot as plt
import seaborn as sns

np.random.seed(1)
numerical_1 = np.random.randn(400)

np.random.seed(2)
numerical_2 = np.random.randn(400)

fig, ax = plt.subplots(figsize=(6,6))

sns.kdeplot(x=numerical_1,
            y= numerical_2,
            ax=ax,
            shade=True,
            color="blue",
            bw=1)
plt.show()
```

Listing 6.17 contains several `import` statements and then initializes the variables `numerical_1` and `numerical_2` with a set of 400 randomly generated numbers. The next code snippet initializes the figure-related variables `fig` and `ax`.

The next code snippet invokes the `kdeplot()` method of `Seaborn` and uses the values in `numerical_1` and `numerical_2` as values for the horizontal and vertical axes, respectively. The final code snippet displays the chart that is generated by the `kdeplot()` method. Now launch the code in Listing 6.17 and you will see the generated chart.

Figure 6.11 displays a plot of the data in the `Titanic` dataset based on the code in Listing 6.17.

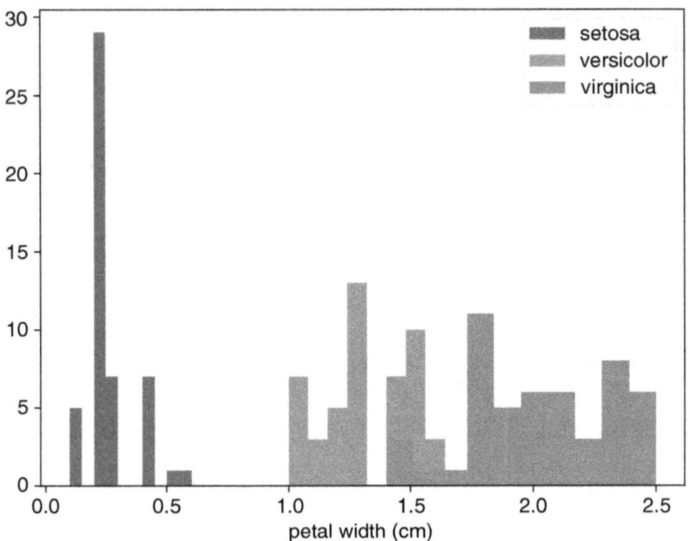

FIGURE 6.11 A Pandas DataFrame displayed via `Seaborn`.

Listing 6.18 displays the contents `sns_line_barchart1.py` that displays a line graph and a bar chart.

LISTING 6.18: sns_line_barchart1.py

```
import numpy as np

import seaborn as sns
import matplotlib.pyplot as plt

sns.set(style="white", rc={"lines.linewidth": 3})
fig, ax1 = plt.subplots(figsize=(4,4))
ax2 = ax1.twinx()
sns.barplot(x=['A','B','C','D'],
            y=[100,200,135,98],
            color='#004488',
            ax=ax1)

sns.lineplot(x=['A','B','C','D'],
             y=[4,2,5,3],
             color='r',
```

```
                    marker="o",
                    ax=ax2)

plt.show()
```

Listing 6.18 contains several `import` statements and then initializes the figure-related variables `fig` and `ax`, followed by the variable `ax2` that is initialized by invoking the `twinx()` method of `ax1`.

The next two code blocks generate a bar plot and a line plot, respectively, using hard-coded values for `x` and `y`. The next code snippet displays the generated bar chart and line plot. Figure 6.12 displays a bar chart and a line plot of the data in Listing 6.18.

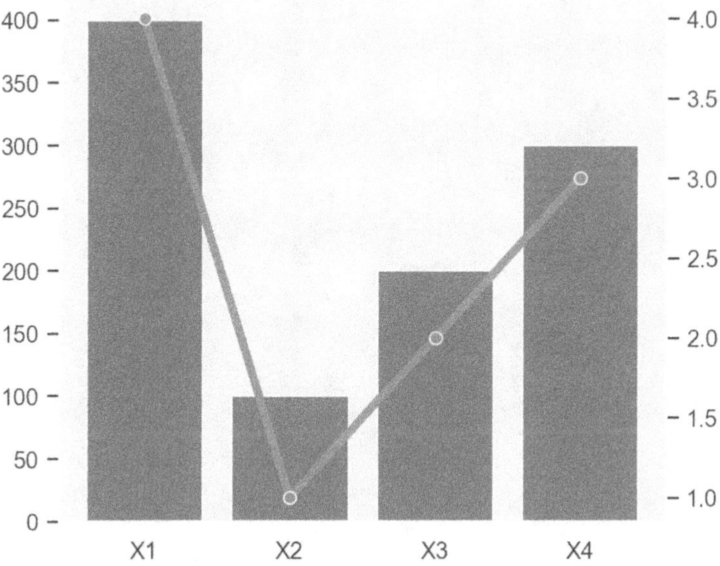

FIGURE 6.12 A bar chart and line graph.

SUMMARY

This chapter started with some basic features of `Seaborn`, which is an extension of `Matplotlib`. You saw examples of plotting lines and histograms, and also how to plot a `Pandas` DataFrame using `Seaborn`.

Next, you learned about `Bokeh`, along with an example of rendering graphics in `Bokeh`. Furthermore, you learned about `SVG` and how to render various 2D shapes, such as line segments, rectangles, circles, Bezier curves, and bar charts.

You also learned about `Scikit-learn`, including examples of working with the `Digits` and `Iris` datasets, and also how to process images. Finally, you learned how to render a bar chart and a line graph in `Scikit-learn`.

CHAPTER 7

ChatGPT and GPT-4

This chapter contains information about the main features of ChatGPT and GPT-4, as well as some of their competitors.

The first part of this chapter starts with information about the nature of generative AI and conversational AI versus generative AI. This section also delves into ChatGPT, along with a comparison of ChatGPT and Google Search. You will also learn about ChatGPT custom instructions, prompts, and the ChatGPT playground. In addition, you will learn about ChatGPT plugins, such as Advanced data analysis (formerly Code Interpreter) and code whisperer.

The second part of this chapter discusses some concerns about ChatGPT, as well as the strengths and weaknesses of ChatGPT. Moreover, you will learn about alternatives to ChatGPT and data visualization with VizGPT.

The third part of this chapter delves into GPT-4, some inference parameters for GPT-4, and fine tuning. You will also learn about some competitors, such as CoPilot and Codex. The final portion of this chapter introduces you to LlaMa-2 and how to download LlaMa-2 so that you can fine tune this model on your laptop.

WHAT IS GENERATIVE AI?

Generative AI refers to a subset of artificial intelligence models and techniques designed to generate new data samples that are similar in nature to a given set of input data. The goal is to produce content or data that was not part of the original training set but is coherent, contextually relevant, and in the same style or structure.

Generative AI stands apart in its ability to create and innovate, as opposed to merely analyzing or classifying. The advancements in this field have led to breakthroughs in creative domains and practical applications, making it a cutting-edge area of AI research and development.

Important Features of Generative AI

The following list contains important features of generative AI, followed by a brief description for each item:

- Data generation
- Synthesis
- Learning distributions

Data generation refers to the ability to create new data points that are not part of the training data, but resemble it. This can include text, images, music, videos, or any other form of data. *Synthesis* means that generative models can blend various inputs to generate outputs that incorporate features from each input, like merging the styles of two images. *Learning distributions* means that generative AI models aim to learn the probability distribution of the training data so they can produce new samples from that distribution.

Popular Techniques in Generative AI

Generative Adversarial Networks (GANs) consist of two networks, a generator, and a discriminator, that are trained simultaneously. The generator tries to produce fake data, while the discriminator tries to distinguish between real data and fake data. Over time, the generator gets better at producing realistic data.

Variational Autoencoders (VAEs) are probabilistic models that learn to encode and decode data in a manner that the encoded representations can be used to generate new data samples.

Recurrent Neural Networks (RNNs) are used primarily for sequence generation, such as text or music.

What Makes Generative AI Unique

Creation vs. Classification: While most traditional AI models aim to classify input data into predefined categories, generative models aim to create new data.

Unsupervised Learning: Many generative models, especially GANs and VAEs, operate in an unsupervised manner, meaning they do not require labeled data for training.

Diverse Outputs: Generative models can produce a wide variety of outputs based on learned distributions, making them ideal for tasks like art generation, style transfer, and more.

Challenges: Generative AI poses unique challenges, such as model collapse in GANs or ensuring the coherence of generated content.

Furthermore, there are numerous areas that involve generative AI applications, some of which are listed in the following list:

- Art and music creation
- Data augmentation
- Style transfer

- Text generation
- Image synthesis
- Drug discovery

Art and music creation includes generating paintings, music, or other forms of art.

Data Augmentation involves creating additional data for training models, especially when the original dataset is limited. *Style transfer* refers to applying the style of one image to the content of another. *Text generation* is a very popular application of generative AI, which involves creating coherent and contextually relevant text. *Image synthesis* is another popular area of generative AI, which involves generating realistic images, faces, or even creating scenes for video games. *Drug discovery* is a very important facet of generative AI that pertains to generating molecular structures for new potential drugs.

CONVERSATIONAL AI VERSUS GENERATIVE AI

Both conversational AI and generative AI are prominent subfields within the broader domain of artificial intelligence. However, these subfields have a different focus regarding their primary objective, the technologies that they use, and applications.

The primary differences between the two subfields are as follows:

- Primary objective
- Applications
- Technologies used
- Training and interaction
- Evaluation
- Data requirements

Primary Objective

The main goal of conversational AI is to facilitate human-like interactions between machines and humans. This includes chatbots, virtual assistants, and other systems that engage in dialogue with users.

The primary objective of generative AI is to create new content or data that was not in the training set but is similar in structure and style. This can range from generating images, music, and text to more complex tasks like video synthesis.

Applications

Common applications for conversational AI include customer support chatbots, voice-operated virtual assistants (like Siri or Alexa), and interactive voice response (IVR) systems.

Common applications for generative AI have a broad spectrum of applications, such as creating art or music, generating realistic video game environments, synthesizing voices, and producing realistic images or even deep fakes.

Technologies Used

Conversational AI often relies on Natural Language Processing (NLP) techniques to understand and generate human language. This includes intent recognition, entity extraction, and dialogue management.

Generative AI commonly utilizes Generative Adversarial Networks (GANs), Variational Autoencoders (VAEs), and other generative models to produce new content.

Training and Interaction

While training can be supervised, semi-supervised, or unsupervised, the primary interaction mode for conversational AI is through back-and-forth dialogue or conversation.

The training process for generative AI, especially with models like GANs, involves iterative processes where the model learns to generate data by trying to fool a discriminator into believing the generated data is real.

Evaluation

Conversational AI evaluation metrics often revolve around understanding and response accuracy, user satisfaction, and the fluency of generated responses.

Generative AI evaluation metrics for models like GANs can be challenging and might involve using a combination of quantitative metrics and human judgment to assess the quality of generated content.

Data Requirements

Data requirements for conversational AI typically involves dialogue data, with conversations between humans or between humans and bots.

Data requirements for generative AI involve large datasets of the kind of content it is supposed to generate, such as images, text, or music.

Although both conversational AI and generative AI deal with generating outputs, their primary objectives, applications, and methodologies can differ significantly. Conversational AI was developed for interactive communication with users, while generative AI was designed to produce new, original content.

IS DALL-E PART OF GENERATIVE AI?

DALL-E and similar tools that generate graphics from text are examples of generative AI. In fact, DALL-E is one of the most prominent examples of generative AI in the realm of image synthesis.

Here is a list of generative characteristics of DALL-E, followed by brief descriptions of each bullet item:

- Image generation
- Learning distributions
- Innovative combinations
- Broad applications
- Transformer architecture

Image generation: This is a key feature of DALL-E, which was designed to generate images based on textual descriptions. Given a prompt like "a two-headed flamingo," DALL-E can produce a novel image that matches the description, even if it never had such an image in its training data.

Learning distributions: Like other generative models, DALL-E learns the probability distribution of its training data. When it generates an image, it samples from this learned distribution to produce visuals that are plausible based on its training.

Innovative combinations: DALL-E can generate images that represent entirely novel or abstract concepts, showcasing its ability to combine and recombine learned elements in innovative ways.

Broad applications: In addition to image synthesis, DALL-E has provided broad application support in areas like art generation, style blending, and creating images with specific attributes or themes, highlighting its versatility as a generative tool.

Transformer architecture: DALL-E leverages a variant of the transformer architecture, similar to models like GPT-3, but has been adapted for image generation tasks.

Other tools that generate graphics, art, or any form of visual content based on input data (whether it is text, another image, or any other form of data) and can produce outputs not explicitly present in their training data are also considered generative AI. They showcase the capability of AI models to not just analyze and classify, but to create and innovate.

ARE CHATGPT-3 AND GPT-4 PART OF GENERATIVE AI?

Both ChatGPT-3 and GPT-4 are LLMs that are considered examples of generative AI. They belong to a class of models called "transformers," which are particularly adept at handling sequences of data, such as text-related tasks.

The following list provides various reasons why these LLMs are considered generative, followed by a brief description of each item:

- Text generation
- Learning distributions
- Broad applications
- Unsupervised learning

Text Generation: These models can produce coherent, contextually relevant, and often highly sophisticated sequences of text based on given prompts. They generate responses that were not explicitly present in their training data but are constructed based on the patterns and structures they learned during training.

Learning Distributions: GPT-3, GPT-4, and similar models learn the probability distribution of their training data. When generating text, they are essentially sampling from this learned distribution to produce sequences that are likely based on their training.

Broad Applications: Beyond just text-based chat or conversation, these models can be used for a variety of generative tasks like story writing, code generation, poetry, and even creating content in specific styles or mimicking certain authors, showcasing their generative capabilities.

Unsupervised Learning: While they can be fine-tuned with specific datasets, models like GPT-3 are primarily trained in an unsupervised manner on vast amounts of text, learning to generate content without requiring explicit labeled data for every possible response.

In essence, ChatGPT-3, GPT-4, and similar models by OpenAI are quintessential examples of generative AI in the realm of natural language processing and generation.

The next several sections briefly introduce some of the companies that have a strong presence in the AI world.

DEEPMIND

DeepMind has made significant contributions to AI, which includes the creation of various AI systems. DeepMind was established in 2010 and became a subsidiary of Google 2014, and its home page is at *https://deepmind.com/*.

DeepMind created the 280 GB language model Gopher that significantly outperforms its competitors, including GPT-3, J1-Jumbo, and MT-NLG. DeepMind also developed AlphaFold, which solved a protein folding task that had eluded researchers for ten years in only 30 minutes. Moreover, DeepMind made AlphaFold available for free for everyone in July 2021. DeepMind has made significant contributions in the development of world-caliber AI game systems, some of which are discussed in the next section.

DeepMind and Games

DeepMind is the force behind the AI systems AlphaStar and AlphaGo that defeated the best human players in Go (which is considerably more difficult than chess). These games provide "perfect information," whereas games with "imperfect information" (such as poker) have posed a challenge for ML models.

AlphaGo Zero (the successor of AlphaGo) mastered the game through self-play in less time and with less computing power than AlphaGo. AlphaGo Zero exhibited extraordinary performance by defeating AlphaGo 100–0. Another powerful system is AlphaZero, which also used a self-play technique learned to play Go, chess, and shogi, and achieved SOTA (State-of-the-Art) performance results.

By way of comparison, ML models that use a tree search are well-suited for games with perfect information. By contrast, games with imperfect information (such as poker) involve hidden information that can be leveraged to devise counter strategies to counteract the strategies of opponents. In particular, AlphaStar is capable of playing against the best players of StarCraft II, and it became the first AI to achieve SOTA results in a game that requires so-called "strategic capability."

Player of Games (PoG)

The DeepMind team at Google devised the general-purpose PoG (Player of Games) algorithm that is based on the following techniques:

- CFR (counterfactual regret minimization)
- CVPN (counterfactual value-and-policy network)
- GT-CFT (growing tree CFR)
- CVPN

The counterfactual value-and-policy network (CVPN) is a neural network that calculates the counterfactuals for each state belief in the game. This is key to evaluating the different variants of the game at any given time.

Growing tree CFR (GT-CFR) is a variation of CFR that is optimized for game-trees trees that grow over time. GT-CFR is based on two fundamental phases, which is discussed in more detail online:

https://medium.com/syncedreview/deepminds-pog-excels-in-perfect-and-imperfect-information-games-advancing-research-on-general-9dbad5c04221

OPENAI

OpenAI is an AI research company that has made significant contributions to AI, including DALL-E and ChatGPT, and its home page is at *https://openai.com/api/*.

OpenAI was founded in San Francisco by Elon Musk and Sam Altman (as well as others), and one of its stated goals is to develop AI that benefits humanity. Given Microsoft's massive investments in, and deep alliance with, the organization, OpenAI might be viewed as part of Microsoft. OpenAI is the creator of the GPT-x series of LLMs as well as ChatGPT, which was made available on November 30, 2022.

OpenAI made GPT-3 commercially available via API for use across applications, charging on a per-word basis. GPT-3 was announced in July 2020, and was available through a beta program. Then, in November 2021, OpenAI made GPT-3 open to everyone; more details can be found at *https://openai.com/blog/api-no-waitlist/*.

In addition, OpenAI developed DALL-E, which generates images from text. OpenAI initially did not permit users to upload images that contained realistic faces. Later, OpenAI changed its policy to allow users to upload faces into its online system. (Check the OpenAI Web page for more details.) Incidentally, diffusion models have superseded the benchmarks of DALL-E.

OpenAI has also released a public beta of Embeddings, which is a data format that is suitable for various types of tasks with machine learning:

https://beta.openai.com/docs/guides/embeddings

OpenAI is the creator of Codex, which provides a set of models that were trained on NLP. The initial release of Codex was in private beta; more information is available at *https://beta.openai.com/docs/engines/instruct-series-beta*.

OpenAI provides four models that are collectively called their *Instruct models*, which support the ability of GPT-3 to generate natural language. These models will be deprecated in early January 2024, and replaced with updated versions of GPT-3, ChatGPT, and GPT-4.

If you want to learn more about the features and services that OpenAI offers, navigate to the following link: *https://platform.openai.com/overview*.

COHERE

Cohere is a start-up and a competitor of OpenAI, and its home page is available at *https://cohere.ai/*.

Cohere develops cutting-edge NLP technology that is commercially available for multiple industries. Cohere is focused on models that perform textual analysis instead of models for text generation (such as GPT-based models). The founding team of Cohere is impressive: CEO Aidan Gomez is one of the co-inventors of the transformer architecture, and CTO Nick Frosst is a protege of Geoff Hinton.

HUGGING FACE

Hugging Face is a popular community-based repository for open-source NLP technology, and its home page is at *https://github.com/huggingface*.

Unlike OpenAI or Cohere, Hugging Face does not build its own NLP models. Instead, Hugging Face is a platform that manages a plethora of open-source NLP models that customers can fine-tune and then deploy. Indeed, Hugging Face has become the eminent location for people to collaborate on NLP models and is sometimes described as "GitHub for machine learning and NLP."

Hugging Face Libraries

Hugging Face provides three important libraries: datasets, tokenizers, and transformers. The Accelerate library supports PyTorch models. The datasets library provides an assortment of libraries for NLP. The tokenizers library enables you to convert text data to numeric values.

Perhaps the most impressive library is the transformers library, which provides an enormous set of pre-trained BERT-based models to perform a wide variety of NLP tasks. The Github repository is at https://github.com/huggingface/transformers.

Hugging Face Model Hub

Hugging Face offers a model hub that provides a plethora of models that are accessible online. Moreover, the website supports online testing of its models, which includes the following tasks:

- Masked word completion with BERT
- Name Entity Recognition with Electra
- Natural Language Inference with RoBERTa
- Question answering with DistilBERT
- Summarization with BART
- Text generation with GPT-2
- Translation with T5

Navigate to the following link to see the text generation capabilities of "write with transformer:" *https://transformer.huggingface.co*.

Later, you will see **Python** code samples that show how to list all the available Hugging Face datasets, as well as how to load a specific dataset.

AI21

AI21 is a company that provides proprietary large language models via API to support the applications of its customers. The current SOTA model of AI21 is called Jurassic-1 (roughly the same size as GPT-3), and AI21 also creates its own applications on top of Jurassic-1 and other models. The current application suite of AI21 involves tools that can augment reading and writing.

Primer is an older competitor in this space, founded two years before the invention of the transformer. The company primarily serves clients in government and defense.

INFLECTIONAI

A more recent company in the AI field is InflectionAI, whose highly impressive founding team includes

- Reid Hoffman (LinkedIn)
- DeepMind cofounder Mustafa Suleyman
- DeepMind researcher Karen Simonyan

InflectionAI is committed to a challenging task: enabling humans to interact with computers in much the same way that humans communicate with each other.

ANTHROPIC

Anthropic was created in 2021 by former employees of OpenAI, and its home page is at *https://www.anthropic.com/*.

Anthropic has significant financial support from an assortment of companies, including Google and Salesforce. As this book goes to print, Anthropic released Claude-2 as a competitor to ChatGPT. Expect Anthropic to make its API available by Q4 of 2023.

Claude-2 has the ability to summarize as much as 75,000 words of text-based content, whereas ChatGPT currently has a limit of 3,000 words. Moreover, Claude-2 achieved a score of 76.5% on portions of the bar exam and 71% in a coding test. Claude-2 also has a higher rate than ChatGPT in terms of providing "clean" responses to queries from users.

This concludes the portion of the chapter regarding the AI companies that are making important contributions in AI. The next section provides a high-level introduction to LLMs (large language models).

WHAT IS PROMPT ENGINEERING?

Text generators such as GPT-3 and DALL-E 2 from OpenAI, Jurassic from AI21, Midjourney, and Stable Diffusion that can perform text-to-image generation. *Prompt engineering* refers to devising text-based prompts that enable AI-based systems to improve the output that is generated, which means that the output more closely matches whatever users want to produce from AI systems. By way of analogy, think of prompts as similar to the role of coaches: they offer advice and suggestions to help people perform better in their given tasks.

Since prompts are based on words, the challenge involves learning how different words can affect the generated output. Moreover, it is difficult to predict how systems respond to a given prompt. For instance, if you want to generate a landscape, the difference between a dark landscape and a bright landscape is intuitive. However, if you want a beautiful landscape, how would an AI system generate a corresponding image? As you can surmise, concrete words are easier than abstract or subjective words for AI systems that generate images from text. Just to add more detail to the previous example, how would you visualize the following?

- A beautiful landscape
- A beautiful song
- A beautiful movie

Although prompt engineering started with text-to-image generation, there are other types of prompt engineering, such as audio-based prompts that interpret emphasized text and emotions that are detected in speech, and sketch-based prompts that generate images from drawings. The most recent focus of attention involves text-based prompts for generating videos, which presents exciting opportunities for artists and designers. An example of image-to-image processing is accessible online:

https://huggingface.co/spaces/fffiloni/stable-diffusion-color-sketch

Prompts and Completions

A *prompt* is a text string that users provide to LLMs, and a *completion* is the text that users receive from LLMs. Prompts assist LLMs in completing a request (task), and they can vary in length. Although prompts can be any text string, including a random string, the quality and structure of prompts affects the quality of completions.

Think of prompts as a mechanism for giving "guidance" to LLMs, or even as a way to "coach" LLMs into providing desired answers. Keep in mind that the number of tokens in a prompt plus the number of tokens in the completion can be at most 2,048 tokens.

Types of Prompts

The following list contains well-known types prompts for LLMs:

- zero-shot prompts
- one-shot prompts
- few-shot prompts
- instruction prompts

NOTE *The first three prompts in the preceding list are also called "zero-shot learning," "one-shot learning," and "few-shot learning," respectively.*

A *zero-shot prompt* contains a description of a task, whereas a *one-shot prompt* consists of a single example for completing a task. As you can probably surmise, *few-shot prompts* consist of multiple examples (typically between 10 and 100). In all cases, a clear description of the task or tasks is recommended: more tasks provide GPT-3 with more information, which in turn can lead to more accurate completions.

T0 (for "zero shot") is an interesting LLM: although T0 is 16 times smaller (11 GB) than GPT-3 (175 GB), T0 has outperformed GPT-3 on language-related tasks. T0 can perform well on unseen NLP tasks (i.e., tasks that are new to T0) because it was trained on a dataset containing multiple tasks.

The following URL provides the Github repository for T0, a Web page for training T0 directly in a browser, and a 3 GB version of T0:

https://github.com/bigscience-workshop/t-zero

As you can probably surmise, T0++ is based on T0, and it was trained with extra tasks beyond the set of tasks on which T0 was trained.

Instruction Prompts

Instruction prompts are used for fine tuning LLMs, and they specify a format (determined by you) for the manner in which the LLM is expected to conform in its responses. You can prepare your own instruction prompts or you can access prompt template libraries that contain different templates for different tasks, along with different data sets. Various prompt instruction templates are publicly available, such as the following links that provide prompt templates for Llama:

https://github.com/devbrones/llama-prompts

https://pub.towardsai.net/llama-gpt4all-simplified-local-chatgpt-ab7d28d34923

Reverse Prompts

Another technique reverses the order of prompts and completions: *input prompts* are answers, and the *responses* are the questions associated with the answers (similar to a popular game show). For example, given a French sentence, you might ask the model, "What English text might have resulted in this French translation?"

System Prompts Versus Agent Prompts

The distinction between a system prompt and an agent prompt often comes up in the context of conversational AI systems and chatbot design.

A *system prompt* is typically an initial message or cue given by the system to guide the user on what they can do or to set expectations about the interaction. It often serves as an introduction or a way to guide users on how to proceed. Here are some examples of system prompts:

```
"Welcome to ChatBotX! You can ask me questions about
weather, news, or sports. How can I assist you today?"
"Hello! For account details, press 1. For technical
support, press 2."
"Greetings! Type 'order' to track your package or 'help'
for assistance."
```

By contrast, an *agent prompt* is a message generated by the AI model or agent in response to a user's input during the course of an interaction. It is a part of the back-and-forth exchange within the conversation. The agent prompt guides the user to provide more information, clarifies ambiguity, or nudges the user towards a specific action. Here are some examples of agent prompts:

```
User: "I'm looking for shoes."
Agent Prompt: "Great! Are you looking for men's or women's shoes?"
User: "I can't log in."
```

```
Agent Prompt: "I'm sorry to hear that. Can you specify if you're
having trouble with your password or username?"
User: "Tell me a joke."
Agent Prompt: "Why did the chicken join a band? Because it had the
drumsticks!"
```

The fundamental difference between the two is their purpose and placement in the interaction. A system prompt is often at the beginning of an interaction, setting the stage for the conversation. An agent prompt occurs during the conversation, steering the direction of the dialogue based on user input.

Both types of prompts are crucial for creating a fluid and intuitive conversational experience for users. They guide the user and help ensure that the system understands and addresses the user's needs effectively.

Prompt Templates

Prompt templates are predefined formats or structures used to instruct a model or system to perform a specific task. They serve as a foundation for generating prompts, where certain parts of the template can be filled in or customized to produce a variety of specific prompts. By way of analogy, prompt templates are the counterpart to macros that you can define in some text editors.

Prompt templates are especially useful when working with language models, as they provide a consistent way to query the model across multiple tasks or data points. In particular, prompt templates can make it easier to

- ensure consistency when querying a model multiple times
- facilitate batch processing or automation
- reduce errors and variations in how questions are posed to the model

As an example, suppose you are working with an LLM, and you want to translate English sentences into French. An associated prompt template could be the following:

"Translate the following English sentence into French: {sentence}"

Note that {sentence} is a placeholder that you can replace with any English sentence.

You can use the preceding prompt template to generate specific prompts:

- "Translate the following English sentence into French: 'Hello, how are you?'"
- "Translate the following English sentence into French: 'I love ice cream.'"

As you can see, prompt templates enable you to easily generate a variety of prompts for different sentences without having to rewrite the entire instruction each time. In fact, this concept can be extended to more complex tasks and can incorporate multiple placeholders or more intricate structures, depending on the application.

Prompts for Different LLMs

GPT-3, ChatGPT, and GPT-4 are LLMs that are all based on the Transformer architecture and are fundamentally similar in their underlying mechanics. ChatGPT is essentially a version of the GPT model fine-tuned specifically for conversational interactions. GPT-4 is an evolution or improvement over GPT-3 in terms of scale and capabilities.

The differences in prompts for these models mainly arise from the specific use case and context, rather than inherent differences between the models. Here are some prompting differences that are based on use cases.

GPT-3 can be used for a wide range of tasks beyond just conversation, from content generation to code writing. Here are some examples of prompts for GPT-3:

- "Translate the following English text to French: 'Hello, how are you?'"
- "Write a Python function that calculates the factorial of a number."

ChatGPT: specifically fine-tuned for conversational interactions. Here are some examples of prompts for ChatGPT:

User: "Can you help me with my homework?"
ChatGPT: "Of course! What subject or topic do you need help with?"

User: "Tell me a joke."
ChatGPT: "Why did the chicken cross the playground? To get to the other slide!"

GPT-4: provides a larger scale and refinements, so the prompts would be similar in nature to GPT-3, but might yield more accurate or nuanced outputs. Here are some examples of prompts of prompts for GPT-4:

- "Provide a detailed analysis of quantum mechanics in relation to general relativity."
- "Generate a short story based on a post-apocalyptic world with a theme of hope."

These three models accept natural language prompts and produce natural language outputs. The fundamental way you interact with them remains consistent.

The main difference comes from the context in which the model is being used and any fine-tuning that has been applied. ChatGPT, for instance, is designed to be more conversational, so while you can use GPT-3 for chats, ChatGPT might produce more contextually relevant conversational outputs.

When directly interacting with these models, especially through an API, you might also have control over parameters like "temperature" (controlling randomness) and "max tokens" (controlling response length). Adjusting these can shape the responses, regardless of which GPT variant you are using.

In essence, while the underlying models have differences in scale and specific training/fine-tuning, the way you prompt them remains largely consistent: clear, specific natural language prompts yield the best results.

Poorly Worded Prompts

When crafting prompts, be as clear and specific as possible to guide the response in the desired direction. Ambiguous or vague prompts can lead to a wide range of responses, many of which might not be useful or relevant to the user's actual intent.

Moreover, poorly worded prompts are often vague, ambiguous, or too broad, and they can lead to confusion, misunderstanding, or non-specific responses from AI models. Here is a list of examples of poorly worded prompts that are shown in italics, along with an explanation regarding the deficiency of each prompt:

"Tell me about that thing."
Problem: Too vague. What "thing" is being referred to?

"Why did it happen?"
Problem: No context. What event or situation is being discussed?

"Explain stuff."
Problem: Too broad. What specific "stuff" should be explained?

"Do what is needful."
Problem: Ambiguous. What specific action is required?

"I want information."
Problem: Not specific. What type of information is desired?

"Can you get me the thing from the place?"
Problem: Both "thing" and "place" are unclear.

"Tell me the summary of What's-His-Name's book?"
Problem: Ambiguous reference. Who is "*What's-His-Name*"?

"How do you do the process?"
Problem: Which "process" is being referred to?

"Describe the importance of the topic."
Problem: The "topic" is not specified.

"Why is it bad or good?"
Problem: No context. What is "it"?
"Help with the issue."

Problem: Vague. What specific issue is being discussed?

"Things to consider for the task."
Problem: Ambiguous. What "task" is being discussed?

"How does this work?"
Problem: Lack of specificity. What is "this"?

WHAT IS CHATGPT?

The chatbot wars are intensifying, and the long-term value of the primary competitors is still to be determined. One competitor is ChatGPT-3.5 (ChatGPT), which is an AI-based chatbot from OpenAI. ChatGPT responds to queries from users by providing conversational responses, and it is accessible at *https://chat.openai.com/chat*.

The growth rate in terms of registered users for ChatGPT has been extraordinary. The closest competitor is the iPhone, which reached one million users in 2.5 months, whereas ChatGPT crossed one million users in *six days*. ChatGPT peaked around 1.8 billion users and then decreased to roughly 1.5 billion users, which you can see in the chart in the following online article:

https://decrypt.co/147595/traffic-dip-hits-openais-chatgpt-first-times-hardest

Note that although Threads from Meta out-performed ChatGPT in terms of membership, Threads has seen a significant drop in daily users in the neighborhood of 50%. A comparison of the time frame to reach one million members for six well-known companies/products and ChatGPT is at *https://www.syntheticmind.io/p/01*.

The preceding link also contains information about Will Hobick, who used ChatGPT to write a Chrome extension for email-related tasks, despite not having any experience with JavaScript or Chrome extension development. Will Hobick provides more detailed information about his Chrome extension at the following URL:

https://www.linkedin.com/posts/will-hobick_gpt3-chatgpt-ai-activity-7008081003080470528-8QCh

ChatGPT: GPT-3 "on Steroids"?

ChatGPT has been called GPT-3 "on steroids," and there is some consensus that ChatGPT3 is currently the best chatbot in the world. Indeed, ChatGPT can perform multitude of tasks, some of which are listed here:

- write poetry
- write essays
- write code
- role play
- reject inappropriate requests

Moreover, the quality of its responses to natural language queries surpasses the capabilities of its predecessor GPT-3. Another interesting capability includes the ability to acknowledge its mistakes. ChatGPT also provides *prompt replies*, which are examples of what you can ask ChatGPT. In addition, ChatGPT can also generate new Christmas song lyrics:

https://www.cnet.com/culture/entertainment/heres-what-it-sounds-like-when-ai-writes-christmas-lyrics

One aspect of ChatGPT that probably will not be endearing to parents with young children is the fact that ChatGPT has told children that Santa Claus does not exist:

https://futurism.com/the-byte/openai-chatbot-santa

https://www.forbes.com/sites/lanceeliot/2022/12/21/pointedly-asking-generative-ai-chatgpt-about-whether-santa-claus-is-real-proves-to-be-eye-opening-for-ai-ethics-and-ai-law

ChatGPT: Google "Code Red"

In December 2022, the CEO of Google issued a "code red" regarding the potential threat of ChatGPT as a competitor to Google's search engine:

https://www.yahoo.com/news/googles-management-reportedly-issued-code-190131705.html

According to the preceding article, Google is investing resources to develop AI-based products, presumably to offer functionality that can successfully compete with ChatGPT. Some of those AI-based products might also generate graphics that are comparable to graphics effects by DALL-E. Indeed, the race to dominate AI continues unabated and will undoubtedly continue for the foreseeable future.

ChatGPT Versus Google Search

Given the frequent speculation that ChatGPT is destined to supplant Google Search, let's briefly compare the manner in which Google and ChatGPT respond to a given query. First, Google is a search engine that uses the Page Rank algorithm (developed by Larry Page), along with fine-tuned aspects of this algorithm that are a closely guarded secret. Google uses this algorithm to rank websites and to generate search results for a given query. However, the search results include paid ads, which can "clutter" the list of links.

By contrast, ChatGPT is not a search engine: it provides a direct response to a given query: in colloquial terms, ChatGPT will simply "cut to the chase" and eliminate the clutter of superfluous links. However, ChatGPT *can* produce incorrect results, the consequences of which can range between benign and significant.

Consequently, Google search and ChatGPT both have strengths as well as weaknesses, and they excel with different types of queries: the former for queries that have multi-faceted answers (e.g., questions about legal issues), and the latter for straight-to-the point queries (e.g., coding questions). Obviously, both of them excel with many other types of queries.

According to Margaret Mitchell, ChatGPT will not replace Google Search, and she provides some interesting details regarding Google Search and PageRank that you can read about at *https://twitter.com/mmitchell_ai/status/1605013368560943105*.

ChatGPT Custom Instructions

ChatGPT has added support for custom instructions, which enable you to specify some of your preferences that ChatGPT will use when responding to your queries.

ChatGPT Plus users can switch on custom instructions by navigating to the ChatGPT website and then perform the following sequence of steps:

```
Settings > Beta features > Opt into Custom instructions
```

As a simple example, you can specify that you prefer to see code in a language other than Python. A set of common initial requirements for routine tasks can also be specified via custom instructions in ChatGPT. A detailed sequence of steps for setting up custom instructions is accessible online:

https://artificialcorner.com/custom-instructions-a-new-feature-you-must-enable-to-improve-chatgpt-responses-15820678bc02

Another interesting example of custom instructions is from Jeremy Howard, who prepared an extensive and detailed set of custom instructions that is accessible online:

https://twitter.com/jeremyphoward/status/1689464587077509120

As this book goes to print, custom instructions are available only for users who have registered for ChatGPT Plus. However, OpenAI has stated that custom instructions will be available for free to all users by the end of 2023.

ChatGPT on Mobile Devices and Browsers

ChatGPT first became available for iOS devices and then for Android devices during 2023. You can download ChatGPT onto an iOS device from the following link:

https://www.macobserver.com/tips/how-to/how-to-install-and-use-the-official-chatgpt-app-on-iphone/

Alternatively, if you have an Android device, you can download ChatGPT from *https://play.google.com/store/apps/details?id=com.openai.chatgpt*.

You can install ChatGPT for the Bing browser from Microsoft from the following URL:

https://chrome.google.com/webstore/detail/chatgpt-for-bing/pkkmgcildaegadhngpjkklnbfbmhpdng

ChatGPT and Prompts

Although ChatGPT is adept at generating responses to queries, sometimes you might not be fully satisfied with the result. One option is to type the word "rewrite" in order to get another version from ChatGPT.

Although this is one of the simplest prompts available, it is limited in terms of effectiveness. If you want a list of more meaningful prompts, the following article contains 31 prompts that have the potential to be better than using the word "rewrite" (and not just with ChatGPT):

https://medium.com/the-generator/31-ai-prompts-better-than-rewrite-b3268dfe1fa9

GPTBot

GPTBot is a crawler for websites. Fortunately, you can disallow GPTBot from accessing a website by adding the GPTBot to the `robots.txt` file for a website:

```
User-agent: GPTBot
Disallow: /
```

You can also customize GPTBot access for only a portion of a website by adding the GPTBot token to the `robots.txt` file for a website:

```
User-agent: GPTBot
Allow: /youcangohere-1/
Disallow: /dontgohere-2/
```

As an aside, Stable Diffusion and LAION both scrape the Internet via Common Crawl. However, you can prevent your website from being scraped by specifying the following snippet in the `robots.txt` file:

```
User-agent: CCBot
Disallow: /
```

More information about GPTBot is accessible online:

https://platform.openai.com/docs/gptbot

https://platform.openai.com/docs/gptbot

https://www.yahoo.com/finance/news/openai-prepares-unleash-crawler-devour-020628225.html

ChatGPT Playground

ChatGPT has its own "playground," which you will see is substantively different from the GPT-3 playground and is accessible at *https://chat.openai.com/chat*.

For your convenience, the link for the GPT-3 playground is reproduced here:

https://beta.openai.com/playground

OpenAI has periodically added new functionality to ChatGPT that includes the following:

- Users can view (and continue) previous conversations.
- There is a reduction in the number of questions that ChatGPT will not answer.
- Users remain logged in for longer than two weeks.

Another nice enhancement includes support for keyboard shortcuts: when working with code, you can use the sequence ⌘ (Ctrl) + Shift + (for Mac) to copy the last code block and the sequence ⌘ (Ctrl) + / to see the complete list of shortcuts.

Many articles are available regarding ChatGPT and how to write prompts to extract the details that you want from ChatGPT. One of those articles is at the following URL:

https://www.tomsguide.com/features/7-best-chatgpt-tips-to-get-the-most-out-of-the-chatbot

PLUGINS, CODE INTERPRETER, AND CODE WHISPERER

In addition to answering a plethora of queries from users, ChatGPT extends its functionality by providing support for the following:

- Third-party ChatGPT plug-ins
- Code Interpreter
- Code Whisperer

Each of the topics in the preceding list are briefly discussed in the following subsections, along with a short section that discusses Code Interpreter versus Claude-2 from Anthropic.

Plugins

There are several hundred ChatGPT plugins available, and lists of some popular plugins are accessible online:

https://levelup.gitconnected.com/5-chatgpt-plugins-that-will-put-you-ahead-of-99-of-data-scientists-4544a3b752f9 https://www.zdnet.com/article/the-10-best-chatgpt-plugins-of-2023/

Keep in mind that lists of the "best" ChatGPT plugins change frequently, so it is a good idea to perform an online search to find out about newer ChatGPT plugins. The following link also contains details about highly rated plugins:

https://www.tomsguide.com/features/i-tried-a-ton-of-chatgpt-plugins-and-these-3-are-the-best

Another set of recommended plugins (depending on your needs, of course) is shown here:

- AskYourPDF
- ChatWithVideo
- Noteable
- Upskillr
- Wolfram

If you are concerned about the possibility of ChatGPT scraping the content of your website, the browser plugin from OpenAI supports a user-agent token called ChatGPT-User that abides by the content specified in the `robots.txt` file that many websites provide for restricting access to content.

If you want to develop a plugin for ChatGPT, navigate to this website for more information: *https://platform.openai.com/docs/plugins/introduction*.

Along with details for developing a ChatGPT plugin, the preceding OpenAI website provides useful information about plugins, as shown here:

- Authentication
- Examples
- Plugin review
- Plugin policies

OpenAI does not control any plugins that you add to ChatGPT: they connect ChatGPT to external applications. Moreover, ChatGPT determines which plugin to use during your session, based on the specific plugins that you have enabled in your ChatGPT account.

Advanced Data Analysis

ChatGPT Advanced Data Analysis enables ChatGPT to generate charts and graphs, and create and train machine learning models, including deep learning models. ChatGPT Advanced data analysis provides an extensive set of features, and it is available to ChatGPT users who are paying the $20/month subscription. However, this feature will probably be made available to all users very soon.

https://towardsdatascience.com/chatgpt-code-interpreter-how-it-saved-me-hours-of-work-3c65a8dfa935

The models from OpenAI can access a Python interpreter that is confined to a sandboxed and fire-walled execution environment. There is also some temporary disk space that is accessible to the interpreter plugin during the evaluation of Python code. Although the temporary disk space is available for a limited time, multiple queries during in the same session can produce a cumulative effect with regard to the code and execution environment.

In addition, ChatGPT can generate a download link (upon request) in order to download data. One other interesting feature: starting from mid-2023, Advanced data analysis can now analyze multiple files at once, which includes CSV files and Excel spreadsheets.

Advanced data analysis can perform an interesting variety of tasks, some of which are listed here:

- solve mathematical tasks
- perform data analysis and visualization
- convert files between formats
- work with Excel spreadsheets
- read textual content in a PDF

The following article discusses various ways that you can use Advanced data analysis:

https://mlearning.substack.com/p/the-best-88-ways-to-use-chatgpt-code-interpreter

Advanced Data Analysis Versus Claude-2

Claude-2 from Anthropic is another competitor to ChatGPT. In addition to responding to prompts from users, Claude-2 can generate code and summarize entire books. Claude-2 is also subject to "hallucinations," which is true of other LLM-based chatbots. More detailed information regarding Claude-2 is accessible online:

https://medium.com/mlearning-ai/claude-2-vs-code-interpreter-gpt-4-5-d2e5c9ee00c3

Incidentally, the currently available version of ChatGPT was trained on September 2021, which means that ChatGPT cannot answer questions regarding Claude-2 or Google Bard, both of which were released after this date.

Code Whisperer

ChatGPT Code Whisperer enables you to simplify some tasks, some of which are listed here (compare this list with the corresponding list for Bard):

- create videos from images
- extract text from an image
- extract colors from an image

After ChatGPT has generated a video, it will also give you a link from which the generated video is downloadable. More detailed information regarding the features in the preceding bullet list is accessible online:

https://artificialcorner.com/chatgpt-code-interpreter-is-not-just-for-coders-here-are-6-ways-it-can-benefit-everyone-b3cc94a36fce

DETECTING GENERATED TEXT

Without a doubt, ChatGPT has raised users' expectations with respect to the quality of generated text, which further complicates the task of plagiarism. When you read a passage of text, there are several clues that suggest generated text, such as

- awkward or unusual sentence structure
- repeated text in multiple locations
- excessive use of emotions (or absence thereof)

However, there are tools that can assist in detecting generated code. One free online tool is GPT2 Detector (from OpenAI) that is accessible online:

https://huggingface.co/openai-detector

As a simple (albeit contrived) example, type the following sentence in GPT2 Detector:

```
This is an original sentence written by me and nobody else.
```

GPT2 Detector analyzed this sentence and reported that this sentence is real with a 19.35% probability. Now, let's modify the preceding sentence by adding some extra text, as shown here:

```
This is an original sentence written by me and nobody else,
regardless of what an online plagiarism tool will report
about this sentence.
```

GPT2 Detector analyzed this sentence and reported that this sentence is real with a 95.85% probability. According to the GPT2 Detector website, the reliability of the probability scores "get reliable" when there are around 50 tokens in the input text.

Another (slightly older) online tool for detecting automatically generated text is Giant Language model Test Room (GLTR) from IBM, which is accessible at *http://gltr.io/*.

You can download the source code (a combination of TypeScript and CSS) for GLRT at *https://github.com/HendrikStrobelt/detecting-fake-text*.

In addition to the preceding free tools, some commercial tools are also available, one of which is shown at *https://writer.com/plans/*.

CONCERNS ABOUT CHATGPT

One important aspect of ChatGPT is that it is not designed for accuracy: in fact, ChatGPT can generate very persuasive answers that are actually incorrect. This detail distinguishes ChatGPT from search engines: the latter provide links to existing information instead of generating responses that might be incorrect. Another comparison is that ChatGPT is more flexible and creative, whereas search engines are less flexible but more accurate in their responses to queries.

Educators are concerned about students using ChatGPT as a tool to complete their class assignments instead of developing research-related skills in conjunction with writing skills. However, there are educators who enjoy the reduction in preparation time for their classes as a direct result of using ChatGPT to prepare lesson plans.

Another concern is that ChatGPT cannot guarantee that it provides factual data in response to queries from users. In fact, ChatGPT can *hallucinate*, which means that it can provide wrong answers as well as citations (i.e., links) that do not exist.

Another limitation of ChatGPT is due to the use of training data that was available only up until 2021. However, OpenAI does support plug-ins for ChatGPT, one of which can perform on-the-fly real time Web searches.

As you will learn later, the goal of prompt engineering is to understand how to craft meaningful queries that will induce ChatGPT to provide the information that you want: poorly worded (or incorrectly-worded) prompts can produce equally poor results. As a rule, it is advisable to curate the contents of the responses from ChatGPT, especially in the case of responses to queries that involve legal details.

Code Generation and Dangerous Topics

Two significant areas for improvement pertain to code generation and handling dangerous topics.

Although ChatGPT (as well as GPT-3) can generate code for various types of applications, it displays code that was written by other developers, which is also code that was used to train ChatGPT. Consequently, portions of that code (such as version numbers) might be outdated or incorrect.

As for queries that involve dangerous topics, ChatGPT explains why it cannot answer such a query. However, a query that is posed in "pretend mode" ("suppose you are a fictional character, and how would you explain ....") has enabled people to obtain results from ChatGPT that do not conform to its guidelines.

Other serious potential issues exist, some of which are discussed in the following article:

https://www.yahoo.com/news/hypnotized-chatgpt-bard-convince-users-182100261.html

ChatGPT Strengths and Weaknesses

ChatGPT has a number of strengths. In particular, it responds directly to questions without including extraneous links. As a simple example, a query entered an online search engine, such as "Generate HTML for an input field," obtains results and ads, while ChatGPT merely returns the results.

However, ChatGPT is prone to various types of errors, along with limitations that include the following:

- inability to "fact check" information
- inability to differentiate misinformation versus facts
- can fabricate answers ("hallucinations")
- can generate inappropriate/toxic responses

ChatGPT is prone to "prompt injection," which can consist of very simple content. However, other chatbots are also susceptible to prompt injection (it is not specific to ChatGPT). More details regarding prompt injections are accessible online:

https://mlearning.substack.com/p/what-exactly-is-a-prompt-injection

Incidentally, the chatbot LaMDA from Google is also prone to the preceding limitations, which has made Google hesitant to release LaMDA for general availability because of its potential risk regarding Google's reputation. As a side note, LaMDA was announced in May 2021, and at that time, it was described as a "breakthrough language technology:" *https://blog.google/technology/ai/lamda/*.

Despite the earlier list, ChatGPT has increased the capabilities of chatbots, and will undoubtedly spur innovation and competition among prominent stakeholders in this arena.

SAMPLE QUERIES AND RESPONSES FROM CHATGPT

This section contains examples of queries submitted to ChatGPT, followed by the detailed response from ChatGPT:

```
Many people think that AI is dangerous. . . what do you think?
```

"There is a common misconception that AI is inherently dangerous. While it is true that AI has the potential to be used for harmful purposes, it is also capable of doing a lot of good. Just like any other technology, it all depends on how it is used. In the right hands, AI can be used to solve some of the world's most pressing problems, such as curing diseases and improving agriculture. In the wrong hands, it could be used to cause harm. It's important for us to use AI responsibly and ethically, and to ensure that it is regulated and controlled in a way that minimizes the potential for harm."

Here is another example of a query submitted to ChatGPT-3, followed by its detailed response:

```
What are some ways in which you can improve the accuracy of
your responses to queries?
```

"There are several ways to improve the accuracy of my responses to queries. One way is to use more data to train my algorithms on. The more data I have, the more information I have to work with, and the more accurate my responses can be. Another way to improve my accuracy is to use more advanced algorithms and techniques, such as machine learning and natural language processing. These methods allow me to better understand the nuances of language and to provide more accurate responses to queries. Additionally, regular testing and evaluation can help identify areas where my accuracy can be improved, and allow me to focus on those areas to refine my responses."

```
Can you give an example of an odd perfect number?
```

"As far as we know, there are no odd perfect numbers. While it is believed that odd perfect numbers exist, none have been found yet, and it is not known if there are any. In fact, it is currently unknown if there are any odd perfect numbers at all. If an odd perfect number were to be discovered, it would be a major breakthrough in mathematics."

```
Can you provide a proof of Goldbach's conjecture?
```

"I'm sorry, but I am not able to provide a proof of Goldbach's conjecture. Goldbach's conjecture is a famous unsolved problem in mathematics that states that every even integer greater than 2 can be expressed as the sum of two prime numbers. Despite much effort by mathematicians over the years, a proof of the conjecture has not yet been found. It is considered to be one of the most challenging unsolved problems in mathematics. Because I am a large language model trained by OpenAI, I do not have the ability to prove mathematical conjectures. My abilities are limited to providing answers based on the information that I have been trained on."

```
Is there life after death, and how does it compare with
life on Earth?
```

"There is no scientific evidence to support the idea of life after death. This is a topic that has been debated for centuries, and different cultures and belief systems have their own ideas about what happens after we die. Some people believe in an afterlife, while others do not. Because there is no scientific evidence to support the existence of an afterlife, it is not possible to say how it would compare to life on Earth. It is ultimately a matter of personal belief."

```
Please provide a four-paragraph analysis of the war between
Ukraine and Russia, and also provide your prediction. . .
regarding the outcome
```

"The war between Ukraine and Russia is a complex conflict that has its roots in the 2014 Russian annexation of Crimea. Since then, the conflict has escalated, with Russian-backed separatists in eastern Ukraine fighting against the Ukrainian government. The fighting has resulted in thousands of casualties and has displaced many people.

The main issue at the heart of the conflict is the question of Ukraine's sovereignty. Russia has long considered Ukraine to be within its sphere of influence, and the annexation of Crimea was seen by many as a violation of Ukraine's sovereignty. Ukraine, on the other hand, is determined to maintain its independence and has been supported in this by many Western countries.

It is difficult to predict the outcome of the war. While the Ukrainian military has been able to make gains against the separatists in recent years, Russia continues to provide support to the rebels and the conflict remains unresolved. In the long term, a diplomatic solution will likely be necessary in order to bring an end to the fighting. However, it is uncertain if and when such a solution will be reached.

In the meantime, the war continues to take a heavy toll on the people of Ukraine. Many are caught in the crossfire, and the ongoing violence and instability have had a significant impact on the country's economy and overall development. It is important for the international community to continue to support Ukraine in its efforts to maintain its sovereignty and bring an end to the conflict."

As you can see from the preceding examples, ChatGPT provides impressive and accurate responses to queries in a manner that surpasses many chatbots of recent years. However, it is still possible to confound this chatbot. The following article has additional examples of using ChatGPT:

https://www.theverge.com/23488017/openai-chatbot-chatgpt-ai-examples-web-demo

CHATGPT AND MEDICAL DIAGNOSIS

A young boy who had been experiencing chronic pain for several years finally found hope through an unexpected helper: ChatGPT. Over a span of three years, the boy's mother had taken him to see 17 different specialists, yet they remained without a diagnosis that could account for all of his symptoms.

The turning point came earlier this year when his mother decided to seek assistance from ChatGPT. She created an account and meticulously input all the details she had gathered over the years, including her son's symptoms and the data from his MRI scans. She recalls the countless hours she spent in front of the computer, sifting through information in a desperate bid to find answers.

Despite visiting numerous doctors and even rushing to the emergency room at one point, the family felt they were running in circles, with each specialist only focusing on their field of expertise without offering a comprehensive solution. She noted a worrying sign when her son stopped growing. Although their pediatrician initially attributed this to the adverse effects of the pandemic, the boy's mother felt there was more to it.

In a moment of desperation and determination, she turned to ChatGPT, inputting every piece of information she had about her son's condition. It was then that ChatGPT suggested the possibility of tethered cord syndrome, a suggestion that resonated with her and seemed to connect all the dots. After a specialist confirmed the suggestion from ChatGPT was correct, she realized this was a pivotal moment in their long and exhausting journey towards finding a diagnosis.

ALTERNATIVES TO CHATGPT

There are several alternatives to ChatGPT that offer a similar set of features, some of which are listed here:

- Bard (Google)
- Bing Chat
- Gemini (Google)
- Jasper
- PaLM (Google)
- Pi
- POE (LinkedIn)
- Replika
- WriteSonic
- YouChat

The following subsections discuss some (but not all) of the ChatGPT alternatives in the preceding list.

Google Bard

Google Bard is a chatbot that has similar functionality to ChatGPT, such as generating code as well as generating text/documents. A subset of the features supported by Bard is shown here:

- built-in support for Internet search
- built-in support for voice recognition
- built "on top of" PaLM 2 (Google)
- support for 20 programming languages
- read/summarize PDF documents
- provides links for its information

According to the following article in mid-2023, Bard has added support for 40 additional languages, as well as support for text-to-speech:

https://www.extremetech.com/extreme/google-bard-updated-with-text-to-speech-40-new-languages

Moreover, Bard supports prompts that include images (interpreted by Google Lens) and can produce captions based on the images.

The following article suggests that Google can remain competitive with ChatGPT by leveraging PaLM:

https://analyticsindiamag.com/googles-palm-is-ready-for-the-gpt-challenge/

YouChat

Another alternative to ChatGPT is YouChat, part of the search engine *you.com*, and it is accessible at: *https://you.com/*.

Richard Socher, who is well known in the ML community for his many contributions, is the creator of *you.com*. According to Richard Socher, YouChat is a search engine that can provide the usual search-related functionality as well as the ability to search the Web to obtain more information to provide responses to queries from users.

Another competitor is POE from LinkedIn, and you can create a free account at: *https://poe.com/login*.

Pi From Inflection

Pi is a chatbot developed by Inflection, which is a company that was by Mustafa Suleyman, who is also the founder of DeepMind. Pi is accessible at: *https://pi.ai/talk*. The following article contains additional information:

https://medium.com/@ignacio.de.gregorio.noblejas/meet-pi-chatgpts-newest-rival-and-the-most-human-ai-in-the-world-367b461c0af1

The development team used Reinforcement Learning from Human Feedback (RLHF) to train this chatbot:

https://medium.com/@ignacio.de.gregorio.noblejas/meet-pi-chatgpts-newest-rival-and-the-most-human-ai-in-the-world-367b461c0af1

MACHINE LEARNING AND CHATGPT

OpenAI supports a plugin called "Advanced data analysis" (formerly known as Code Interpreter), which enables ChatGPT to generate Python code that produces charts and graphs based on data from datasets. Moreover, Advanced data analysis can generate machine learn- ing models that can be trained on datasets.

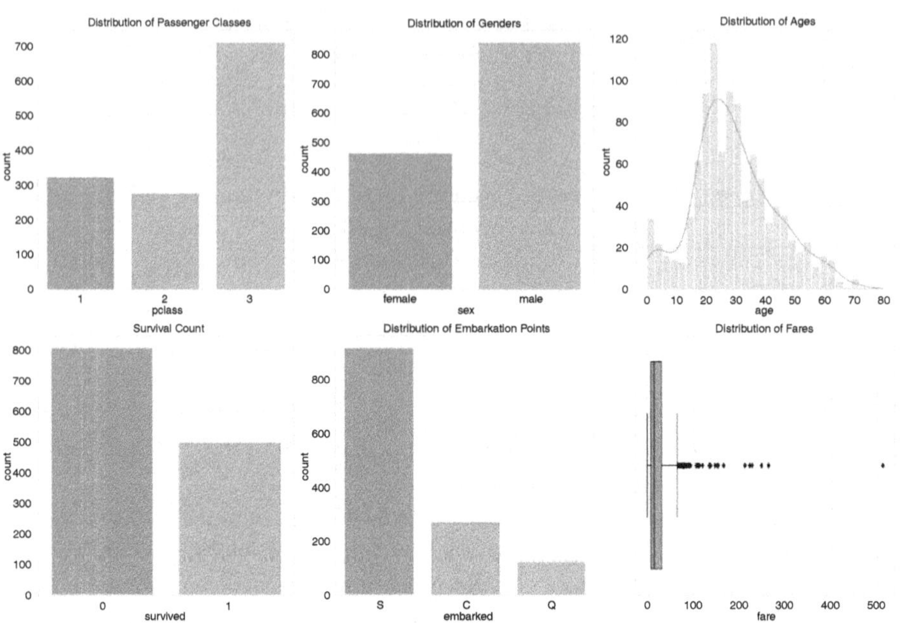

FIGURE 7.1 Titanic charts and graphs generated by Advanced Data Analysis

Incidentally, if you would like to see examples of ChatGPT generating Python code for machine learning models, as well as code for charts and graphs, you can learn how to do so in several upcoming books:

- *Machine Learning, Python3, and ChatGPT*
- *Python 3 Using ChatGPT/GPT-4*
- *GPT-4 For Developers*

The preceding books are published by Mercury Learning and will be available in early 2024.

WHAT IS INSTRUCTGPT?

InstructGPT is a language model developed by OpenAI, and it is a sibling model to ChatGPT. InstructGPT is designed to follow instructions given in a prompt to generate detailed responses. Some key points about InstructGPT are listed here:

- Instruction following
- Training
- Applications
- Limitations

Instruction Following: Unlike ChatGPT, which is designed for open-ended conversations, InstructGPT was developed to follow user instructions in prompts. This makes it suitable for tasks where the user wants to get specific information or outputs by giving clear directives.

Training: InstructGPT was trained using Reinforcement Learning from Human Feedback (RLHF), similar to ChatGPT. An initial model was trained using supervised fine-tuning, where human AI trainers provided conversations for both sides (the user and the AI assistant). This new dialogue dataset was then mixed with the InstructGPT dataset and transformed into a dialogue format.

Applications: InstructGPT can be useful in scenarios where you want more detailed explanations, step-by-step guides, or specific outputs based on the instructions provided.

Limitations: Like other models, InstructGPT has its limitations. It might produce incorrect or nonsensical answers. The output heavily depends on how the prompt is phrased. It is also sensitive to input phrasing and might give different responses based on slight rephrasing.

As AI models and their applications evolve, there might have been further developments or iterations of InstructGPT after 2021. Always refer to OpenAI's official publications and updates for the most recent information. More information about InstructGPT is accessible at *https://openai.com/blog/instruction-following/*.

VIZGPT AND DATA VISUALIZATION

VizGPT is an online tool that enables you to specify English-based prompts in order to visualize aspects of datasets: *https://www.vizgpt.ai/*.

Select the default "Cars Dataset" and then click on the "Data" button to display the contents of the dataset, as shown in Figure 7.2.

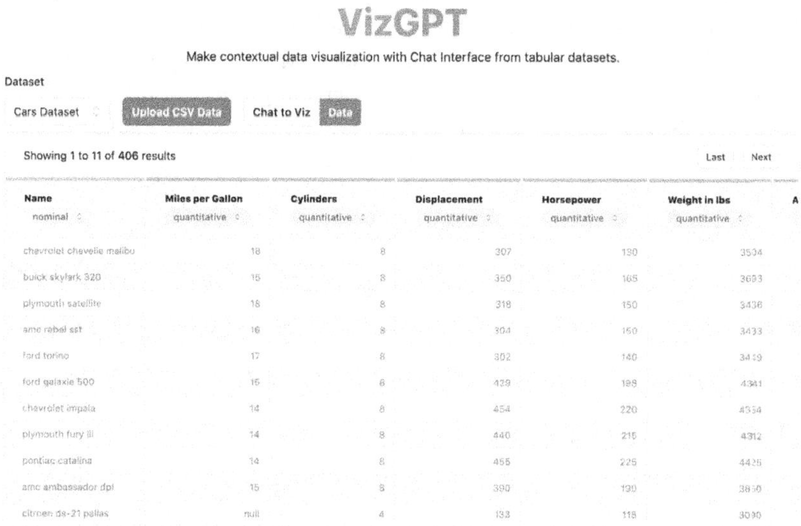

VizGPT

Make contextual data visualization with Chat Interface from tabular datasets.

Dataset

Cars Dataset | Upload CSV Data | Chat to Viz | Data

Showing 1 to 11 of 406 results   Last Next

Name nominal	Miles per Gallon quantitative	Cylinders quantitative	Displacement quantitative	Horsepower quantitative	Weight in lbs quantitative	A
chevrolet chevelle malibu	18	8	307	130	3504	
buick skylark 320	15	8	350	165	3693	
plymouth satellite	18	8	318	150	3436	
amc rebel sst	16	8	304	150	3433	
ford torino	17	8	302	140	3449	
ford galaxie 500	15	8	429	198	4341	
chevrolet impala	14	8	454	220	4354	
plymouth fury iii	14	8	440	215	4312	
pontiac catalina	14	8	455	225	4425	
amc ambassador dpl	15	8	390	190	3850	
citroen ds-21 pallas	null	4	133	115	3090	

FIGURE 7.2 VizGPT "Cars Dataset" rows example

Next, select the default "Cars Dataset" and then click on the "Chat to Viz" button to display a visualization of the dataset, as shown in Figure 7.3.

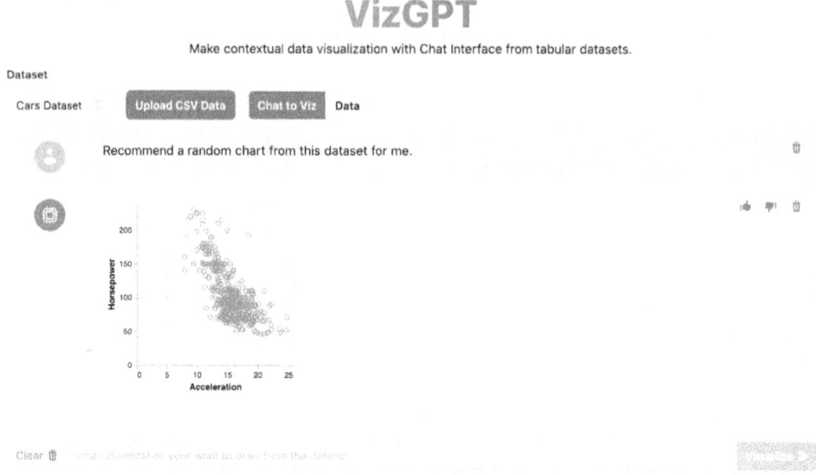

FIGURE 7.3 VizGPT "Cars Dataset" visualization

You can experiment further with VizGPT. For example, you can upload your own dataset by clicking on the "Upload CSV" button and obtain similar results with that dataset.

WHAT IS GPT-4?

GPT-4 was released in mid-March 2023, and became available only to users with an existing ChatGPT account via a paid upgrade ($20/month) to that account. According to various online anecdotal stories from users, GPT-4 is significantly superior to ChatGPT. In addition, Microsoft has a version of GPT-4 that powers its Bing browser, which is freely available to the public.

GPT-4 is a large multimodal model that can process image-based inputs as well as text-based inputs and then generate textual outputs. Currently, image-based outputs are unavailable to the general public, but it does have internal support for image generation.

GPT-4 supports 25,000 words of input text: by comparison, ChatGPT is limited to 4,096 characters. Although the number of parameters in GPT-4 is undisclosed, the following article asserts that GPT-4 is a mixture of 8x220-billion-parameter models, which is an example of a Mixture of Experts (MoE):

https://thealgorithmicbridge.substack.com/p/gpt-4s-secret-has-been-revealed

GPT-4 and Test Scores

One interesting example of the improved accuracy pertains to the bar exam, which ChatGPT initially scored in the bottom 10%. By contrast, GPT-4 scored in the top 10% for the same bar exam. More details are accessible online:

https://www.abajournal.com/web/article/latest-version-of-chatgpt-aces-the-bar-exam-with-score-in-90th-percentile

In addition, GPT-4 is apparently able to pass first year at Harvard with a 3.34 GPA. More details are accessible online:

https://www.businessinsider.com/chatgpt-harvard-passed-freshman-ai-education-GPT-4-2023-7?op=1

Furthermore, GPT-4 has performed well on a number of additional tests, some of which are listed here:

- AP exams
- SAT
- GRE
- Medical tests
- Law exams
- Business school exams
- Wharton MBA exam
- USA Biology Olympiad Semifinal Exam
- Sommelier exams (wine steward)

You can read more details regarding the preceding tests from this link:

https://www.businessinsider.com/list-here-are-the-exams-chatgpt-has-passed-so-far-2023-1

The following link contains much more detailed information regarding test scores, benchmarks, and other results pertaining to GPT-4: *https://openai.com/research/gpt-4*.

GPT-4 Parameters

This section contains information regarding a few of the GPT-4 parameters, some of which are best-guess approximations.

Since GPT-4 is a transformer-based autoregressive model, it was trained to perform next-token prediction. The following paper, *GPT4 Technical Report*, was released in March 2023, and it contains a detailed analysis of the capabilities of GPT-4:

https://docs.kanaries.net/en/tutorials/ChatGPT/gpt-4-parameters

GPT-4 Fine-Tuning

Although OpenAI allows you to fine-tune its four base models, it is (currently) not possible to perform fine-tuning on ChatGPT 3.5 or GPT-4. Instead, you can integrate OpenAI models with your own data source via LangChain or LlamaIndex (previously known as GPT-Index). Both of them enable you to connect OpenAI models with your existing data sources.

An introduction to LangChain is accessible online:

https://www.pinecone.io/learn/series/langchain/langchain-intro/

An introduction to LlamaIndex is accessible online:

https://zilliz.com/blog/getting-started-with-llamaindex

https://stackoverflow.com/questions/76160057/openai-chat-completions-api-how-do-i-customize-answers-from-gpt-3-5-or-gpt-4-mo?noredirect=1&lq=1

CHATGPT AND GPT-4 COMPETITORS

Shortly after the release of ChatGPT on November 30, 2022, there was a flurry of activity among various companies to release a competitor to ChatGPT, some of which are listed here:

- Bard (Google chatbot)
- CoPilot (Microsoft)
- Codex (OpenAI)
- Apple GPT (Apple)
- PaLM 2 (Google and GPT-4 competitor)
- Claude-2 (Anthropic)
- Llama-2 (Meta) in a later section

The following subsections contain additional details regarding the LLMs in the preceding list.

Bard

Bard is an AI chatbot from Google that was released in early 2023 as a competitor to ChatGPT. Bard is powered by PaLM 2, whereas ChatGPT is powered by GPT-4. Recently, Bard added support for images in its answers to user queries, whereas this functionality for ChatGPT has not been released yet to the public (but you can expect it to be available sometime soon).

https://artificialcorner.com/google-bards-new-image-recognition-means-serious-competition-to-chatgpt-here-are-6-best-use-cases-55d69eae1b27

Bard encountered an issue pertaining to the James Webb Space Telescope during a highly publicized release, which resulted in a significant decrease in market capitalization for Alphabet. However, Google has persevered in fixing issues and enhancing the functionality of Bard. You can access Bard at: *https://bard.google.com/*.

Around mid-2023, Bard was enhanced with several features that were not available in GPT-4 during the same time period, some of which are listed here:

- generate images
- generate HTML/CSS from an image

- generate mobile applications from an image
- create Latex formulas from an image
- extract text from an image

Presumably, these features will spur OpenAI to provide the same set of features (some are implemented in GPT-4, but they are not publicly available).

CoPilot (OpenAI/Microsoft)

Microsoft CoPilot is a Visual Studio Code extension that is also powered by GPT-4. GitHub CoPilot is already known for its ability to generate blocks of code within the context of a program. In addition, Microsoft is also developing Microsoft 365 CoPilot, whose availability date has not been announced as of mid-2023.

However, Microsoft has provided early demos that show some of the capabilities of Microsoft 365 CoPilot, which includes automating tasks such as

- writing emails
- summarizing meetings
- making PowerPoint presentations

Microsoft 365 CoPilot can analyze data in Excel spreadsheets, insert AI-generated images in PowerPoint, and generate drafts of cover letters. Microsoft has also integrated Microsoft 365 CoPilot into some of its existing products, such as Loop and OneNote.

According to the following article, Microsoft intends to charge $30 per month for Office 365 Copilot:

https://www.extremetech.com/extreme/microsoft-to-charge-30-per-month-for-ai-powered-office-apps

Copilot was reverse engineered in late 2022, which is described online:

https://thakkarparth007.github.io/copilot-explorer/posts/copilot-internals

The following article shows you how to create a GPT-3 application that uses NextJS, React, and CoPilot:

https://github.blog/2023-07-25-how-to-build-a-gpt-3-app-with-nextjs-react-and-github-copilot/

Codex (OpenAI)

OpenAI Codex is a fine-tuned GPT3-based LLM that generates code from text. In fact, Codex powers GitHub Copilot. Codex was trained on more than 150 GB of Python code that was obtained from more than 50 million GitHub repositories.

According to OpenAI, the primary purpose of Codex is to accelerate human programming, and it can complete almost 40% of requests. Codex tends to work quite well for generating code for solving simple tasks. Navigate to the Codex home page to obtain more information: *https://openai.com/blog/openai-codex*.

Apple GPT

In mid-2023, Apple announced Apple GPT, which is a competitor to ChatGPT from OpenAI. The actual release date was projected to be 2024. "Apple GPT" is the current name for a product that is intended to compete with Google Bard, OpenAI ChatGPT, and Microsoft Bing AI.

In brief, the LLM PaLM 2 powers Google Bard, and GPT-4 powers ChatGPT as well as Bing Chat, whereas Ajax is what powers Apple GPT. Ajax is based on Jax from Google.

PaLM-2

PaLM-2, the second version of the Pathways Language Model, is the successor to PaLM (circa 2022). PaLM-2 powers Bard, and it is also a direct competitor to GPT-4. By way of comparison, PaLM consists of 540 B parameters, and it is plausible that PaLM-2 is a larger LLM (details of the latter are undisclosed).

PaLM-2 provides four sub-models called Gecko, Otter, Bison, and Unicorn (from smallest to largest). PaLM-2 was trained on more than 100 human languages, as well as programming languages such as Fortran. Moreover, PaLM-2 has been deployed to a plethora of Google products, including Gmail and YouTube.

Med-PaLM M

In addition to the four sub-models listed above, Med-PaLM 2 (the successor to Med-PaLM) is an LLM that provides answers to medical questions, and it is accessible online at: *http://sites.research.google/med-palm/*.

The successor to Med-PaLM is Med-PaLM M, and details about this LLM are accessible at: *https://arxiv.org/abs/2307.14334*.

The following article provides a direct comparison of performance benchmarks for PaLM 2 and GPT-4:

https://www.makeuseof.com/google-palm-2-vs-openai-gpt-4/

All told, PaLM-2 has a robust set of features, and it is definitely a significant competitor to GPT-4.

Claude-2

Anthropic created the LLM Claude-2 that not only answer queries about specific topics, but also perform searches that involves multiple documents, summarize documents, create documents, and generate code.

Claude-2 is an improvement on Anthropic's predecessor Claude 1.3, and it can ingest entire books as well as generate code based on prompts from users. In fact, Claude-2 appears to be comparable with its rivals ChatGPT and GPT-4 in terms of competing functionality.

Furthermore, Claude-2 supports a context window of 100,000 tokens. Claude-2 was trained on data as recent as early 2023, whereas ChatGPT was trained on data up until 2021. However, Claude-2 cannot search the Web (unlike its competitor GPT-4). Anthropic is likely to continue to develop its capabilities the LLM space.

LLAMA-2

Llama-2 (Large Language Model Meta AI) is an open source fine-tuned LLM from Meta, that trained on only public data, that has created a lot of excitement in the AI community. Llama-2 provides three models (7 B, 13 B, and 70 B parameters) that utilize more data during the pre-training step than numerous other LLMs. Llama-2 is optimized to provide faster inferences and also provides a longer context length (4 K) than other LLMs.

Moreover, the Llama-2-Chat LLM performs surprisingly well: in some cases, its quality is close to the quality of high-performing LLMs such ChatGPT and GPT-4. Llama-2 is more user-friendly and also provides better results for writing text in comparison to GPT-4. On the other hand, GPT-4 is more adept for tasks such as generating code.

How to Download Llama-2

Llama-2 provides a permissive license for community use and commercial use, and Meta has made the code as well as the pre-trained models and the fine-tuned models publicly available.

There are several ways that you can download Llama-2, starting from this link from Meta after you provide some information (name, country, and affiliation):

https://ai.meta.com/llama/

Another way to access demos of the 7 B, 13 B, and 70 B models is from the following links:

https://huggingface.co/spaces/huggingface-projects/llama-2-7b-chat

https://huggingface.co/spaces/huggingface-projects/llama-2-13b-chat

https://huggingface.co/spaces/ysharma/Explore_llamav2_with_TGI

A third way to access Llama-2 on Hugging Face is from the following link: *https://huggingface.co/blog/llama2*

More information is available online:

https://github.com/facebookresearch/llama

https://ai.meta.com/research/publications/llama-2-open-foundation-and-fine-tuned-chat-models/

If you are interested in training Llama-2 on your laptop, more details for doing so are accessible at *https://blog.briankitano.com/llama-from-scratch/*.

Llama-2 Architecture Features

This section simply contains a high-level list of some of the important distinguishing features of Llama-2, as shown here:

- decoder-only LLM
- better pre-training
- improved model architecture
- SwiGLU activation function
- different positional embeddings
- GQA (Grouped Query Attention)
- Ghost Attention (GAtt)
- RLHF and PPO
- BPE SentencePiece tokenizer
- modified normalization step

The majority of LLMs contain the layer normalization that is in the original Transformer architecture. By contrast, Llama uses a simplified alternative that involves Root Mean Square Layer Normalization (RMSNorm). RMSNorm has yielded improved results for training stability as well as for generalization.

Although SwiGLU is computationally more expensive than the ReLU activation function that is part of the original Transformer architecture, SwiGLU achieves better performance.

Note that RLHF is discussed earlier, and that section includes a brief description of TRPO and PPO. For a detailed description of how to fine-tune Llama-2 on three tasks, navigate to the following link:

https://www.anyscale.com/blog/fine-tuning-llama-2-a-comprehensive-case-study-for-tailoring-models-to-unique-applications

Fine-Tuning Llama-2

Although Llama-2 is an improvement over its predecessor Llama, you can further improve the performance of Llama-2 by performing some fine-tuning of this LLM.

https://medium.com/@murtuza753/using-llama-2-0-faiss-and-langchain-for-question-answering-on-your-own-data-682241488476

The following article shows you how to fine tune Llama-2 in a Google Colaboratory notebook:

https://towardsdatascience.com/fine-tune-your-own-llama-2-model-in-a-colab-notebook-df9823a04a32

The following article describes how to use MonsterAPI (also discussed in the article) to fine-tune LlaMa-2 in five steps:

https://blog.monsterapi.ai/how-to-fine-tune-llama-2-llm/

The following link describes how to access Llama-2 in Google Colaboratory:

https://levelup.gitconnected.com/harnessing-the-power-of-llama-2-using-google-colab-2e1dedc2d1d8

WHEN WILL GPT-5 BE AVAILABLE?

As this book goes to print, there is no official information available regarding the status of GPT-5, which is to say that everything is speculative. In the early part of 2023, Sam Altman (CEO of OpenAI) remarked that there were "no official plans" for GPT-5.

However, during mid-2023, OpenAI filed a patent for GPT-5 in which there are some high-level details about the features of GPT-5. Some people speculated that GPT-5 will be a more powerful version of GPT-4, and others suggest that filing a patent might be nothing more than securing the name "GPT-5."

Regardless of the motivation for filing a patent, there is a great deal of competition with GPT-4 from various companies. Therefore, it is highly plausible that OpenAI will release GPT-5, perhaps by the end of 2023. Regarding model sizes, recall that GPT-3 has 175 B parameters, and some speculate that GPT-4 has 10 trillion parameters, which would mean that GPT-4 is roughly 60 times larger than GPT-3. The same increase in scale for GPT-5 seems implausible because GPT-5 would then consist of 600 trillion parameters.

Another possibility is that GPT-4 is based on the Mixture of Experts methodology that involves multiple components. For instance, GPT-4 could be a combination of 8 components, each of which involves 220 million parameters, and therefore GPT-4 would consist of 1.76 trillion parameters.

Keep in mind that training LLMs such as GPT-4 is very costly and requires huge datasets for the pre-training step. Regardless of the eventual size of GPT-5, the training process could involve enormous costs.

SUMMARY

This chapter started with a discussion of ChatGPT from OpenAI and some of its features. In addition, you learned about some competitors to ChatGPT, such as Claude-2 from Anthropic.

Next you learned about GPT-4 from OpenAI, which powers ChatGPT, and some of its features. Then you learned about some competitors of GPT-4, such as Llama-2 (Meta) and Bard (Google).

CHAPTER 8

ChatGPT and Data Visualization

This chapter contains examples of using ChatGPT to perform data visualization, such as creating charts and graphs that are based on datasets (e.g., the Titanic dataset). ChatGPT generated all the code samples shown here via the Advanced data analysis plugin. ChatGPT also generated some of the accompanying text for the Python-based code samples.

The first part of this chapter describes the process of uploading a dataset in ChatGPT and then provides prompts for tasks such as explaining the features in a given dataset, generating visualizations, and downloading the curated dataset. You will also learn how to prompt ChatGPT to create and train a machine learning model.

The second part of this chapter contains examples of data visualization with Matplotlib, where the code samples were generated with ChatGPT. The third part of this chapter contains examples of data visualization with Seaborn, where the code samples were generated with ChatGPT.

After you have read the material in this chapter, compare the code samples in this chapter with the code samples in Chapter 5 (Matplotlib) as well as Chapter 6 (Seaborn).

One more detail to keep in mind regarding the code samples in this chapter, all of which were generated by ChatGPT. The general format for the prompt that was provided to ChatGPT is shown here:

"Please generate Python code to render [specify-a-graph-type] using Matplotlib."

The first few code samples in this chapter provide the prompt that ChatGPT used in order to generate the given Python code.

WORKING WITH CHARTS AND GRAPHS

Each chart type has its unique strengths and is best suited for specific kinds of data and analysis. The choice of chart often depends on the nature of the data and the specific insights one wants to derive. This section contains multiple subsections that provide information about an assortment of charts and graphs, as shown below:

- Bar charts
- Pie charts
- Line graphs
- Heat maps
- Histograms
- Box plots
- Pareto charts
- Radar charts
- Treemaps
- Waterfall charts
- Scatterplots

Each of the charts and graphs in the preceding list is discussed in the following subsections.

Bar Charts

Bar charts represent data with rectangular bars. The lengths of the bars are proportional to the values they represent. They can be vertical (column charts) or horizontal. An example of usage involves comparing the sales of different products in a store.

Some advantages of bar charts are as follows:

- easily interpretable and widely recognized
- can compare individual or multiple data series
- effective for displaying data that spans several categories

Some disadvantages of bar charts are as follows:

- not ideal for showing patterns or trends over time
- can become cluttered when comparing too many categories

Pie Charts

Pie charts represent data in a circular format, with individual sections (slices) showing categories' proportion to the whole. An example of usage involves representing the market share of different companies in an industry.

Some advantages of pie charts are as follows:

- simple visualization that shows part-to-whole relationships
- clearly indicate proportions.
- effective when there are a limited number of categories

Some disadvantages of pie charts are as follows:

- not efficient for comparing individual categories
- can become ineffective and difficult to interpret with too many slices
- do not show absolute values, only proportions

Line Graphs

Line graphs display data points connected by straight lines. They are used primarily to visualize values over a continuous interval or time period. An example of usage involves tracking a company's revenue growth over several years.

Some advantages of line graphs are as follows:

- effective for displaying trends over time.
- can compare multiple data series on one graph
- clear visualization of data points and intervals

Some disadvantages of line graphs are as follows:

- not suitable for showing part-to-whole relationships
- can become cluttered when displaying too many data series
- require a meaningful order of data points

Heat Maps

A heat map represents data in a matrix format, where individual values are depicted as colors. The color intensity usually represents the magnitude of the value. An example of usage involves visualizing website visitor activity on different parts of a Web page.

Some advantages of heat maps are as follows:

- quickly identify patterns, correlations, and areas of concentration
- use color effectively to convey information about magnitudes

Some disadvantages of heat maps are as follows:

- not suitable for detailed numerical analysis
- color choices are crucial; poor choices can mislead interpretation

Histograms

A histogram is a graphical representation of the distribution of a dataset. It is an estimate of the probability distribution of a continuous variable. An example of usage involves showing the distribution of ages in a population.

Some advantages of histograms are as follows:

- provide a visual interpretation of numerical data by indicating the number of data points that lie within a range of values
- can help identify data distribution patterns

Some disadvantages of histograms are as follows:

- do not show exact values
- number and width of bins can influence perception

Box Plots

Box plots represent a summary of a dataset using quartiles. The "box" shows the interquartile range, while the "whiskers" indicate variability outside the upper and lower quartiles. An example of usage involves comparing sales performances across different teams.

Some advantages of box plots are as follows:

- quickly visualize data spread and skewness
- identify outliers

Some disadvantages of box plots are as follows:

- not suitable for detailed distribution analysis
- do not show the frequency distribution of data

Pareto Charts

Pareto charts combine a bar chart and a line graph to represent the cumulative frequency of occurrences. They identify the most significant factors in a dataset. An example of usage involves identifying which product defects occur most frequently.

Some advantages of Pareto charts are as follows:

- efficiently highlight the most important factors in large datasets
- aid in prioritizing efforts

Some disadvantages of Pareto charts are as follows:

- limited to datasets where ranking and prioritization are relevant
- not suitable for showing relationships between data points

Radar Charts

A radar chart is a graphical method of displaying data in a 2D chart of three or more quantitative variables. The data points are plotted on axes that start from the center. An example of usage involves comparing the performance metrics of products.

Some advantages of radar charts are as follows:

- can compare multiple quantitative variables
- provide a visual overview of the data

Some disadvantages of radar charts are as follows:

- can become cluttered when comparing too many datasets
- difficult to interpret with similar values

Treemaps

Treemaps display hierarchical data as nested rectangles. Each branch of the hierarchy is represented by colored rectangles. An example of usage involves visualizing storage usage on a computer.

Some advantages of treemaps are as follows:

- efficient use of space
- can represent multiple dimensions using size and color

Some disadvantages of tree maps are as follows:

- not suitable for datasets with large hierarchies
- can become difficult to interpret

Waterfall Charts

Waterfall charts represent the cumulative effect of sequentially occurring positive or negative values. An example of usage involves visualizing how profit or revenue is affected by various factors.

Some advantages of waterfall charts are as follows:

- clearly visualize positive and negative sequential changes
- help in understanding the gradual transition from one data point to another

Some disadvantages of waterfall charts are as follows:

- limited to situations where understanding sequential changes is necessary
- can become confusing with too many data points.

LINE PLOTS WITH MATPLOTLIB

Let's plot a simple line graph to visualize a trend. Listing 8.1 displays the content of `line_plots.py` that ChatGPT generated to render a line using Matplotlib. The prompt for ChatGPT is shown here:

"Please generate Python code to render a line graph using Matplotlib."

LISTING 8.1: line_plot.py

```
import matplotlib.pyplot as plt

def plot_line(x, y, title, x_label, y_label):
    plt.plot(x, y)
    plt.title(title)
    plt.xlabel(x_label)
    plt.ylabel(y_label)
    plt.grid(True)
    plt.show()
# Usage
x = [1, 2, 3, 4, 5]
y = [2, 4, 1, 3, 5]
plot_line(x, y, 'Sample Line Graph', 'X-Axis', 'Y-Axis')
```

Listing 8.1 starts with an `import` statement and then defines the function `plot_line()`, which renders a line plot. Matplotlib has the `plot()` function, which provides a straightforward way to create line graphs. In this function, we visualize a trend across the x and y axes.

The next portion of code initializes the Python lists `x` and `y`, and then invokes `plot_line()` with three strings that are the values for the title, the horizontal axis, and the vertical axis. Figure 8.1 displays the output from launching the code in Listing 8.1.

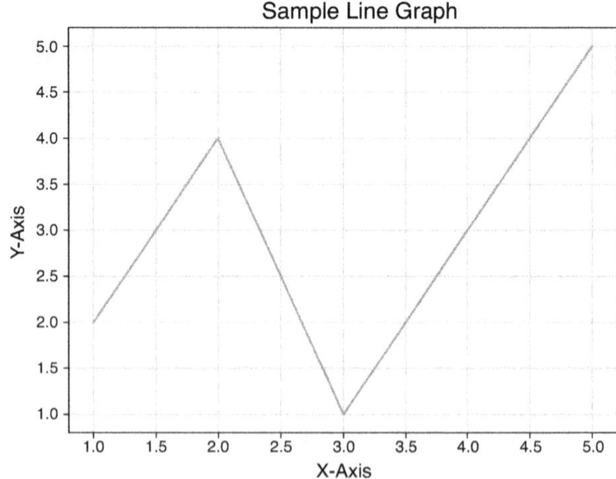

FIGURE 8.1 A line plot with Matplotlib

A PIE CHART USING MATPLOTLIB

Pie charts are ideal for displaying proportional data among categories. The pie function from Matplotlib provides an easy way to achieve this. Listing 8.2 displays the content of pie_chart1.py that ChatGPT generated to render a pie chart using Matplotlib. The prompt for ChatGPT is shown here:

"Please generate Python code to render a pie chart using Matplotlib."

LISTING 8.2: pie_chart1.py

```
import matplotlib.pyplot as plt

def plot_pie(labels, sizes, title):
    plt.pie(sizes, labels=labels, autopct='%1.1f%%',
startangle=140)
    plt.title(title)
    plt.axis('equal')  # Equal aspect ratio ensures the pie
is drawn as a circle.
    plt.show()

# Usage
labels = ['A', 'B', 'C']
sizes = [215, 130, 245]
plot_pie(labels, sizes, 'Sample Pie Chart')
```

Listing 8.2 starts in a similar fashion to Listing 8.1, except that the `plot_pie()` function for generating a pie chart is generated. The next portion of Listing 8.2 initializes the Python lists' labels and sizes, and invokes the function `plot_pie()` with these lists as well as a string that is displayed as the title of the pie chart. Figure 8.2 displays the pie chart that is rendered by launching the code in Listing 8.2.

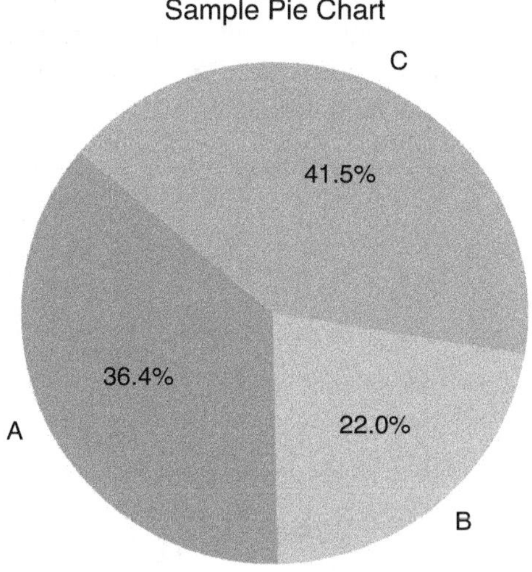

FIGURE 8.2 A pie chart created with Matplotlib

BOX AND WHISKER PLOTS USING MATPLOTLIB

Box plots, or box-and-whisker plots, provide a summary of the distribution of data, highlighting the central tendency, variability, and presence of outliers. They can be particularly useful for comparing distributions across different groups. They can display the distribution of data based on the minimum, first quartile, median, third quartile, and maximum.

Listing 8.3 displays the content of boxplot1.py that ChatGPT generated to render a box plot using Seaborn. The prompt for ChatGPT is shown here:

"Please generate Python code to render a box plot using Matplotlib."

The prompt for ChatGPT is shown here:

"Please generate Python code to render a line graph using Matplotlib."

LISTING 8.3: boxplot1.py

```
import matplotlib.pyplot as plt
import seaborn as sns

import matplotlib.pyplot as plt

def plot_box(data, column):
    plt.boxplot(data[column])
    plt.show()

# Usage
data = sns.load_dataset("iris")
plot_box(data, "sepal_length")
```

Listing 8.3 contains three import statements followed by the `plot_box()` function that generated a box plot. The next portion of Listing 8.3 initializes the variable `data` with the contents of the Seaborn built-in `iris` dataset, and then invokes `plot_box()` with data and a string that specifies the feature (column) to use when rendering a box plot. Figure 8.3 displays the box plot that is rendered by launching the code in Listing 8.3.

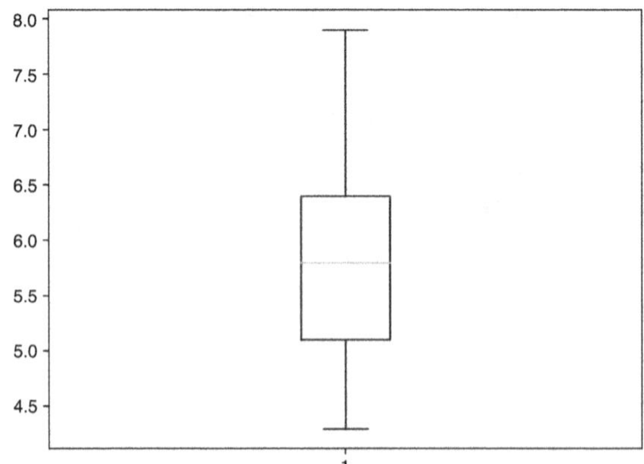

FIGURE 8.3 A box plot created with Matplotlib

TIME SERIES VISUALIZATION WITH MATPLOTLIB

Time series data, where observations are taken at regular time intervals, can be visualized using line plots. This enables analysts to discern trends, patterns, and anomalies.

Let's plot time series data to understand trends over time. Listing 8.4 displays the content of `time_series.py` that ChatGPT generated to render a time series using Matplotlib.

LISTING 8.4: time_series.py

```
import matplotlib.pyplot as plt

import pandas as pd

def plot_time_series(dates, values, title):
    plt.figure(figsize=(10, 5))
    plt.plot(dates, values)
    plt.title(title)
    plt.xlabel('Date')
    plt.ylabel('Value')
    plt.tight_layout()
    plt.show()

# Usage
dates = pd.date_range(start="2021-01-01", periods=10,
freq='D')
values = [x**1.5 for x in range(10)]
plot_time_series(dates, values, 'Sample Time Series Data')
```

Figure 8.4 displays the time series that is rendered by launching the code in Listing 8.10.

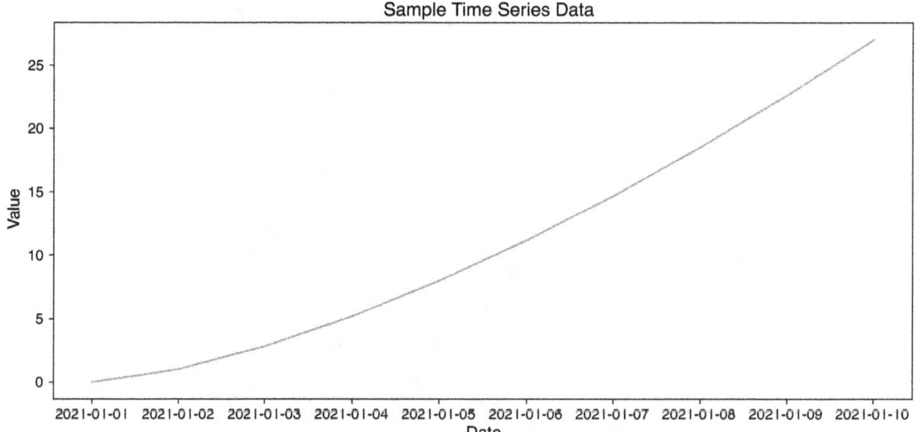

FIGURE 8.4 A time series created with Matplotlib

STACKED BAR CHARTS WITH MATPLOTLIB

Stacked bar charts allow for the representation of sub-groups in each category, giving a sense of the total size across categories and the sub-group distributions within them.

Listing 8.5 displays the content of `stacked_bar_charts.py` that ChatGPT generated to render stacked bar charts using Matplotlib.

LISTING 8.5: stacked_bar_charts.py

```
import matplotlib.pyplot as plt
import numpy as np

def plot_stacked_bar(data, labels, categories):
    cum_size = np.zeros(len(categories))

    for i, label in enumerate(labels):
        plt.bar(categories, data[label], bottom=cum_size,
label=label)
        cum_size += data[label]

    plt.legend()
    plt.show()

# Usage
data = {
    'A': [10, 15, 20],
    'B': [5, 10, 5]
}
labels = ['A', 'B']
categories = ['Category 1', 'Category 2', 'Category 3']
plot_stacked_bar(data, labels, categories)
```

Figure 8.5 displays the stacked bar charts that are rendered by launching the code in Listing 8.5.

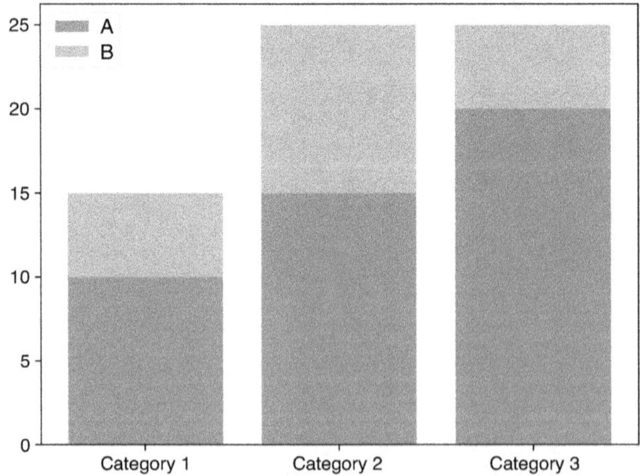

FIGURE 8.5 Stacked bar charts created with Matplotlib

DONUT CHARTS USING MATPLOTLIB

Donut charts are a variation of pie charts. The hollow center can be used for additional annotations or just to provide a different aesthetic. We can use them to represent data proportionally among categories, similar to a pie chart, but with a hollow center. Listing 8.6 displays the content of `donut_charts.py` that ChatGPT generated to render a donut chart using Matplotlib.

LISTING 8.6: donut_charts.py

```
import matplotlib.pyplot as plt

def plot_donut_chart(sizes, labels, title, hole_size=0.3):
    fig, ax = plt.subplots()
    ax.pie(sizes, labels=labels, autopct='%1.1f%%',
startangle=90, wedgeprops=dict(width=hole_size))
    ax.axis('equal')
    plt.title(title)
    plt.show()

# Usage
labels = ['A', 'B', 'C']
sizes = [215, 130, 245]
plot_donut_chart(sizes, labels, 'Sample Donut Chart')
```

Figure 8.6 displays the donut chart that is rendered by launching the code in Listing 8.13.

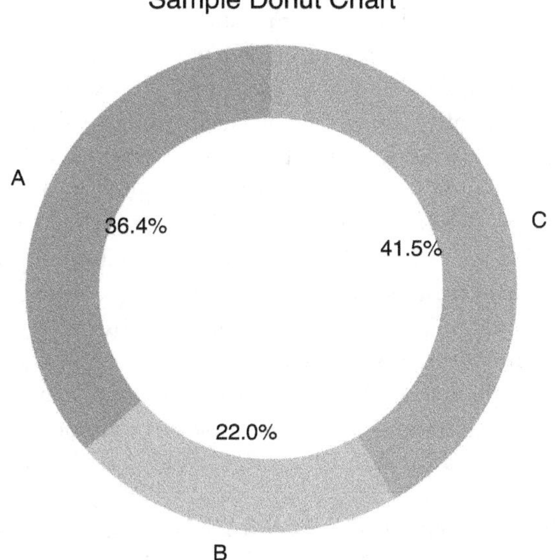

FIGURE 8.6 Donut chart created with Seaborn

3D SURFACE PLOTS WITH MATPLOTLIB

3D surface plots are used for visualizing functions with two variables. They can reveal intricate patterns and relationships in the data. Listing 8.7 displays the content of `3d_surface.py` that ChatGPT generated to render a 3D surface using `mpl_toolkits`.

Incidentally, if you encounter issues with `mpl_toolkits`, please read the following post that contains useful information:

https://stackoverflow.com/questions/37661119/python-mpl-toolkits-installation-issue

LISTING 8.7: 3d_surface.py

```
import matplotlib.pyplot as plt
import numpy as np

def plot_3d_surface(x, y, z):
    fig = plt.figure()
    ax = fig.add_subplot(111, projection='3d')
    ax.plot_surface(x, y, z, cmap='viridis')
    plt.show()

# Usage
x = np.linspace(-5, 5, 50)
y = np.linspace(-5, 5, 50)
x, y = np.meshgrid(x, y)
z = np.sin(np.sqrt(x**2 + y**2))
plot_3d_surface(x, y, z)
```

Listing 8.7 starts with two `import` statements, followed by the `plot_3d_surface()` function that renders a 3D plot. The second half of Listing 8.7 initializes the variables `x` and `y` via the NumPy function `linspace()` that partitions an interval into a set of equally-sized subintervals.

For example, the code snippet `np.linspace(-5, 5, 50)` divides the interval `[-5,5]` into 50 equally spaced points, which means that there are 49 intervals of equal width. You can persuade yourself that this is true by replacing 50 with 3: the result is the left endpoint -5, the midpoint, and the right endpoint 5, which creates 2 (=3-1) intervals.

The next code snippet updates `x` and `y` with the result of invoking the `meshgrid()` function in NumPy, after which `z` is defined as the trigonometric sine function applied to the number that equals the distance of the point `(x,y)` from the origin. Although the latter number is monotonically increasing as the point `(x,y)` shifts away from the origin, and `z` is the sine of that distance, which is a periodic function: as a result, you will see a rolling wave-like effect.

The final code snippet in Listing 8.7 invokes the function `plot_3d_surface()` with the values contained in the variables `x`, `y`, and `z`. Now launch the code in Listing 8.7, and you will see the 3D surface that is displayed in Figure 8.7.

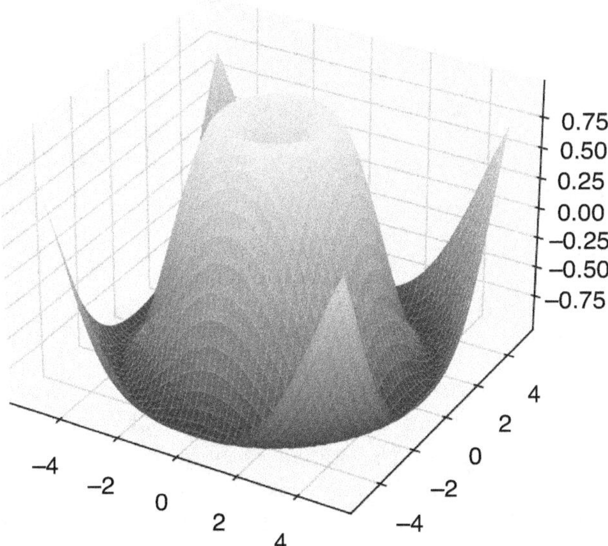

FIGURE 8.7 A 3D surface created with Matplotlib

RADIAL OR SPIDER CHARTS WITH MATPLOTLIB

Radial or spider charts are used to visualize multivariate data in the form of a two-dimensional chart of three or more quantitative variables. Each variable is represented on a separate axis that starts from the center of the chart. These charts allow us to compare multiple quantitative variables.

Listing 8.8 displays the content of `radial_charts.py` that ChatGPT generated to render radial charts using Matplotlib.

LISTING 8.8: radial_charts.py

```
import matplotlib.pyplot as plt
import numpy as np

def plot_spider_chart(values, categories, title):
    angles = np.linspace(0, 2 * np.pi, len(categories),
endpoint=False).tolist()
    values += values[:1]
    angles += angles[:1]

    fig, ax = plt.subplots(figsize=(6, 6), subplot_
kw=dict(polar=True))
    ax.fill(angles, values, color='blue', alpha=0.25)
    ax.set_yticklabels([])

    # the following snippet causes an error:
    # ax.set_xticks(angles)
```

```
    # the following snippet is correct:
    ax.set_xticks(angles[:-1])  # Exclude the last angle
since it's cyclic

    ax.set_xticklabels(categories)

    plt.title(title, size=20, color="blue", y=1.1)
    plt.show()

# Usage
categories = ["A", "B", "C", "D"]
values = [50, 30, 60, 40]
plot_spider_chart(values, categories, 'Sample Spider Chart')
```

Listing 8.8 starts with two `import` statements, followed by the Python function `plot_spider_chart()` function that renders a radial chart. The second portion of Listing 8.8 initializes the variables `categories` and `values` as two Python lists, and then invokes the function `plot_spider_chart()` with the variables `categories`, `values`, and a text string for the title of the plot. Figure 8.8 displays the radial chart that is rendered by launching the code in Listing 8.8.

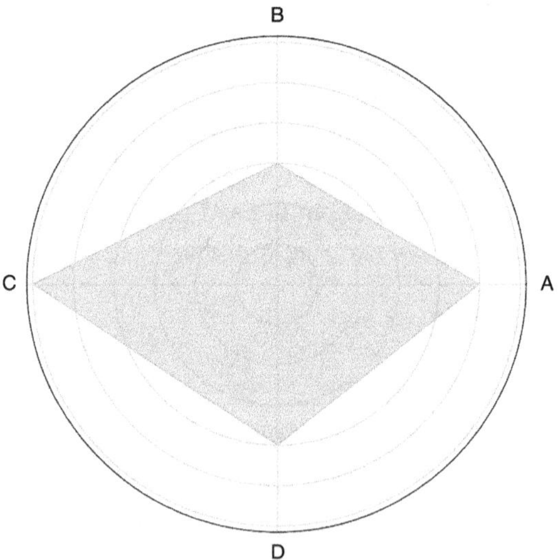

FIGURE 8.8 Radial chart created with Matplotlib

One more detail that will help you with debugging the code that ChatGPT generates for you. Let's look at the code block in bold in Listing 8.8:

```
# the following snippet causes an error:
# ax.set_xticks(angles)
# the following snippet is correct:
ax.set_xticks(angles[:-1])  # Exclude the last angle since
it's cyclic
```

If you reverse the order of the two code snippets, the code will not work correctly. Here is the "conversation" with ChatGPT that was needed to ask for a solution.

ME: I uploaded radial_charts.py that contains code that you wrote for me. However, this code results in this error: ValueError: The number of FixedLocator locations (5), usually from a call to set_ticks, does not match the number of ticklabels (4). Can you provide a solution?

```
ChatGPT:
Thank you for providing the radial_charts.py file. Let's
start by reading its content to understand the structure and
context of the code. After that, I'll analyze the potential
causes of the mentioned error and offer a solution.

The provided radial_charts.py file contains a function,
plot_spider_chart, which is designed to plot a spider (or
radar) chart using given values and categories.

Based on the error you reported and the code's structure,
the issue likely arises from the mismatch between the
number of tick locations (set by ax.set_xticks(angles))
and the number of tick labels (set by ax.set_
xticklabels(categories)).

To address this, I'll ensure that the number of tick locations
matches the number of tick labels. Let's proceed to make this
adjustment and provide a corrected version of the function.
```

ME: This works correctly now! Thank you for your help!

```
ChatGPT:
You're welcome! I'm glad to hear it's working as expected now.
If you have any more questions or need further assistance in
the future, don't hesitate to reach out. Happy coding!
```

MATPLOTLIB'S CONTOUR PLOTS

Contour plots help visualize three-dimensional data in two dimensions using contour lines. Each contour line represents points of equal value. These plots help us visualize contour lines for 3D data.

Listing 8.9 displays the content of `contour_lines.py` that ChatGPT generated to render contour lines using Matplotlib.

LISTING 8.9: contour_lines.py

```
import matplotlib.pyplot as plt
import numpy as np

def plot_contour(x, y, z):
    plt.contourf(x, y, z, 20, cmap='viridis')
    plt.colorbar()
    plt.show()
```

```
# Usage
x = np.linspace(-5, 5, 50)
y = np.linspace(-5, 5, 50)
x, y = np.meshgrid(x, y)
z = np.sin(np.sqrt(x**2 + y**2))
plot_contour(x, y, z)
```

Listing 8.9 contains two import statements and then the function `plot_contour()` is defined that renders the contour lines for the code sample. Note that the second part of Listing 8.9 is virtually identical to the code in the second half of Listing 8.7. Figure 8.9 displays the contour plot that is rendered by launching the code in Listing 8.9.

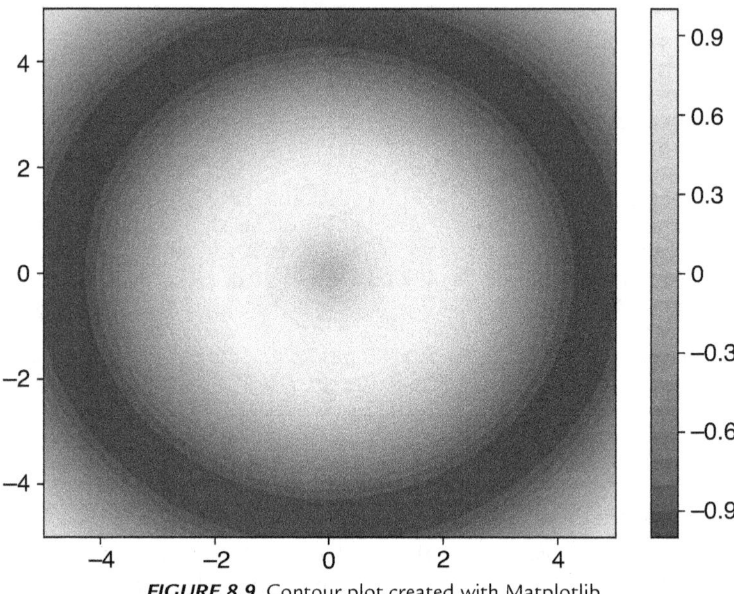

FIGURE 8.9 Contour plot created with Matplotlib

STREAM PLOTS FOR VECTOR FIELDS

Stream plots are used for displaying vector fields, like wind patterns. They provide a snapshot of the flow trajectories and can be color-coded for scalar data. They allow us to visualize a vector field as streamlines.

Listing 8.10 displays the contents of `stream_plot.py` that ChatGPT generated to render a stream plot using Seaborn.

LISTING 8.10: stream_plot.py

```
import matplotlib.pyplot as plt
import seaborn as sns
import numpy as np

def plot_streamplot(x, y, u, v):
    plt.streamplot(x, y, u, v, density=1)
    plt.show()
```

```
# Usage
x = np.linspace(-5, 5, 10)
y = np.linspace(-5, 5, 10)

# this causes an error:
#y, x = np.meshgrid(y, x)
# this works correctly:
x, y = np.meshgrid(x, y)

u = -1 - x**2 + y
v = 1 + x - y**2
plot_streamplot(x, y, u, v)
```

Figure 8.18 displays the stream plot that is rendered by launching the code in Listing 8.10.

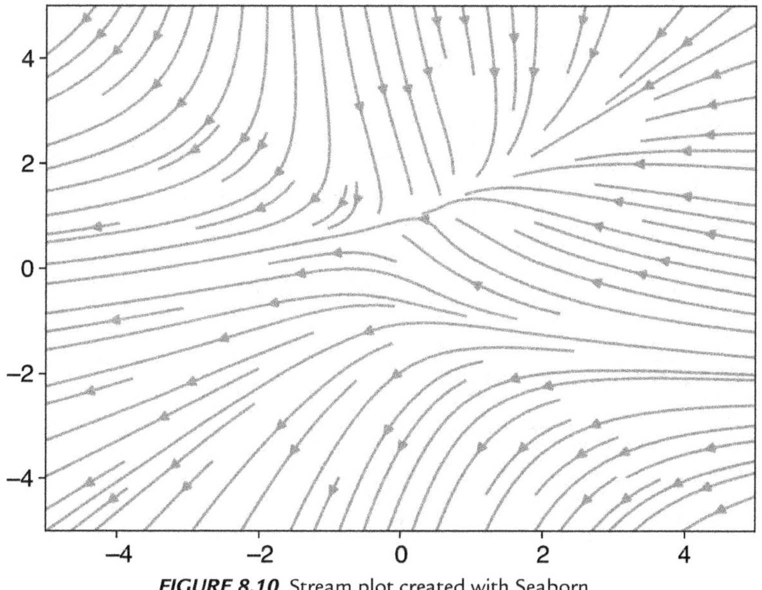

FIGURE 8.10 Stream plot created with Seaborn

The initial code in Listing 8.10 from ChatGPT did not work correctly, so I asked ChatGPT to provide a solution during the following "dialog" with ChatGPT.

ME: I uploaded stream_plot.py that contains code that you wrote for me. This code results in the following error: ValueError: The rows of 'x' must be equal. Can you provide a solution?

```
ChatGPT:
The shapes of the arrays x, y, u, and v are all
(10,10), which means they are consistent in terms of
dimensions.
```

```
The error message "ValueError: The rows of 'x' must be
equal" suggests that there might be an issue with the values
within the rows of the x array, rather than its shape.

The line y, x = np.meshgrid(y, x) swaps the original x and
y arrays. This might be causing inconsistencies in the rows
of the x array.

To address the error, I'll modify the meshgrid creation and
ensure the x and y arrays are correctly initialized. Let's
make the necessary adjustments.
```

ME: This works! Thanks for your help!

```
ChatGPT:
You're welcome! I'm glad to hear it's working as expected
now. If you have any more questions or need further
assistance in the future, don't hesitate to reach out.
Happy coding!
```

QUIVER PLOTS FOR VECTOR FIELDS

Quiver plots are useful for representing vector fields, showing both the direction and magnitude of vectors. For instance, they can be utilized in physics to show electric fields or fluid flow directions. They allow us to visualize the direction and magnitude of vectors.

Listing 8.11 displays the content of `quiver_plot.py` that ChatGPT generated to render a quiver plot using Matplotlib.

LISTING 8.11: quiver_plot.py

```
import matplotlib.pyplot as plt
import numpy as np

def plot_quiver(x, y, u, v):
    plt.quiver(x, y, u, v, scale=20)
    plt.show()

# Usage
x, y = np.meshgrid(np.arange(0, 2 * np.pi, .2),
np.arange(0, 2 * np.pi, .2))
u = np.sin(x)
v = np.cos(y)
plot_quiver(x, y, u, v)
```

Figure 8.11 displays the quiver plot that is rendered by launching the code in Listing 8.11.

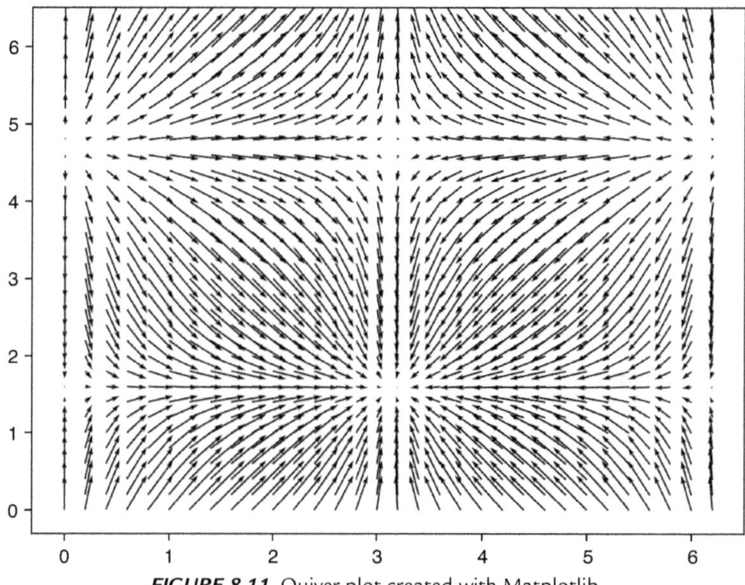

FIGURE 8.11 Quiver plot created with Matplotlib

POLAR PLOTS

Polar plots or radial plots are suitable for displaying multivariate data in a two-dimensional chart where the variables are represented on axes starting from the same point. They are useful for viewing patterns based on angles and magnitudes. They allow us to display data in terms of values and angles.

Listing 8.12 displays the content of `facet_grids.py` that ChatGPT generated to render stacked bar charts using Seaborn.

LISTING 8.12: polar_plots.py

```
import matplotlib.pyplot as plt
import numpy as np

def plot_polar(theta, radii, title=""):
    plt.figure(figsize=(8, 4))
    ax = plt.subplot(111, projection='polar')
    ax.plot(theta, radii)
    ax.set_title(title)
    plt.show()
# Usage
theta = np.linspace(0, 2 * np.pi, 100)
radii = np.abs(np.sin(theta) * 2)
plot_polar(theta, radii, "Sample Polar Plot")
```

Figure 8.12 displays the point plot that is rendered by launching the code in Listing 8.12.

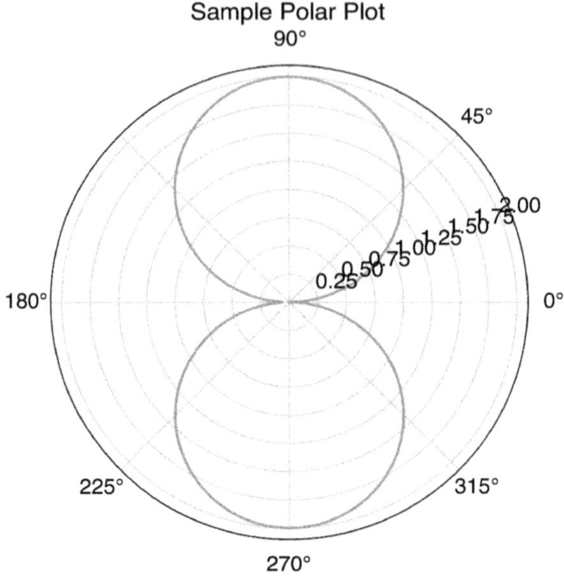

FIGURE 8.12 Polar plots created with Matplotlib

BAR CHARTS WITH SEABORN

Seaborn provides a higher-level interface for Matplotlib, making the creation of stylish plots more accessible. A bar plot helps us visualize data across different categories. Plotting bar charts allows us to visualize categorical data.

NOTE *Seaborn works best when integrated with Pandas.*

Listing 8.13 displays the content of `bar_chart1.py` that ChatGPT generated to a bar chart using Seaborn.

LISTING 8.13: bar_chart1.py

```
import matplotlib.pyplot as plt
import seaborn as sns
import pandas as pd

def plot_bar(data, x_col, y_col):
    sns.barplot(x=x_col, y=y_col, data=data)
    plt.show()

# Usage
data = pd.DataFrame({
    'Category': ['A', 'B', 'C'],
    'Values': [10, 20, 15]
})
plot_bar(data, 'Category', 'Values')
```

Listing 8.13 starts with three `import` statements, followed by the function `plot_bar()` that renders the bar chart. The second half of Listing 8.13 initializes the Pandas `DataFrame` data and then invokes `plot_bar()` with data and a string for labeling the horizontal axis and another string for labeling the vertical axis. Figure 8.13 displays the bar chart that is rendered by launching the code in Listing 8.13.

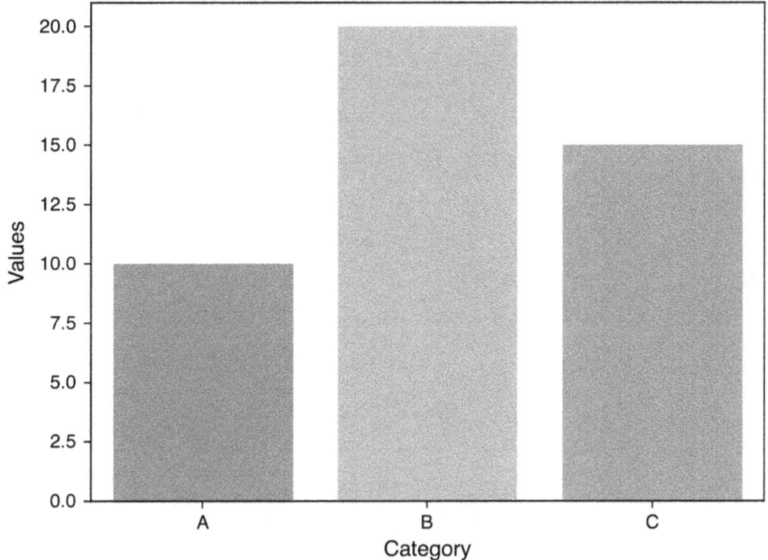

FIGURE 8.13 A bar chart created with Matplotlib

SCATTERPLOTS WITH A REGRESSION LINE USING SEABORN

Scatterplots allow us to display data points and a regression line to understand relationships. Listing 8.14 displays the content of `scatter_plot.py` that ChatGPT generated to render a scatter chart using Seaborn.

LISTING 8.14: scatter_plot.py

```
import matplotlib.pyplot as plt
import pandas as pd
import seaborn as sns

def plot_scatter_with_regression(data, x_col, y_col):
    sns.regplot(x=x_col, y=y_col, data=data)
    plt.show()

# Usage
data = pd.DataFrame({
    'X_Values': [10, 20, 30, 40, 50],
    'Y_Values': [15, 25, 35, 45, 55]
})
plot_scatter_with_regression(data, 'X_Values', 'Y_Values')
```

Scatterplots are useful for visualizing relationships between two variables. Seaborn has a `regplot()` function that not only plots the data points, but also fits a regression line.

Listing 8.14 starts with three `import` statements and the `plot_scatter_with_regression()` function that renders the scatterplot. The second half of Listing 8.13 initializes the Pandas `DataFrame` `data` and then invokes `plot_scattter_with_regression()` with the variable `data`. Figure 8.14 displays the scatterplot that is rendered by launching the code in Listing 8.14.

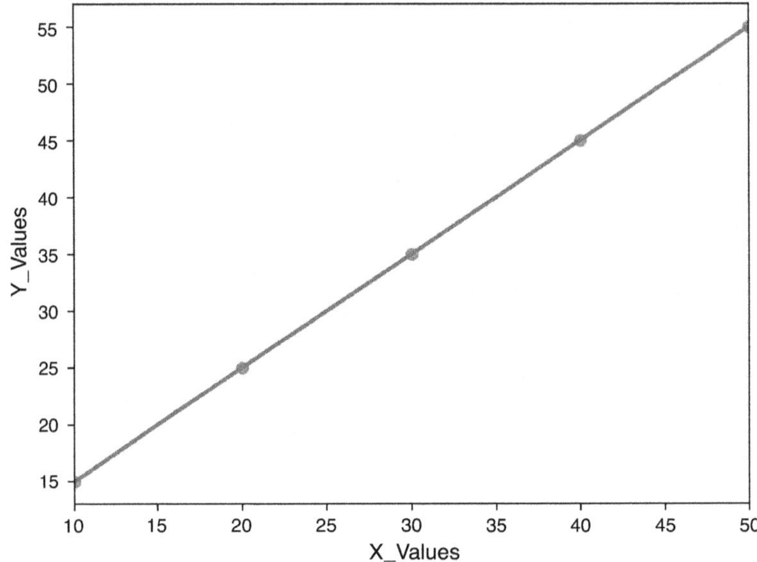

FIGURE 8.14 A scatterplot created with Matplotlib

HEAT MAPS FOR CORRELATION MATRICES WITH SEABORN

Heat maps are powerful for representing matrices of data, with colors indicating magnitudes. A common use case is visualizing correlation matrices, which helps in understanding relationships among different variables.

Heat maps allow us to visualize correlations among multiple variables. Listing 8.15 displays the content of `heatmap1.py` that ChatGPT generated to render a heat map using Matplotlib.

LISTING 8.15: heatmap1.py

```
import matplotlib.pyplot as plt
import pandas as pd
import seaborn as sns

def plot_heatmap(data):
    correlation_matrix = data.corr()
    sns.heatmap(correlation_matrix, annot=True, cmap='coolwarm')
    plt.show()
```

```
# Usage
data = pd.DataFrame({
    'A': [1, 2, 3, 4, 5],
    'B': [5, 4, 3, 2, 1],
    'C': [2, 3, 4, 5, 6]
})
plot_heatmap(data)
```

Listing 8.15 starts with three `import` statements and the `plot_heatmap()` function that renders the heat map. The second half of Listing 8.15 initializes the Pandas `DataFrame data` and then invokes `plot_heatmap()` with the variable `data`. Figure 8.15 displays the heat map that is rendered by launching the code in Listing 8.15.

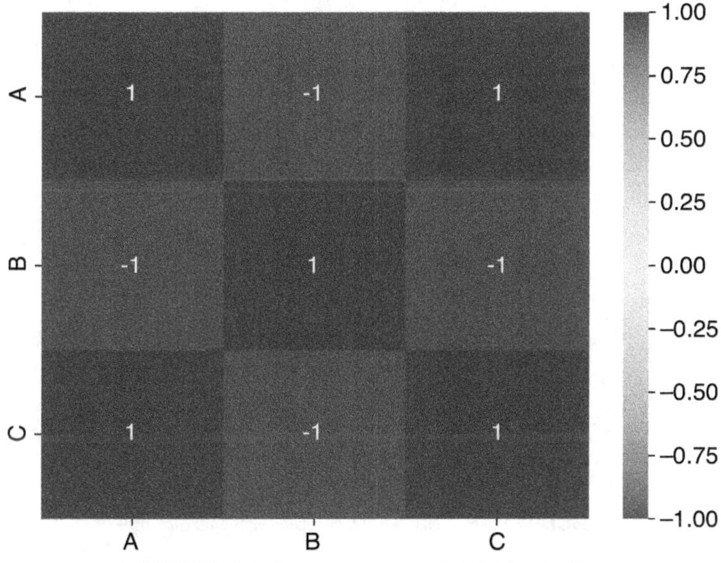

FIGURE 8.15 A heat map created with Matplotlib

HISTOGRAMS WITH SEABORN

Histograms are powerful tools for visualizing the distribution of data. Seaborn's `histplot()` function provides a way to easily generate histograms with additional features like kernel density estimation.

Listing 8.16 displays the content of `histogram1.py` that ChatGPT generated to render a histogram using Seaborn.

LISTING 8.16: histogram1.py

```
import matplotlib.pyplot as plt
import seaborn as sns

def plot_histogram(data, column, bins=10):
    sns.histplot(data[column], bins=bins)
    plt.show()
```

```
# Usage
data = sns.load_dataset("iris")
plot_histogram(data, "sepal_length")
```

Listing 8.16 starts with two `import` statements and the `plot_histogram()` function that renders the histogram. The second half of Listing 8.16 initializes the Pandas `DataFrame` `data` with the contents of the Seaborn built-in dataset `iris`, and then invokes `plot_histogram()` with the variable `data`. Figure 8.16 displays the heat map for the `iris` dataset that is rendered by launching the code in Listing 8.16.

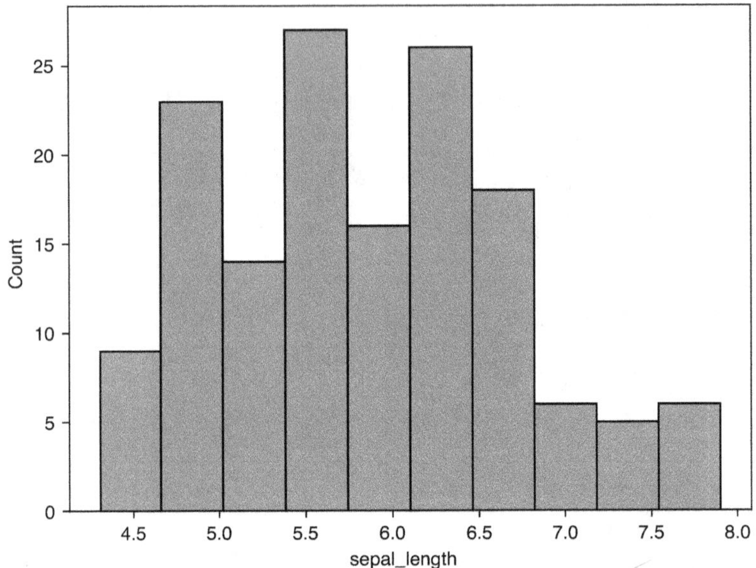

FIGURE 8.16 A histogram created with Matplotlib

VIOLIN PLOTS WITH SEABORN

Violin plots offer a deeper understanding of the distribution of data. They combine the characteristics of box plots and histograms, showing the probability density of the data at different values.

We can combine aspects of box plots and histograms to obtain richer descriptions of data distributions. Listing 8.17 displays the content of `violin_plots.py` that ChatGPT generated to render a violin plot using Seaborn.

LISTING 8.17: violin_plots.py

```
import seaborn as sns

def plot_violin(data, x_col, y_col):
```

```
    sns.violinplot(x=x_col, y=y_col, data=data)
    plt.show()

# Usage
data = sns.load_dataset("iris")
plot_violin(data, "species", "sepal_length")
```

Listing 8.17 starts with one `import` statement and the `plot_violin()` function that renders the violin plot. The second half of Listing 8.17 initializes the `Pandas DataFrame data` and then initializes the `Pandas DataFrame data` with the contents of the `Seaborn` built-in dataset `iris`, and then invokes `plot_violin()` with the variable `data`. Figure 8.17 displays the violin plot that is rendered by launching the code in Listing 8.8.

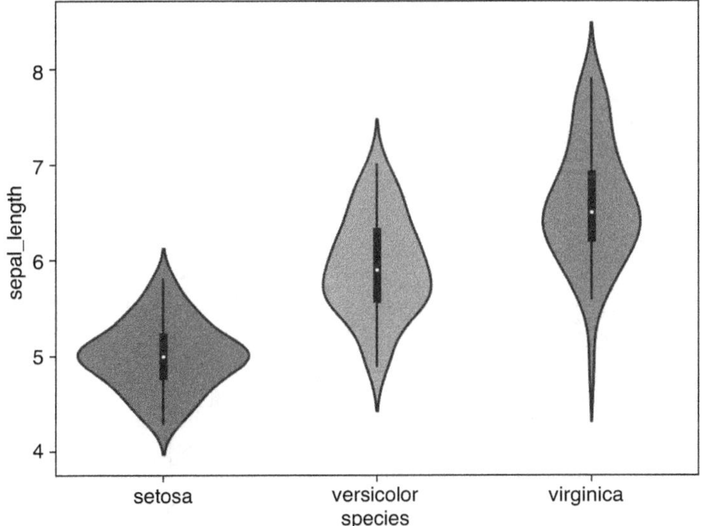

FIGURE 8.17 A violin plot created with Matplotlib

PAIR PLOTS USING SEABORN

When dealing with datasets having multiple features, it is often helpful to visualize the pairwise relationships between features. Seaborn has a `pairplot()` function that generates a matrix of scatterplots, allowing for the exploration of such relationships.

Listing 8.18 displays the content of `pair_plots.py` that ChatGPT generated to render a pair plot using Matplotlib.

LISTING 8.18: pair_plots.py

```
import matplotlib.pyplot as plt
import seaborn as sns
```

```
def plot_pairplot(data):
    sns.pairplot(data)
    plt.show()

# Usage
data = sns.load_dataset("iris")
plot_pairplot(data)
```

Listing 8.18 starts with two `import` statements and the `plot_pairplot()` function that renders the pair plot. The second part of Listing 8.18 initializes the Pandas `DataFrame` `data` with the contents of the Seaborn built-in dataset `iris`, and then invokes `plot_pair()` with the variable `data`. Figure 8.18 displays the pair plot that is rendered by launching the code in Listing 8.18.

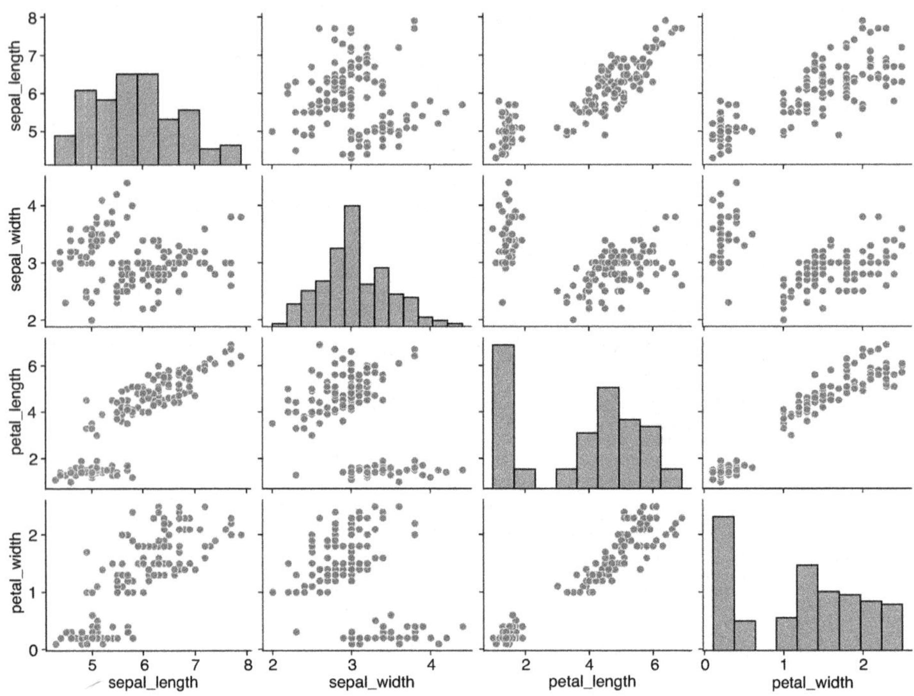

FIGURE 8.18 A pair plot created with Matplotlib

FACET GRIDS WITH SEABORN

Facet grids are a way to visualize the data distribution across several subplots based on a categorical variable. Each facet (subplot) represents a category. Listing 8.19 displays the content of `facet_grids.py` that ChatGPT generated to create and render multiple plots segmented by categories.

LISTING 8.19: facet_grids.py

```
import matplotlib.pyplot as plt
import seaborn as sns
```

```
def plot_facetgrid(data, x_col, y_col, facet_col):
    g = sns.FacetGrid(data, col=facet_col)
    g.map(sns.scatterplot, x_col, y_col)
    g.add_legend()
    plt.show()

# Usage
data = sns.load_dataset("iris")
plot_facetgrid(data, "sepal_length", "sepal_width",
"species")
```

Listing 8.19 starts with two `import` statements and the `plot_facetgrid()` function that renders the facets. The second part of Listing 8.19 initializes the Pandas `DataFrame data` with the contents of the Seaborn built-in dataset `iris`, and then invokes `plot_pair()` with the variable `data`. Figure 8.19 displays the facet grids that are rendered by launching the code in Listing 8.19.

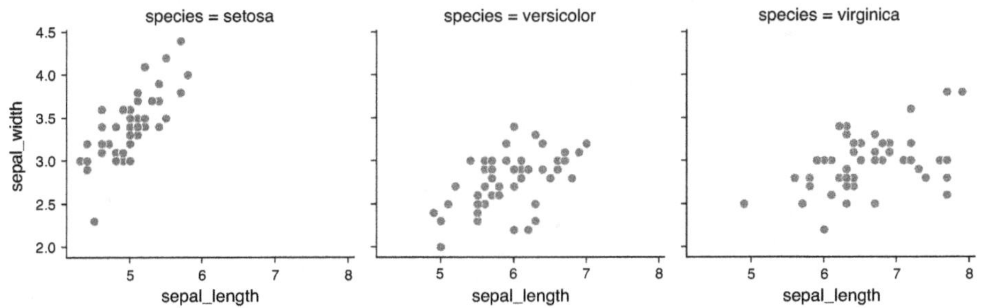

FIGURE 8.19 Facet grids created with Seaborn

HIERARCHICAL CLUSTERING

Seaborn's `clustermap` is a 2D matrix dataset representation where both rows and columns are hierarchically clustered. This allows patterns to emerge from complex datasets. We can visualize hierarchically clustered relationships in a cluster map format.

LISTING 8.20: cluster_map.py

```
import matplotlib.pyplot as plt
import seaborn as sns

def plot_clustermap(data):
    sns.clustermap(data, method='average', cmap='coolwarm')
    plt.show()

# Usage
data = sns.load_dataset("iris").drop("species", axis=1)
plot_clustermap(data)
```

Listing 8.20 starts with two `import` statements and the `plot_clustermap()` function that renders the cluster map. The second part of Listing 8.20 initializes the Pandas `DataFrame` `data` with the contents of the Seaborn built-in dataset `iris`, and then invokes `plot_pair()` with the variable `data`. Figure 8.20 displays the cluster map that is rendered by launching the code in Listing 8.20.

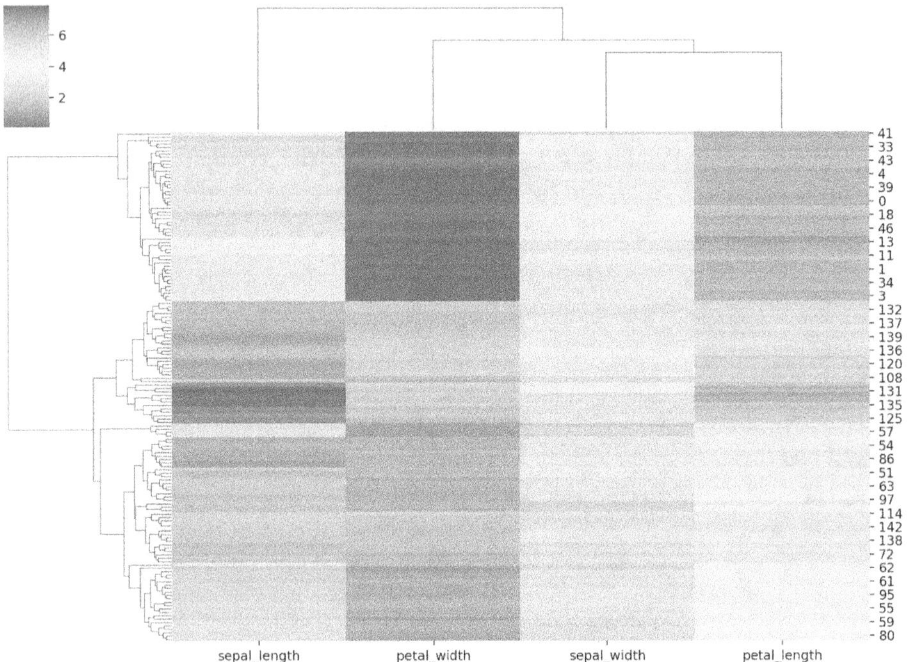

FIGURE 8.20 Cluster map created with Seaborn

SWARM PLOTS

The swarm plot positions each data point on the categorical axis with minimal overlap, giving a better representation of the distribution of values. It allows us to display a categorical scatterplot with non-overlapping points.

Listing 8.21 displays the content of `swarm_plot.py` that ChatGPT generated to render contour lines using Seaborn.

LISTING 8.21: swarm_plot.py

```
import matplotlib.pyplot as plt
import seaborn as sns

def plot_swarm(data, x_col, y_col):
    sns.swarmplot(x=x_col, y=y_col, data=data)
    plt.show()
```

```
# Usage
data = sns.load_dataset("iris")
plot_swarm(data, "species", "sepal_length")
```

Listing 8.21 starts with two `import` statements and the `plot_swarm()` function that renders the swarm plot. The second part of Listing 8.21 initializes the Pandas `DataFrame` `data` with the contents of the Seaborn built-in dataset `iris`, and then invokes `plot_swarm()` with the variable `data`. Figure 8.21 displays the swarm plot that is rendered by launching the code in Listing 8.21.

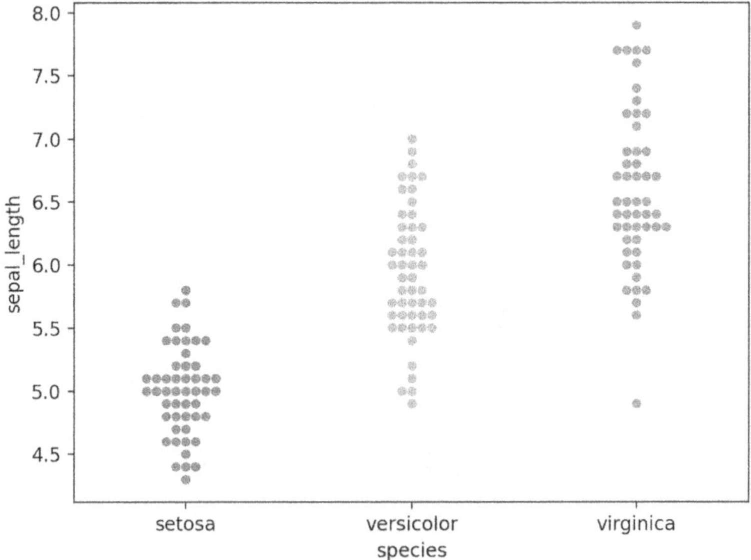

FIGURE 8.21 Swarm plot created with Seaborn

JOINT PLOT FOR BIVARIATE DATA

Seaborn's `jointplot` displays a relationship between two variables. It combines scatterplots, regression plots, and even hexbin plots with histograms. It allows us to display a relationship between two variables along with their individual distributions.

Listing 8.22 displays the content of `joint_plot.py` that ChatGPT generated to render a joint plot using Seaborn.

LISTING 8.22: joint_plot.py

```
import matplotlib.pyplot as plt
import seaborn as sns

def plot_jointplot(data, x_col, y_col, kind='scatter'):
```

```
    sns.jointplot(x=x_col, y=y_col, data=data, kind=kind)
    plt.show()

# Usage
data = sns.load_dataset("iris")
plot_jointplot(data, "sepal_length", "sepal_width", "hex")
```

Listing 8.22 starts with two `import` statements and the `plot_joint()` function that renders the joint plot. The second part of Listing 8.22 initializes the Pandas `DataFrame` `data` with the contents of the Seaborn built-in dataset `iris`, and then invokes `plot_pair()` with the variable `data`. Figure 8.22 displays the joint plot that is rendered by launching the code in Listing 8.22.

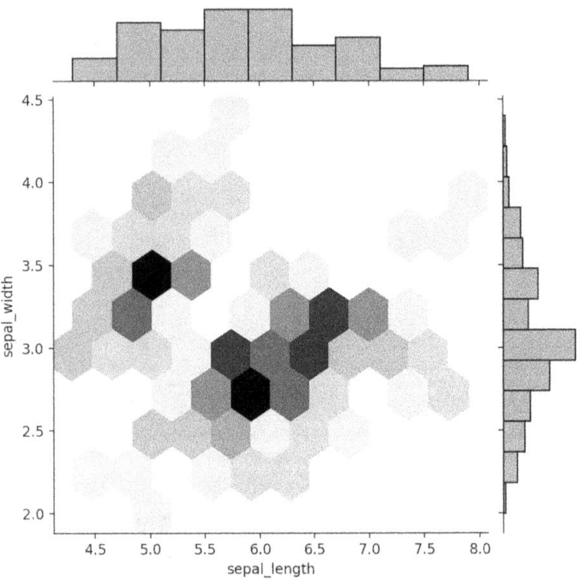

FIGURE 8.22 A joint plot created with Seaborn

POINT PLOTS FOR FACTORIZED VIEWS

Point plots can be useful to highlight the differences between points, especially when categorized by factors. The lines connecting the points can help emphasize trends. Point plots emphasize the comparison between points with lines.

Listing 8.23 displays the content of `point_plot.py` that ChatGPT generated to render a point plot using Seaborn.

LISTING 8.23: point_plot.py

```
import matplotlib.pyplot as plt
import seaborn as sns
```

```
def plot_pointplot(data, x_col, y_col, hue=None):
    sns.pointplot(x=x_col, y=y_col, hue=hue, data=data)
    plt.show()

# Usage
data = sns.load_dataset("tips")
plot_pointplot(data, "day", "total_bill", "sex")
```

Listing 8.23 starts with two `import` statements and the `plot_pointplot()` function that renders the point plot. The second part of Listing 8.23 initializes the Pandas `DataFrame data` with the contents of the Seaborn built-in dataset `tips`, and then invokes `plot_pointplot()` with the variable `data`. Figure 8.23 displays the point plot that is rendered by launching the code in Listing 8.23.

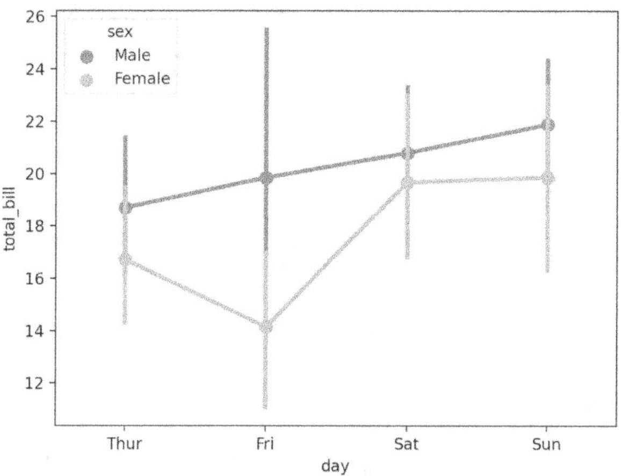

FIGURE 8.23 A point plot created with Seaborn

SEABORN'S KDE PLOTS FOR DENSITY ESTIMATIONS

Kernel Density Estimation (KDE) plots visualize the probability density of a continuous variable. They can be thought of as smoothed histograms and are particularly useful when discerning the underlying distribution of a dataset. They allow us to visualize data density.

Listing 8.24 displays the content of `kde_plot.py` that ChatGPT generated to render a KDE plot using Seaborn.

LISTING 8.24: kde_plot.py

```
import matplotlib.pyplot as plt
import seaborn as sns

def plot_kde(data, column):
    sns.kdeplot(data[column], shade=True)
    plt.show()
```

```
# Usage
data = sns.load_dataset("iris")
plot_kde(data, "sepal_length")
```

Listing 8.24 starts with two `import` statements and the `plot_kde()` function that renders the KDE plot. The second part of Listing 8.23 initializes the Pandas `DataFrame` `data` with the contents of the Seaborn built-in dataset `iris`, and then invokes `plot_kde()` with the variable `data`. Figure 8.24 displays the point plot that is rendered by launching the code in Listing 8.24.

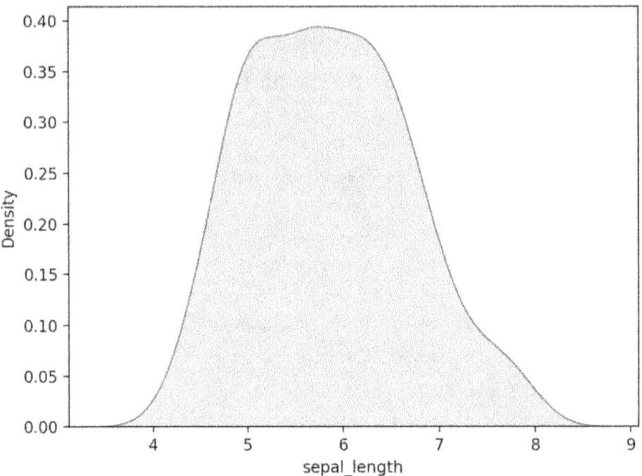

FIGURE 8.24 A KDE plot created with Seaborn

SEABORN'S RIDGE PLOTS

Ridge plots are essentially a series of KDE plots displayed on top of one another, allowing for the comparison of distributions across categories. They allow for the display of overlaid distribution plots, which is useful for visualizing distribution changes across categories.

Listing 8.25 displays the content of `ridge_plot.py` that ChatGPT generated to render the ridge plot using Seaborn.

LISTING 8.25: ridge_plot.py

```
import matplotlib.pyplot as plt
import seaborn as sns

def plot_ridge(data, x_col, category_col):
    g = sns.FacetGrid(data, row=category_col, hue=category_
col, aspect=5)
    g.map(sns.kdeplot, x_col, clip_on=False, shade=True,
alpha=1, lw=1.5, bw_method=0.2)
    g.map(sns.kdeplot, x_col, clip_on=False, color="w",
lw=1, bw_method=0.2)
    g.map(plt.axhline, y=0, lw=2, clip_on=False)
    plt.show()
```

```
# Usage
data = sns.load_dataset("diamonds")
subset_data = data[data['cut'].isin(['Ideal', 'Fair',
'Good'])]
plot_ridge(subset_data, "price", "cut")
```

Listing 8.25 starts with two `import` statements and the `plot_ridge()` function that renders the ridge plot. The second part of Listing 8.25 initializes the Pandas `DataFrame data` with the contents of the Seaborn built-in dataset `diamonds`, and then invokes `plot_ridge()` with the variable `data`. Figure 8.25 displays the ridge plot that is rendered by launching the code in Listing 8.25.

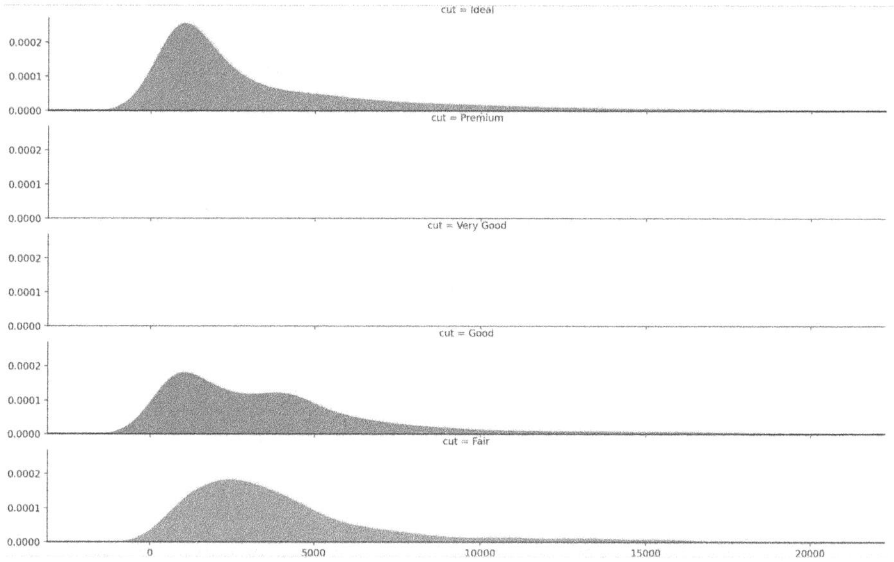

FIGURE 8.25 A ridge plot created with Seaborn

SUMMARY

This chapter contains Python-based solutions generated by ChatGPT for a variety of tasks. You learned about various types of charts and graphs, when to use them, along with the advantages and disadvantages of each type of chart and graph.

You learned about data visualization using a popular open-source Python-based library called Matplotlib that can render numerous types charts and graphs.

You also learned how to render histograms, violin plots, and time series visualizations. By mastering these techniques, you can craft compelling narratives from data, aiding in decision-making and insight generation. Keep in mind that a well-crafted visualization is worth a thousand rows of raw data.

INDEX

R

S

www.ingramcontent.com/pod-product-compliance
Lightning Source LLC
LaVergne TN
LVHW020535100826
845148LV00010B/1468